Praise for *Running: A Love Story*

"*Running: A Love Story* is Jen's ultimate faith healer, restoring belief not only in herself but life's possibilities."
— Bart Yasso, Chief Running Officer of
Runner's World magazine and author of *My Life on the Run*

"Once, I was running with Jen Miller in Philly when a crusty guy on the sidewalk yelled at her, 'You run like a GIRL!' I had no idea what he meant, but in this inspiring, honest and fierce book, Jen finally explains it."
—Peter Sagal, host of NPR's *Wait Wait…Don't Tell Me* and
columnist for *Runner's World* magazine

"*Running: A Love Story* is a frank and sometimes gritty look inside Jen Miller's heart. She speaks for a lot of us as she reveals her self-doubts, and then finds the confidence to quiet them through running. How running does that to us is, like love, very simple yet totally mysterious. But here's the bottom line: It works for everyone."
— Kathrine Switzer, author of *Marathon Woman* and
the first woman to officially run the Boston Marathon

"A contemporary coming of age story that will speak to a generation of women, *Running: A Love Story* is the candid memoir of a young woman's painful but triumphant search for her place in the world. Skillfully crafted and unsparingly honest, *Running* is a courageous memoir written straight from the heart."
— Amy Hill Hearth, *New York Times* and
Washington Post bestselling author

"Millions of everyday men and women have a love affair with running. No book I've read captures the richness and complexity of this widely shared experience—the exhilaration and heartbreak and everything in between—more faithfully than Jen Miller's lovely memoir, *Running: A Love Story*."
— Matt Fitzgerald, author of more than 20 endurance sports books,
including *How Bad Do You Want It? Mastering the Psychology of Mind Over Muscle*

"*Running: A Love Story* is a ballad for anyone looking to discover themselves. Jen Miller is remarkably honest, candid, and approachable in her writing style. She narrates in a way that makes you feel like the two of you are tucked in the corner of a tapas restaurant sharing stories way into the late hours. As someone who has never been "good" at running, I was delighted to find this book to be about so much more than sneakers and mile marks. This is a book about finding love, discovering your breaking points, and letting go. Jen pieces together a moral I think the world needs: only when we fully let go can we finally grip tight to the stuff that really matters."
—Hannah Brencher, author of *If You Find This Letter*

Running

a love story

Running

a love story

10 YEARS, 5 MARATHONS, AND 1 LIFE-CHANGING SPORT

JEN A. MILLER

SEAL PRESS

For my grandmother, Dorothy Miller
Bums!

Running: A Love Story

Copyright © 2016 Jennifer Miller

ISBN 9781580056106

Miller, Jen A.
Running: a love story / Jen A. Miller.
LCCN 2015040211 I ISBN 9781580056106
Miller, Jen A. I Runners (Sports)--United States--Biography.
LCC GV1061.15.M55 A3 2015 I DDC 796.42092--dc23

Published by
Seal Press
A Member of the Perseus Books Group
1700 Fourth Street
Berkeley, California
Sealpress.com

Cover design by Jeff Miller, Faceout Studios
Interior design by Amber Pirker
Printed in the United States of America
Distributed by Publishers Group West

Author's Note: The author has changed the names and personal details of some individuals mentioned in this book to protect their privacy. Some timelines have been condensed for clarity.

Ay me! for aught that I could ever read,
Could ever hear by tale or history,
The course of true love never did run smooth.

William Shakespeare
A Midsummer Night's Dream

Pain is inevitable. Suffering is optional.

Haruki Murakami
What I Talk About When I Talk About Running

chapter 1

WARM-UP

MAY 5, 2013

New Jersey Marathon

I closed my eyes as we approached the staging area. Mom drove, silent. She knew not to talk to me before races, and the only noise was me softly giving directions to Monmouth Park. It's normally a thoroughbred horse race track, but that day it was the start line of the New Jersey Marathon and Long Branch Half Marathon.

Under my sweatpants and sweatshirt, I wore an outfit I had tested in my sixth Ocean Drive 10-Miler five weeks before: two-toned blue tank top, black compression shorts (and Body Glide spread liberally on unmentionable areas that would otherwise chafe over the next four-plus hours), blue knee-high compression socks, black gloves, Timex sports watch. My yellow visor rounded out the ensemble. On my feet were the blue and orange Mizuno Musha 5s that I hoped would carry me over 26.2 miles in under four hours and thirty-five minutes.

I first signed up to run this race back in 2010. It would have been my first marathon, but I ran myself into the ground and quit halfway through training. That year, temperatures had topped out at a humidity-soaked 89 degrees. This time around, the race was on a freak May cold day, with a forecast high of 53 degrees. If I was planning to blame the weather for not reaching my goal that day, I lost that out. I couldn't have asked for a better day or better conditions to try, in my third marathon, to put together a race—one where I could take pride in the results, one where I didn't crash and burn and beg and cry and almost crawl to the finish line in the final miles.

I had eighteen weeks of training in my legs and lungs. I'd prepared using a controversial marathon training method blasted as dangerous, unhealthy, and unproven. It put me, a middle-of-the-pack amateur, through high-intensity workouts, topping out at fifty-seven miles a week—a volume that had sent me into daily naps and two dinners a night. One of my editors—a longtime runner—wished me luck with the training as if I were about to paddle a canoe into the Bermuda Triangle. I ran that schedule fresh out of a breakup with the man I thought I was going to marry, and somehow kept it up through living with my mother, re-settling my home, trips to Seattle, Florida, Las Vegas—white-knuckle clinging to those runs to keep me from falling over the edge into the black tar pit of my mind that kept telling me I was a failure.

I had pushed my body to the brink to outrun my pain. And as I planted myself among the thousands of runners who would test themselves in either a half or full marathon that day, I felt more prepared than I had before my last two marathons. My body was humming. My muscles were in tune. I had panicked before most of the races I'd run in the last seven years–dozens of 5Ks and 10Ks and ten-milers and half marathons–but this time my breathing was steady and I was strong, like a horse set to charge out of the gate.

Except for one thing: Doubt. Would this marathon end like the Philadelphia and Chicago marathons? Maybe I hadn't rested enough in the taper, or the ankle that was sore last week would give out, or the training method I used really was snake oil, and I'd end up a carcass being picked over by seagulls on the streets of Long Branch.

No, I told myself. *No. Stop.* That wasn't going to happen. That could not happen. I had no excuses. That day was do or be humiliated. I had the training. All I had to do was push my mind out of the way, get the hell out there, and run.

Mom stopped just short of the entrance to Monmouth Park. I got out of the car, said goodbye to her with a squeeze of her hand, and walked to the start.

Teenage me would be more stunned to see me at the starting line of a marathon than if I'd grown up to become a mermaid, a unicorn, a professional baseball player, or a mermaid riding a unicorn picking off runners at first base.

I detested running growing up, though "detested" might be

too kind a description. How about loathed, despised, hated with
the burning of a white-hot fire?

I wasn't anti-sport. I ran a lot, but that running had a
purpose: to chase after a soccer ball or someone with a soccer
ball, to get to first base, second, third, home. I was good, too. I
was never that big or that tall, but I was stocky and solid, the
inheritor of the bone structure of women who, for generations
in Italy and Slovakia and Ireland and Scotland relied on their
wide hips and matching shoulders to survive both harsh living
conditions and birthing the requisite six to twelve children each.
I have a huge family on my mother's side—twenty cousins—so
most of the girls and women I knew were related to me and
built more or less the same, and I thought all women were like
that. I kept up with the boys in games of tag or red light, green
light played on the Bellmawr, New Jersey, cul-de-sac where I
grew up—or I beat them.

I knew how to throw my weight around, and was proud of
it. I started playing soccer when I was five, the kind of soccer
where players on both teams herd after the ball while kicking
at each other's shins. I had no qualms about shoving my way
through the herd. I was never the fastest player through middle
and high school, but I would still be standing, and running,
deep into the game. By then, the skinny offensive players on
the other team, who were usually given that role because of
their speed rather than their stamina, started to flag. While my
ball-handling skills weren't great, that didn't matter if I could
still physically put myself between an offender and the ball, and

if need be, knock her over with a well-placed shoulder to the chest. I was a wall of a defensive player in basketball, too, but gave up that sport because I didn't like playing indoors.

My best game was softball. I picked it up in third grade, made the town league's all-star team that year and then every year after. I wasn't the quickest in getting down the first base line, but no one on my team could beat me in the haul from first to third. Having the leadoff batter on third base to start the game isn't a bad place to be.

Despite all the running in softball and soccer games and practices, I never ran for the sake of running except when forced. That happened either through punishment of laps or suicide sprints for game errors, or from my dad deciding that I needed to get in better shape two weeks before the first high school soccer practice of the year. He expected me to get a scholarship to play softball in college, which is why I went to camps and batting cages in the off-season. Soccer would be a backup if softball didn't work out, and I needed to be ready for the upcoming season.

I spent most of my summer in a campground at the Jersey Shore with my mom and siblings while my dad worked during the week and came down on weekends. By late August we'd come back home to get ready for the next school year. Those days, I'd be stretched across the couch after a long day of swimming in our above-ground pool that we jumped into via a step ladder, biking endless loops around our town looking for dirt trails, lawn mowing, or, when it was too hot to do anything, reading a book, usually from the *Sweet Valley High* oeuvre.

"Jenny!" my dad would yell when he walked in the front door, his dress shoes clicking on the tiled foyer floor. "Go run a lap!"

"It's too hot!" I'd yell back. My father came home from work every day at 5:30 PM, which sounds like a cooler time of day to run, but heat plus humidity plus August in New Jersey meant muck—still—that late in the afternoon. It's not uncommon for temperatures to be stuck in the 90s until sunset. Going outside was like getting a hot, wet washcloth stuffed into your mouth.

"You need to start conditioning for soccer!"

No, he didn't call it running. Conditioning. The name comes from the training boxers did to get ready for the ring. "Jog" first appeared in *The Taming of the Shrew*, but it wasn't applied to running until done so by New Zealand running coach Arthur Lydiard. "Jogging" made its way to the U.S. in the 1960s after University of Oregon track coach and Nike founder Bill Bowerman went to New Zealand to meet Lydiard. Bowerman brought the word back with him, and slapped it on his 1966 running book called—aptly—*Jogging*.

When I was a teenager in the mid-1990s, only skinny weirdos in tiny split shorts and calf-high white cotton socks "jogged." I looked at joggers the same way I did guys who freaked out that my high school chemistry class had Mac computers and/or played Dungeons and Dragons: antisocial losers with bad hair and a special interest in antisocial behaviors, who self-selected to stay away from other people, especially girls.

Running wasn't exactly popular then, not like it is now. In 1995, there were 239,000 finishers in U.S. marathons and 420,000 in half marathons. By 2014, those numbers ballooned to 550,600 marathon finishers and 2.05 *million* half marathon finishers.

The 1995 New York City Marathon had just over 26,000 finishers. By the time I ran it in 2014, I was one of more than 50,000—and thousands more had tried to get in (in 2015, runners had an 18 percent chance of making it into the race through a lottery system, according to the New York Road Runners, the nonprofit organization that puts on the race). Back in ye olden 1990s, when Pearl Jam was young and our family computer didn't have a hard drive, there was no such thing as Couch to 5K or Color Runs, or even regular running groups that would have had people like me as a member.

And by people like me, I mean women. I didn't see women run anywhere other than my high school's track. TV coverage of running was mostly limited to the Olympics, and marathons were condensed for broadcast. So even if I caught sight of women distance runners, they weren't on TV for long. Today, according to Running USA, women make up 57 percent of all U.S. road race finishers, but then? They only dented the sport's fender. Just 26 percent of marathon finishers were women in 1995, and women didn't even have their own Olympic marathon when I was born (that came in 1984 when Joan Benoit Samuelson, with her brown short hair plastered to her face by sweat and white painter's cap in hand, leapt across the finish line in Los Angeles to show that not only could a woman run long distances without passing out, but also that she wouldn't leave her uterus on the track behind her).

Still, running should have appealed to me. I enjoyed activities that were so boring they blanked my mind, like the solo walks I took on the beach in the summer, and weeding. I didn't mind cutting the lawn, not just because I made $20 for doing so, but because it was monotonous. I'd spend the time making up short stories, usually about a poor but not impoverished girl saved from an always-tense family by a handsome man who may or may not have looked like Prince Eric from *The Little Mermaid*.

But running? Never. Why in the world would I want to run just to run? Boring.

Which brings me back to that couch reading about whatever mischief those perfect size sixes Jessica and Elizabeth Wakefield were up to in that particular *Sweet Valley* volume. Of the four Miller kids, I was the most athletic, which is why I was pressed to condition while my two brothers played video games in the family room and my sister locked herself in her bedroom to mimic looks from *YM* and *Seventeen* and belted along to the soundtrack of *Newsies*.

"Go. Now," my father said, nudging me with his foot.

He was not a man to be defied. By the time I was old enough to form memories, I knew my parents as a couple always on the brink of another fight so loud that I'd hide in my room. They'd been high school sweethearts and married after my father finished college. Mom took night classes but didn't finish because that's not what women in her strict Catholic family did when there was the possibility of marriage and babies on the horizon. She had four kids by the time she was thirty-one. When my father hinted he wanted a fifth, she had her tubes tied.

When Mom started a part-time job working for a financial planner, this became the axis around which many of their fights turned, and they launched at each other with gusto (my mother might have been at a disadvantage because she was financially dependent on my father, but she had an Italian temper and a spine of titanium and could more than hold her own). My dad said she didn't need a job and that it looked bad that his wife worked. She said she wanted to work and he should let her. But she wasn't there during the day to scrub the kitchen floor, clean the bathrooms, or do the laundry at perfectly timed intervals, which threw him into a rage, which threw her into a rage right back, which in turn sent toys flying out the back door and me into my room to blast Meat Loaf on my Walkman and bang on a manual typewriter to get down my latest Prince Eric-inspired story.

So as I lay on that couch trying to ignore my dad but hearing the pressure and volume build into his voice, I knew I had to go or that temper would turn on me.

I put on my sneakers without bothering to change my clothes, then opened the front door into the furnace. A lap was one quarter-mile loop, as measured by the odometer on my father's Oldsmobile, around the block that surrounded our cul-de-sac.

I did a few soccer stretches in the driveway, then headed off down our four-house street, turning onto Oakland Avenue. That took me past the home of the mean girl who once told me my thighs looked fat when I sat down. Then a right turn past the house with the dogs that threw themselves against the fence as I ran by, to the corner liquor store, then another right onto the Creek Road, which was a two-lane artery between a couple of two-lane roads that served as alternate routes to the Jersey Shore. I wasn't even halfway there, but already sweat popped out on my forehead and dampened the straps and cups of my training bra.

The sidewalk here was older concrete, pockmarked in places where stones had popped out. Halfway down Creek Road was a convent: the three-story yellow brick residence of the nuns who had taught me up through sixth grade, where I took piano lessons with a scary nun named Sister Anna who had tiny gray teeth and no patience for children (perfect qualities in a piano teacher), where I'd lost countless soccer balls and softballs and baseballs to the yard, some retrieved by climbing onto the roof of our woodshed and jumping over the fence that separated our property from theirs.

By the time I passed the nuns' driveway, the forehead sweat dripped into my eyes, and my bra felt like a bathing suit top after I had jumped into the pool. Maybe if I collapsed on their lawn, one of the nuns—preferably not Sister Anna—would find me while walking their order's poodle and hose me down. I didn't understand pacing. I always started the lap like I was trying to run out a throw to first base, but this was much longer than those 60-foot sprints.

Please, God, just let it be over, I prayed to the statue of Jesus on their front lawn, and put one foot in front of the other, a deep cramp jabbing into my side.

The motion of running itself never hurt. I spent too much time during the summer alternating between body surfing and riding my bike in endless loops to be out of shape. I was strong, and my legs and arms swung along with my intentions, but my lungs could not keep up with the oxygen demand pressed upon them. I short-circuited, gulping for breaths of stuffy air. At least when I biked or swam, I could count on a breeze or the ocean to cool me down. At least when I cut the lawn, I could listen to my Walkman, and move no faster than the mower allowed.

By the time I made the last turn toward home, dragging my feet and wheezing, I was bent over, both sides cramped, sweat running freely down my spine and crack of my butt. My bra and underwear were soaked, shorts and shirt sticking to both.

"Never again!" I yelled when I stomped into the house and slammed the door behind me, then stomped upstairs to strip naked and lie under the ceiling fan until its breeze evaporated the sweat from my skin.

This scene replayed every August before high school soccer season, except my senior year when my parents had separated and my father lived in an apartment near his office. But in those years when he still lived at home, and he'd tell me to do a second lap, I'd strap on my Rollerblades instead and zip out. I didn't care if he'd get mad—I let my mom deal with him. They fought enough. What was one more argument? It was still hot, but at least I was moving fast enough to stay just ahead of that washcloth.

I skated to Barrington, one town over. They had just covered over their old concrete roads with flat black asphalt. I glided over their freshly paved streets, making patterns and shapes on roads with almost no traffic. Just as when I rode my bike, or swam in the ocean, there was something else there to cool me down. The wheels of my skates gave me freedom to move without putting a vise on my lungs. I could cover so much more ground, all with a gentle breeze lapping over my face. *This is so much better,* I thought. *Why would anyone want to run and go so slow?*

The first real runner I knew was Dan, my high school boyfriend. I left Catholic school after sixth grade when my parents paid for me to go to the public high school of Haddonfield, which had better classes, no uniforms, and no girls pointing out that I had fat thighs when I sat down. That's where Dan lived. We met in math class freshman year, and after months of furtive glances thrown at each other during geometry lectures, he professed his love for me in a card he bought for $1 as part of a student government Valentine's Day fund-raiser.

When I met him, he was fluffy. His cheeks looked like those of Chip and/or Dale when they shoved a bunch of nuts in their mouths before running away from Donald Duck. Not that this was a deal breaker—I was thrilled to be one of the girls who had a real, live boyfriend to hold hands with in the hallway. I didn't care what was under his clothes because he kept them on. We were shy, guilty Catholic teenagers, and there wasn't much groping that first year. When I finally saw his penis, the event was more like an unveiling than a lust-inspired display. It was done in the unfinished portion of my basement under fluorescent lights. I didn't touch it, not then. It wasn't very attractive. It looked like a piece of debarked kindling.

I had soccer and softball, but Dan was a golf wunderkind. He went on to be an All-American golfer and a golf management major in college. As a sophomore in high school, he tried out for the cross-country team because he thought running would get him in better shape for swinging and walking and carrying clubs through eighteen holes of golf. I was doubtful. Dan was too short and round to be one of those willowy, antisocial cross-country guys, I thought.

Running unstuffed his cheeks, and by the time I was actually seeing parts of his body unclothed when we were not in his pool, he was compact and lean with a hint of muscles. He was often the sixth man on the cross-country team, which meant that his score rarely counted toward the team's total, but his coach made him co-captain his junior year, then captain his senior year because his teammates said he was so upbeat about running, even when finishing last.

I could not wrap my mind around his running schedule. I saw no problem with hitting hundreds of softballs off a batting tee, but running six, seven, eight miles in one clip? Especially when most of his cross-country races were under five miles? Lunacy. His junior year co-captain would go on to run for a Division I school and then briefly as a pro—he was running 60 miles a week.

One day Dan and a few teammates ran 10 miles. Ten miles! *For fun!* I'd have rather run right over a rusty nail.

"What do you DO for 10 miles next to the same guys you run with all the time?" I asked him one warm afternoon in June while floating in his pool and waiting for his parents to go to dinner so we could make out.

"Talk shit," he said.

"What does he do for 60 miles?"

"I don't know. Think of things to say while talking shit?"

That seemed like too little of a distraction for what I assumed was 60 miles of agony, but I let it go because his parents left soon after, and we threw ourselves at each other. Our time was running out. In a few days, we would graduate high school and he'd be off to start college early, while I was to toil away at my dad's office before shipping off to the University of Tampa.

Dan was a constant that made high school a flat and smooth experience for me, like floating on the bay instead of getting smacked in the face by ocean waves. Haddonfield could be an isolating place if you didn't start there right in kindergarten with your classmates. It was and is the richest town in the county, but while my classmates drove Eddie Bauer Limited Edition Ford Explorers and diesel Mercedes to school, I parked next to them in my mom's Dodge Caravan, beaten down with 180,000 miles. Bellmawr is a town of intersecting highways and a twenty-four-hour post office that at the time was best known as the site of one of the 2001 anthrax attacks. It was a town my classmates were aware of only because they drove through it on the way to their shore houses (except for one classmate whose family's "shore" house was in the Caribbean). We had a shore place, too, but it was a trailer, inland. I had felt so lucky that we had that place, but when I realized that my friends' homes were actual houses on the island, I stopped talking about it, and always told them I was busy if they asked me to meet up with them down the shore.

I was not quite a member of the friend group when I first came to school, but as Dan's girlfriend, I was soon let inside their circle. Dan hadn't grown up in Haddonfield either—his parents moved there from Connecticut when he was in middle school—but he was part of that crowd more than I was simply by living there, and I became one of the group by proxy.

Being with Dan throughout high school meant that I never dealt with boy angst because I'd had Dan and hand-holding and penis grabbing and tying up the phone line with a conversation that stretched nearly four years. I didn't know how to date and I didn't really want to learn. Dan was perfect: smart, polite, respectful. My parents adored him and vice versa. His parents, two former Woodstock hippies, showed me that grown-ups could be married and not throw things out the back door. I didn't want to let him, or them, go. Of course I wanted to go to college. I had worked through high school to get there, and my mother was adamant that all her children would go, but I was envious of Emily Webb, one of the protagonists in *Our Town*, because she locked down George Gibbs soon after they earned their high school diplomas (though I could have done without the dying young part).

The night after graduation, Dan gave me a pair of diamond stud earrings, said he'd love me forever, then broke up with me, because . . . college, following dreams, girls, or something. We were both still virgins, at my insistence, which may have had something to do with his decision. Dan was polite, but he was still an eighteen-year-old virgin going into college where a platter of new, non-Catholic women lay ahead.

I was devastated. Plunging me further into despair, the University of Tampa had not been my first-choice school. Despite being accepted to brand-name schools, despite Tampa's reputation as a big fat zero to anyone north of the Mason–Dixon line, and despite the fact that all the girls with WASP names in my high school class wailed if they had to settle for a place like Colgate, the University of Tampa offered me the most financial aid. My parents didn't have much money to start. They still had to pay Catholic high school tuition for my younger siblings, and the divorce ripped up what college budget my parents had left in a year when my older brother and I would be in college. They told me I was heading south. I was an angry teenager who couldn't see that I was lucky my parents had pushed me to go to college and had saved some money to fund it, and that I was lucky to have earned scholarships, too. But in that moment, when my family life was upending, that shove to Florida seemed like a death blow.

I spent my last summer before Tampa filling in at my dad's office as an accounting clerk for a woman on maternity leave.

There, I shuttled from an office with no windows to a file room with no windows. Every night I went home smelling like carbon paper and played witness to my parents unwinding their lives from each other. My only escape would be moving to a swamp. I was, I thought, doomed.

"Are you sure?" my father asked. He was squinting into the sun outside my dorm, a two-story cinder block box full of smaller boxes that held two people each, and one shower/bathroom area per gender per floor. He had just arrived the night before, and that morning I gave him a tour of my room, which was still a mess of boxes and books—including what I'd brought with me from my stacks of books at home, like *Where the Red Fern Grows* and *Bridge to Terabithia*, and what I had picked up at the college bookstore the day before.

My mother and I had driven my dad's SUV, crammed with my stuff, to Florida, while Dad flew down to meet us and help me move into that dank dorm by the Hillsborough River (which I'd evacuate within the first month of school during my first Florida hurricane). My parents were hammering out their divorce agreement at the time, and were barely talking to each other.

At first, I thought that my dad was asking about my college choice: Am I sure about this school? This weather? This state? *No!* It wasn't even 9:00 AM and we were already roasting. But what he was really referring to was my not playing softball in college. I had been captain of my high school team, which wasn't great but wasn't terrible. I had talked with some college coaches while looking at schools, and my dad had asked me to still consider walking on to the University of Tampa squad.

But I wasn't interested. I'd played on two softball teams for most of high school; that combined with the peer pressure at my über-wealthy high school to get the best grades and SAT scores, even though we couldn't afford the schools that those grades and scores would get me into, meant I was fried. I expected college classes to be hard, too, and I wanted to focus on those without having to read and do homework on buses to and from games played in broiling heat.

When Dad asked me that one last time, we were about to walk to a welcome event for parents, and sweat stains already showed on the underarms of his shirt.

A trickle of sweat ran down my back and into my shorts. "Positive."

Soon after the semester started, though, I found that almost all my freshman classes were easier than those I had taken in high school. With no need to be anywhere after class, I had a lot of time on my hands. I filled part of that time writing for the student newspaper, and the rest pining for my old life. I'd never spent much time away from Bellmawr. I missed Dan, my family, New Jersey, and those touchstones of home that had filled the first eighteen years of my life, like twenty-four-hour diners, fall allergies, leaves that changed colors, and knowing whose hair was in the bottom of the shower drain. Not to mention a breeze. A breeze! My kingdom for a cool breeze!

I went a little nuts.

Some nights I'd lodge myself in front of a computer lab iMac with AOL Instant Messenger open, talking to high school friends and pretending that I was having as much fun as they were, while hoping that Dan would log on too, which he didn't often do. Other nights, when I couldn't stand another night in the lab, I jumped into all those vices I had skipped in high school and tried everything at once. I was like Christian the first time he walked into the Moulin Rouge. I wanted it all: boys and booze and cigarettes-with-booze and black stretch pants and tight tube tops worn to dark bars where I could drink at eighteen years old because I was blond and had a nice rack. I drew male attention I didn't realize would be there until I looked up and saw a dozen possible Dans with a fifth of vodka in hand looking back at me.

I hit straight As my first year of college (except for two ABs in Introduction to Computers and Precalculus). I made friends with some people in my building and on the newspaper staff—editors who worked hard to keep me from transferring to Rutgers University. They gave me the commentary editor job when I decided to stay. But I also spent a lot of hungover mornings sleeping in a library carrel. I napped in the library because my roommate, a weepy girl from Arizona, refused to leave our room in case her boyfriend from back home called. She spent much of that time doing *something* with the guy who lived across the hall.

I did not exercise. I had no desire to do so when New Jersey's August was reality in Florida for nine months out of the year.

Even in the state's weather glory days of December, January, and February, I was too busy relishing things like not sweating and wearing light sweaters to do anything that would reheat my body.

This, plus an introduction to southern cooking, hot wings, and beer, led to the dreaded freshman fifteen. I didn't look terrible. (When I tried to sign up for Weight Watchers, they rejected me because I was too light.) But I didn't feel great about the way I looked either, not when I compared myself to classmates who had picked Tampa because the weather meant they could be as naked as possible as often as possible.

Having a boyfriend ravenous for my body helped buoy my confidence in high school, as did having friends who were all shapes and sizes. One of my best friends in high school was rail thin with no chest or hips; another was Jessica Rabbit-buxom and used her chest to knock the soccer balls out of the air and drop them at her feet. They both considered their shapes an asset. I was a happy middle ground.

But they weren't in my dorm, and Dan wasn't there to worship at the altar of my body. Even if I hadn't lost the sharpness in my muscles that year-round sports had chiseled, I still would have felt like the Hulk when I put myself in a lounge chair next to campus pool bunnies who drank Diet Coke with their cigarettes and talked about how they dared not work out too much or else they'd look too mannish or bulky. (Yes, you could smoke by the college pool then. You could also smoke in dorm rooms, but not all dorm rooms—at the time I thought that partial smoking ban was very progressive.)

It was the fall of 1998. Britney Spears's "Hit Me Baby One More Time" came out that September. The ideal body shape was transitioning from the heroin chic of the early 1990s to cartoons: uber thin with perfect abs and big boobs, highlighted by fake orange tans and super-low-rise jeans.

My sophomore year, I joined a sorority. Although I'd been surrounded by girls on sports teams since I was seven years old, our collective focus there had been on smashing our opponents, no matter how dirty and bloody we left the field. Here, though, everyone was dipped in perfume and covered in body glitter, and I jumped feetfirst into the makeup aisle at CVS to try to keep up. My sorority wasn't the type to shame pledges into losing weight, but we still had a lot of very pretty girls who worried about how they looked all the time. They'd write down everything they ate, pass around diets ripped from exercise magazines, and debate about which one would help them lose the most weight the fastest. They spent hours on the elliptical, flipping through the next issues of those magazines while sweating off the beer binge from the night before. No one shrugged when a sister came back from winter break sporting a new pair of breasts. We didn't have Greek houses, but many of our sisters lived together in on-campus suites. One room featured pictures of Britney that the girls had cut out of magazines with handwritten captions that said, "Hey fatty. Want to look like me? Shut the fridge." They discussed how they could use stress as a way to stop eating, and agreed that the perfect lower body shape meant that your calves and knees touched but nothing else (this was before the term "thigh gap" existed).

Plenty of girls had issues with food and how they looked. I don't blame the sorority for this, because I saw it happen outside of the Greek system too, especially among athletes. But for someone who has a self-esteem gap—me included—that kind of obsession and groupthink can send the mind down a bad road. One of my younger sorority sisters weighed about ninety pounds: Her elbows pushed up against her skin, her hip bones' sharp points poked out above her low-rise jeans. Her blond hair, silky when she started school, thinned and faded, and her face became covered in lanugo, a peach-like fuzz that's a common side effect of anorexia. We all talked about being heavier than we wanted to be, and she did too. But she often obsessed about how no boys would want her at her "heavy weight." She told me she'd never fit into my clothes because she thought I was so skinny. I was horrified—my roommate and I tried to help her realize she had a problem and go to the school's counseling center. Secretly, she became my line in the sand. I didn't feel so bad about my body that I was going to starve it into submission. I might start wearing baggier clothing to class to hide what I thought were my inflating legs and waistline. But as long as I didn't lose touch with reality like she did, I was fine.

One solution was a simple one: running. Running was hard and would burn the most calories quickly. I was too embarrassed to go to the gym because I had never been in a gym before. When I peeked into the one on campus and saw a bunch of machines with weird levers and arms and ramps, I kept on walking. Running didn't need a gym. Plus I had sneakers and workout clothes that I'd bought for dorm lounging, so I didn't need anything new in order to run. So, once or twice every semester, I'd put on my Nike Air Pegasus sneakers, still streaked with paint from making banners for my high school's spirit week, and vow to run around campus.

The University of Tampa may have not been challenging to me, but it does have a gorgeous campus, anchored by Plant Hall, an old Victorian hotel that served as the center of school. Between Plant Hall and the Hillsborough River was Plant Park, which was small but stuffed with tall and squat palm trees, crabgrass, and a sidewalk. That's where I'd always start my run, with a spring in my step and determination to run 3 miles to counteract the plate of nachos I'd had for dinner the night before.

Yes, I am going to do this! Running is great, I will love it! I thought as I bounded away. *Yes! This is . . . hard! And hot! But I am going to love it!* The spring turned into a muted bounce. *Think about something else, like . . . Shakespeare! Or Dan! Or, no, not Dan!* The muted bounce became a shuffle, then a walk, and then I was that teenager again, dragging her feet up the cul-de-sac after thinking it might be nice for a nun to find her passed out on their lawn. I'd make it about a half mile before stopping in a humid mess of sweat and panting. My lungs burned, my clothes stuck to my body, and this time there was no ceiling fan to lie under to cool off, nor rollerblades to strap on—just a window AC unit in a cinder block dorm. I didn't like how I felt when I wasn't working out, but if turning myself into a heaving, sweating heap was the alternative, I had to find another way.

There was one aberration to this pattern. In the spring semester of my junior year, I shipped off to Oxford University as part of the University of Tampa honors program's study abroad exchange, which sent me to study post-World War II British theater and Shakespearean drama at the same cost as my University of Tampa tuition—and I could keep my scholarships. I convinced my parents to let me go after I won another scholarship to pay for my flights to and from the U.K.

I'd like to say that I set out every day to bramble forth through the English meadows and countryside and that's how I fell in love with having time by myself while exercising, but I really walked every day because I didn't have another choice.

The flat I shared with six other Americans was just outside the city center. I didn't have a car or a bike. I didn't come over with much money, and most of that was reserved for bars, so I didn't take taxis, and the only bus I rode was to and from London.

So I walked everywhere: to Tesco, Boots, the library that was once a twelfth-century church, one of the two Gap stores in town, whichever bar the Americans met at that night, meetings with my instructors (I didn't have actual classes; instead I met my professors once a week, go away and do some research, then come back with a six- to eight-page paper on what I'd learned).

I didn't exactly mind all this walking—even in the rain,

which was persistent. Plugging my ears with an iPod while walking wasn't a thing then because iPods didn't exist, so I stepped out the door and walked down High Street each morning with a blank mind. I let it wander around, with thoughts centering on calculating what time it was at home, themes in whatever Shakespeare play I was writing about that week, and that cute guy from the Naval Academy who lived in another American house in our program. I liked showing up with red cheeks, as if I'd accomplished something through the brisk effort of getting there.

When my dad visited (separately from my mom, of course— she had come a few weeks earlier), he went with me on my daily rounds and was agog at how much I walked.

"How do you walk all that way all the time?" he asked after he flopped into one of the two IKEA chairs in our living room. "That must be at least a mile each way. And then you walk everywhere in between."

I'd never thought about it. I did it because I didn't have another option to get from one place to another. Like when I mowed the lawn as a teenager, the brain space was a nice benefit, but one I didn't walk to achieve. I didn't notice a big change in my body, but was surprised that my clothes were a little baggy given the English penchant to drink a lot more throughout the day than I did at home—especially since I was legal at twenty years old—and that our frequent post-bar stop specialized in fries doused with shredded cheese and mayonnaise. English students were also a lot more covered up than my peacocking Tampa peers, draping themselves in layers of sweaters and scarves and raincoats while still managing to look stylish and appealing.

When I returned to America, and to Tampa, I fell back into old habits: feeling like the Hulk and looking for shortcuts to staying thin, then trying to run and flailing around before I stopped that too. After my last attempt to run during the fall of my senior year, I gave up on exercise and instead opted for the black coffee diet: Get a giant cup from the school's brand-new Starbucks and then go as long as I could that day without eating.

This became a place for my former competitive spirit to live. It became a game: How long could I last? How long could I ignore my hunger? If I made it to three o'clock, could I make it to four? Maybe five? Once I made it all the way through dinner.

Playing this stupid game was much easier than trying to find a new kind of exercise that worked for me. I was still flabbier and always tired, but I felt slimmer and chalked up the exhaustion to the vague idea of "college." I was editor of the student newspaper by then, applying to graduate schools and keeping up an active social life. Of course I was tired. Of course I wouldn't have time to eat full meals.

I didn't cover up so much at the pool, and I let my sorority sisters talk me into wearing lower-rise pants, then bought a thong to wear with them. While I had a few shaky moments when I pushed the food timeline too far—like when I nearly blacked out in the middle of the street while walking to my newspaper office—I knew I was not my ninety-pound sorority sister. I can see now that I was already on a dangerous path, but I kept telling myself I wasn't even close to doing to myself what she was doing to herself. The coffee plan worked—for a little while.

chapter 2

RUN FOR THE HEALTH OF IT 5K

JUNE 17, 2006

New Jersey Marathon — Mile 0

After the half marathoners started their race, I sat on the bench of a picnic table and listened to a mix of twelve songs that were played on every radio station at that moment but hadn't grown stale to me yet. I ate half a granola bar. I checked Twitter. There were no lines for the Porta-Potty, and I hit them once, then twice. I pulled off my sweats and stuffed them into the clear plastic bag I would check, ate the other half of the granola bar, and sat back down on the bench.

Police with German shepherds patrolled the start area, and a helicopter buzzed overhead. This race was less than three weeks after the Boston Marathon bombings. I'd been searched before I entered

Monmouth Park, and the finish line was already cordoned off. There would be no wall of screaming fans there to pull me through to the end. Mom planned to hand me a Clif Bar at mile 19.5, then drive to the finish line so she could stand as close to it as she could, despite me begging her to stand anywhere but there. It's not that I thought anything would happen—this race was too small a target, especially when a 32,000-plus-person race was running through Philadelphia in the Broad Street Run on the same day. But my heart was still raw after the bombings, not just because of heavy sorrow, but because the targets of that attack were people like my mom. I couldn't lose Mom. I didn't want to take a chance even if it was a slim one. But she ignored me.

I closed my eyes again and turned up the volume of my iPhone so Icona Pop blasted in my ears. Breathe in, breathe out. I've never been big into warm-ups. I didn't get the point when I was about to expel so much energy in a race. Shouldn't I be saving it? I maintained this despite what every running coach and every running expert has ever told me since I started running in 2006, and then writing about running for *Runner's World* and the *New York Times* in 2010. I wasn't going to change anything on race day, especially this one, when I was about to attempt conquering a distance that had vexed me three times before—once through injury and twice through terrible performances.

I peed one more time, stuffed my phone deep into my bag, slid a sleeve of Clif Shot Bloks—the package already torn slightly open—into my pocket, then hustled over to the gear-check trucks, because I knew they'd pack up when the national anthem started to play. Today the anthem was followed by "Sweet Caroline," in honor of Boston (it's the Red Sox's song). Around me, runners were dressed in neon or shades of blue and yellow, some wearing shirts that read BOSTON: UNITED WE RUN, which had been sold at the expo. I tried not to cry. In the last seven months, Superstorm Sandy had destroyed my favorite place in the world, and my favorite sport had been subjected to terror. And that wasn't even getting into the mess I'd made of my personal life in January.

I was in the last of four corrals. Each corral received the same treatment: A bugle played out "Call to Post," a cheeky reference to the race starting at a horse track, followed by a recording of Bruce Springsteen's "Born to Run" played at the exact moment the front of the corral crossed the starting line timing mat. I'd heard the same song at the start of the Chicago Marathon.

That's when tears pricked my eyes. Not just because of that song in that moment at that time—we were about to run through towns that had been picked up and chucked aside by Superstorm Sandy, and Springsteen wrote "Born to Run" about Asbury Park, which we'd run through twice, but on the street parallel to the ocean instead of the boardwalk because the boards were floating somewhere in the Atlantic. No, tears pricked my eyes because I knew what lay ahead. This wasn't my first race or even my first marathon. I wasn't going in blind. I knew what was coming: Pain. Anguish. A vise squeezed onto my legs, lungs, hips, and everything else in between. The always-hovering threat that I'd poop my pants. And the finish line, where I'd either revel in the glory of crushing my goal time or not. And after eighteen weeks of beating my body into shape for this moment on this day, what if I failed? What if, with all the bad decisions I'd made and how terribly my life had gone in the last seven months, I still couldn't get this one thing right?

"D CORRAL!" an announcer called. We shuffled forward, a swaying mass of nerves and energy with a slight sheen of terror.

"In the day we sweat it out on the streets of a runaway American dream . . ."

And we were off.

Seven years earlier, I stood on another starting line, this one in Medford, New Jersey, with a few hundred instead of a few thousand people. The goal distance was much shorter: 3.1 miles. I didn't run my first 5K because I suddenly realized the joy of prancing around in a sports bra and running shorts, or to raise money for a charity, or experience that mythical runner's high, or even because I was curious as to what all the fuss was about (by 2005, U.S. road races had nearly 9.5 million finishers, about 2.5 million more than in 1995, according to Running USA).

I ran it because a magazine paid me $750 to do it.

After college, I came back to South Jersey to work on a master's degree in English literature at Rutgers University–Camden. I thought I'd like to be an English professor. Twelve out of thirteen PhD programs I applied to thought otherwise. Rutgers let me into their Camden master's program with a promise to look at me again if I did well there—and Camden was a short drive from my mom's house, which meant I could live rent-free. I was still out of shape, and my black-coffee-no-food diet didn't work so well when I was living with a mother who expected me to eat breakfast with her. While going to school at night, I worked part-time again for my dad's company, writing press releases and newsletters for the marketing department, and I could not resist complimentary soft pretzel Fridays.

I tried some of those ridiculous magazine workouts that promised a beach! ready! body! In six! easy! moves! One featured exercises done in bed. The model, who looked like she was fifteen, wore pink menswear-inspired pajamas and did things like . . . stretch her arms in the air. I like stretching in bed, and I dig menswear pajamas, but it took one rotation through a workout of stretching into a yawn and lifting my feet above a pillow and then spreading my legs in what I assumed was something sex-related, wink wink, before I realized it was bullshit and would do nothing to get me back in shape.

And I was single again. After bouncing around between hookups through most of college, I met a medical student training to become an Air Force surgeon the last month of my senior year of college. He walked by my room while I was making cookies with the door open, and stopped to tell me they smelled good. Three weeks later, we took each other's virginity, and we swore we'd make it work while he went to medical school in Maine and I went back to home to New Jersey. As with most long-distance relationships, it didn't last.

I didn't attribute that relationship to anything special about me—sure, he thought I was smart and pretty and fun, as he told me many times, especially when we decided to split—but instead I chalked it up to an accidental meeting and both of us not wanting to leave college virgins.

I re-joined some of my high school friends who'd also moved home after college and went out to bars to survey the men before me, but also to size up the other women. Sure, my sorority sisters had instilled in me some womanly habits like wearing thongs and mascara, but I still felt like I was now swimming in an adult world without having grown up. I didn't know how to straighten my hair or do a smoky eye. Maybe if I lost a little weight, I could overcome those gaps in my knowledge of being a woman.

When I'd almost finished my master's degree, I quit working for Dad and started real full-time employment in the public relations department of a major Philadelphia hospital, a job I quickly despised. It wasn't because of the work, which was fascinating (whenever you hear a news report with the words "researchers have found that"—I interviewed the doctors to write the press releases that led to development of those stories), but because of my boss, who liked to pull my ponytail and call me "Jenny."

I'd also started writing commentaries for the *Philadelphia Inquirer* almost as soon as I moved back home, and had parlayed that into writing for a local South Jersey publication called *SJ Magazine*. The buzz from seeing my name in print in something other than a college newspaper was addictive and soon trumped my desire to become an English professor. I wanted more than three people to read my writing, so I passed on moving up to the PhD program. When the *SJ Magazine* editor quit and asked me to write for her at a new, competing publication, I called her former *SJ* boss and asked for her old job instead.

While editing that local yokel magazine, where I assigned and edited hard-hitting stories like "Top Doctors"(as determined by our advertisers), "Holiday Gift Guide" (as determined by our advertisers), and the "Best of SJ!" (as determined by our advertisers), I wrote articles on the side for cash and broke into a national book magazine, a Philadelphia lifestyle magazine, an airline magazine. Freelancing was my fallback plan since the magazine was under constant threat of closing, especially when I returned from a vacation to find the sales team had moved all of our files and computers out of the office, and I was told to work from home.

When my paycheck bounced ten months into the job, I quit (the magazine's since been sold to new, wonderful owners who seem to have a much better grasp on journalistic ethics *and* have made it a thriving publication). I'd scraped together enough freelance work to cover my $600-a-month rent, a $110-a-month student loan payment, and a few essentials like food and beer, so why not try freelancing while I was twenty-three? If I fell flat on my face, I could blame my failure on being young and stupid and get another office job.

But I didn't fall. I flew. This was in 2005, the go-go days of freelancing when everyone had vats of cash. I wrote an annual report for a state university's college of business; healthy-eating stories for a website published by General Mills; a travel article about places to drive your Jeep in New York City for *Jeep Magazine*, even though I neither owned a Jeep nor enjoyed New York City. I raised my hand, and work high-fived me back. I even wrote for the *Jewish Exponent*. I'm not Jewish. I am a blond-haired, blue-eyed Catholic who knew nothing about Judaism except that pork is not kosher. But another writer referred me to the magazine, and I turned in clean copy on time, so the editor kept giving me work. When he asked if I wanted to go through a fitness boot camp and write about it for the magazine, I said sure, why not? It's not like poking at my stomach was doing anything to firm it back up to high school shape, when I was hitting hundreds of softballs against a fence per day.

Boot camp class met three times a week at 5:30 AM at a playground with a track about a mile from my apartment. This wasn't one of those military porn-lite classes. The guy running the class was a nice man with oversized biceps who also owned a personal training company. He didn't yell or bark. He pushed—nicely—when I said I wanted to quit, and laughed when the class groaned at another session of planks and squats and sprints and burpees and crunches and arm exercises with stretchy bands that moved my muscles in directions they hadn't gone in years.

Boot camp also came with a diet, one that involved no carbs except at lunch, and no fat—period. Our trainer recommended things like fat-free soy nuts and fat-free cheese. I threw out everything in my kitchen that didn't comply, and except for my Saturday sandwich tradition with my mom (bologna and cheese with mayo and pickles on a roll), I stuck to it, applying the same determination that I'd used on my coffee-only college diet. I had incentive to do so. My weight and body fat had been measured before I started boot camp, and would be measured again after. That was the shove I needed for a fitness program to stick. No one wants to read a fitness challenge story where the writer is the same at the end. They wanted to read about progress! Solutions! Results! From a program that didn't seem too hard! I wanted to show readers that boot camp was magic by having the best outcome possible.

The food was disgusting. I assume rubber tastes better and has a nicer consistency than fat-free cheese, and trust me when I say that a fat-free soy nut snack is neither a nut nor really a snack. But it worked. The combination of three-day-a-week workouts and no-fat, no-carb grazing equaled a 6 percent body fat loss in a month. I had biceps and abs, and thighs that still touched but didn't jiggle so much when I walked. After boot camp was over, I joined a gym and started lifting free weights, watching meatheads to see what they were doing and copying their routines.

I knew I looked good. I took the class in the spring, and immediately that summer, I attracted more catalog model-looking men than I had before.

So I didn't mind being a little shallow for a while. I was buoyed by the attention. That summer, I crashed at friends' houses at the Jersey Shore and strutted around the beach in a red string bikini, then hit the bars at night and got numbers and someone to make out with on the beach until the cops came and shooed the dozen or so couples away. These hookups didn't go anywhere—and more often than not I'd wake up the next morning with a strange number and a headache—but I reveled in the fact that these kinds of men wanted me when they hadn't bothered to look at me before. I kept challenging myself to work out harder and cheat less often to see how far I could go, and I dropped another five pounds. *Thank you*, Jewish Exponent, *for that assignment*, I thought.

Not only had boot camp shoved me over my seven-year exercise slump, but that clip gave me enough ammo to pitch a story to a national women's magazine. Topic: running. But not just any running story. The angle was that I, the person who thought running was a socially acceptable form of torture, would train for a 5K. Yes, I would do that for $750 and a clip in a publication I could buy in a grocery store.

Another prong of the pitch was that I would train through this newfangled thing called online training. I signed up for a twelve-week 5K program with a guy named Lowell who ran an online coaching program. Online portals for coaching are the norm now, but this was in 2006, before iPhones and Fitbit and Internet on airplanes. I had only just gotten Wi-Fi in my apartment.

The training package included the following: one consultation phone call, an online training log, and weekly emails. After my boot camp workouts, a 5K didn't sound impossible. I didn't think this assignment would turn me into a runner. I figured my anti-running stance would make for a funny story.

I tried a few treadmill runs before I pitched the story, setting the machine for ten-minute miles and running in place with Guster in my ears and the Phillies on the TV in front of me. It was boring, but steady. I couldn't go out too fast if I was on a belt that did the pacing for me. I knocked out 3 miles in a half hour and didn't wheeze. The most exciting thing that happened in those thirty-minute segments was a squirrel snuck into the gym and ran under the treadmills.

I wanted to start my 5K training on the treadmill, too, but Lowell, in his initial consultation call, insisted that I run outside. The first run he had me do was 2 miles with the goal of pacing myself right so I wouldn't sprint and tire myself out like I had during my attempts running for running's sake in high school and college.

"Go slow, go slow," I repeated to myself as I walked down my apartment stairs to the street, then to the corner where I had set the route's starting line using Google Pedometer. By that time, I was renting the second floor of a house in Collingswood, New Jersey, a town that sat between the wealth of Haddonfield and its cousin Haddon Township and the poverty of Camden. As a result, Collingswood was a medley of grand turn-of-the-century mansions, row homes, bungalows, duplexes, and apartment buildings. For me it was perfect, a step up from my former one-bedroom apartment, but a bargain compared to where my other writer friends lived. I paid only $1,000 for 1,200 square feet. When I had briefly considered moving to New York City, a studio in Brooklyn—and not the nice part—

cost as much. I could write from anywhere, I reasoned, so why not write somewhere that was cheap and close to home?

That first run attempt happened on a pretty, clear day in April, right after I'd walked my dog and had a banana for breakfast. I ran on the treadmill with music to block out other people, but outside I left my iPod at home so I could focus on the task at hand. I had adopted Emily, my four-year-old Jack Russell terrier, the day before I moved into this apartment. She hunted tennis balls but was terrified of empty brown paper bags, and she did not understand why I put on sneakers but left her behind.

I didn't own what I'd call running clothes, instead wearing Target gym shorts, a cotton sports bra, and old college T-shirt. My shoes were the same I'd worn in boot camp: gray New Balances with worn treads that looked vaguely trailish.

"Go slow," I said again as I stood at the corner, finger on the Start button of my Timex sports watch. I took a deep breath, pressed the button, and set off down the street.

Running is controlled falling. Every time your foot hits the ground, your body absorbs three times its own weight. That's a lot of mass to be throwing around, no matter your weight, especially when that movement is new to your body. A treadmill can make the motion a little steadier, but when done outside, everything from a rogue bird to a tree root to a driver rolling through a stop sign can throw off that controlled motion. Running at length for the sake of running was frightening and almost violent: my shirt, my shorts, my arms, my head, my hair, flying up and down at the same time. As I hurled myself forward on that very first training run, I stared at my feet. One gray foot in front of the other, and repeat, repeat, repeat. When I tried to run in high school and college, I focused so much on not wanting to be there, and hating every second, that I didn't think about what I was doing. Then, I could quit if I wanted to, even with my dad waiting for me to come home. Here, I could not. I could not fail, not on my first run. I was scared, both of failing my new editor at the brink of what could be a big break in my writing career, and of my body failing too. What if I didn't get past that first run?

I didn't look up until I hit my first turn, which took me to Knight Park in the middle of town. It had soccer and baseball fields, a playground, and picnic areas, all ringed by a paved trail.

I had to look up, first to cross the street, and second so I didn't ram into one of the many women pushing strollers on the trail. I moved my "Go slow" mantra into my head, too, because I didn't want to scare anyone by talking to myself. I passed them without saying a word, not even a hello. I didn't want to risk adding any sort of movement that could turn into a real fall. As I turned away from the park and back toward home, my breakfast started to make itself known.

Don't puke. You don't want to write about how you puked. Not far now, not far now. How far? Not far. Not far.

When I reached the final corner and stopped my watch, I was panting, my shirt spritzed with sweat. I ran those 2 miles in nineteen minutes, seven seconds. The experience was terrifying. My legs shook, my lungs burned, my mouth tasted like mushed bananas and stomach acid, and I could barely breathe, but I did it, and I did not die.

Over the next twelve weeks, I ran five days a week. The feet-staring and "go slow" muttering stopped, and while I was still running with an aura of terror, I felt a little bit more confident with each workout, even though they didn't get any easier. They couldn't when Lowell had me doing interval training (400-meter sprint followed by 400-meter jog, then repeat) and weekend-long runs went up to six miles. Six! The race was only three!

I started changing up my route so I could see something a little different every day: Once I ran at twilight so I could lap Little League games. Another time I ran two towns over so I could browse yard sales. I stopped defaulting to the treadmill in the rain. I didn't feel like I was wringing out my lungs like a wet rag when I ran anymore, and didn't worry that I'd collapse on the way back to my house in the final mile of a training run. I dirtied up my brand-new red-and-white running shoes, and as I scrubbed mud off my legs I realized this could be fun.

I thrilled in every small victory: every "this is the longest I've ever run" run, every interval training set met, every time I went into a running store and didn't try to tuck my head into my shoulders like a turtle because I felt I didn't belong. I learned that cotton socks give me blisters, that a sports bra appropriate for the elliptical didn't contain anything when I ran, and, when I finally crossed the bridge into the world of Body Glide, that I could avoid stinging red welts on my thighs even though they still touched.

I felt *good* when I met the tasks Lowell laid before me.

Sometimes I stopped thinking about running while running. I looked up and I thought maybe there was something to this thing after all.

For the story, I chose to run the Run for the Health of It 5K in Medford, New Jersey, about a half hour from my apartment. My mom drove me to the race because I was a twitchy bundle of anxiety, and I wanted her there in case I broke myself. I had run further than 3 miles, yes, but never with other people trying to beat me at it. I didn't know how my pace compared to anyone else's. What if I went out too fast? What if I tripped? What if I was hit by a car flying through a police barricade and broke both my legs? Would anyone help me? If I crawled through the finish line, would the magazine let me write the story? Would they still pay me the $750?

What if I finished last?

"What if I finish last?" I asked my mom before shoving in earphones and trying to psych myself up with misogynistic rap. She pulled one ear phone back out. "I don't think that's going to happen. Look around you. There are people here like me." But I couldn't look around. I was still trying to figure out how to pin my bib to my sports bra. The race was in June on an 86-degree day with start temperatures in the 70s, so I didn't want to overheat by bothering with a shirt.

Lowell told me to do a 1-mile warm-up, but I was too nervous, and his request didn't make sense to me. Why tire my legs out before the actual race?

I gave my mother my iPod, made the sign of the cross, and put myself near the start line. Then the official announced the race was delayed while the police closed down the road leading to the finish line. I ran to the bathroom and peed again, made the sign of cross again, put myself near the starting line again. When "GO!" came through a megaphone—for real this time—I pushed off, bringing back my "Go slow" mantra to combat a surge of adrenaline that wanted me to spring out as dozens of runners around me did.

I let them go around me in the first quarter, then half mile. I ran the first mile in seven minutes, thirty-four seconds. I held steady and started passing people who went out too fast and were already Darth Vader-breathing halfway in. I hit mile 2 at fifteen minutes, twenty-two seconds, sweat already damping my sports bra. I passed another batch of runners walking while grabbing their sides, like I had done as a kid running that one-block lap. Between miles 2 and 3 my lungs tightened, and I felt the sun press down on my head and shoulders. I almost stole a water bottle from a spectator. But I didn't want to stop, and kept going, even as my legs and lungs protested. *One more mile, one more mile, one more lap, and you never have to do this again,* I thought. *And DON'T FINISH LAST.*

The end of the race was first set to end in the town park, but it had been moved on the day of the race to finish in a parking lot, which was a surprise uphill. I made the final turn, saw that steep climb, and wanted to weep. My legs already felt like pilings. I didn't know if they could make the climb. But there, at the top of the hill, I saw my mom, jumping up and down like a contestant who just won the Showcase Showdown on the *Price Is Right*.

Just get to Mom, I told myself, lungs and legs on fire. I reached her, and the finish line soon after. I put my hands above my head, which is what I had always done after soccer sprints because my coaches told me it was an easier way to suck in air. It wasn't working just then. I thought I might lie down on the grass and pass out for a little while when my mother caught me.

"I counted ponytails," she said. "I think you won something."

I finished in 22:12, good enough for third place in my age group. I won a mug and a $5 gift certificate to a place called Macho Taco that sold tacos for $6.

"Aren't you excited?" Mom asked at Club Diner, our local spot, after the race while I wolfed down a BLT.

"Um, should I be?" I replied. I was sore and stunned. That was not the outcome I would have expected. I didn't know how to feel.

When I turned in the article, my editor's first comment was that they couldn't publish my time. It was too fast for their readers, she said. I was surprised. I had no idea what was a good or a bad time. I thought I won something because the 5K was a small community race on the border of the Jersey Devil-producing forest of Pine Barrens. Lowell said that if I kept working with him, he could probably get me to under a twenty-minute 5K—whatever that meant (now I know: not pro-level, but pretty good).

I ended the article with the truth: "I don't know if I'll ever be a serious runner. But I know that I can now lace up and go out for a run. That's serene enough for me."

No one ever read it, though, at least not in a magazine. After a flurry of rewrites and revisions and then a check that came three months late, the entire staff at the magazine was fired, and a new crew came in. The article was lost in the shuffle. I was disappointed, but the check cleared, so I moved on to the next assignment.

Despite those moments when running turned to a joy, I didn't expect it to stick, not without a coach paid for by a magazine and a check waiting for me at the finish line. I figured I'd keep running as part of my regular workout routines, all of which were chosen because they burned as many calories as possible in the shortest period of time, and that the mug would be a souvenir of one of those athletic things I could say I tried, like boot camp and Ultimate Frisbee. You know, for that *one time* I ran a 5K.

chapter 3

OCEAN DRIVE 10-MILER

MARCH 30, 2008

New Jersey Marathon — Miles 0–7

With Bruce blasting, runners around me leapt ahead. I held back the urge to go with them, reminding myself that my goal was solid ten-minute miles for the first 20 miles. If I stuck to my plan, I knew that I would start passing a lot of those runners by the halfway point and then–fingers crossed, wood knocked, prayers said to St. Sebastian, the patron saint of athletes–blowing by them in those last 6.2 miles. My training may have been controversial. My longest run topped out at 16 miles instead of 20 as most American training plans do. Taken as a whole, though, the training program was designed to prepare my legs to maintain a pace at the end of the race instead of folding as they had in my last two marathons.

To distract myself, I looked at the crowd around me. I didn't wear headphones that day—I rarely do in races—and knew that ten-minute miles meant I'd be able to keep up a conversation while running. Also, any race longer than a 5K can be a slog. Talking to people keeps the miles interesting, and blocks my brain from obsessing about the pain that lies ahead.

But it will hurt. It will. It will.

In the first mile I fell into step with two thirty-something men who were either friends or brothers. They stared ahead, puzzled looks on their faces. I looked too: It was a young woman whose shorts were either too small or had lost the elasticity in the bottom of the legs. Her butt cheeks kept popping out of the bottom of her shorts, prompting her to pull down on them every thirty seconds.

I could tell the brothers/friends were trying not to look.

"Um," one said.

"Ah," said the other.

"She's going to be sunburned by the end of the race," I said. I'm not a pale person, but I knew that once we passed mile 10 and moved out of the year-round residential towns of the race, we'd lose trees and shade. After I'd dressed that morning, Mom sprayed me with sport-strength 30 SPF sunscreen in the bathroom of our hotel. I still smelled like chemicals, but I hoped I wouldn't have red shoulders by the end of the day.

"Oh, is that what we're looking at?" the taller brother/friend asked.

"How could you not? It's right . . . there," I said.

They both laughed.

"First marathon?" I asked them.

"Yup, and we're running it together," the shorter friend/brother said. "You?"

"Third," I said as we passed the second mile marker and crossed into a residential section of Oceanport, where more than half of the town's 2,400 homes had been damaged by Sandy. The first 7 miles would be a pretzel through residential streets of Monmouth and Oceanport, piling up miles for both the half and the full marathon before turning south.

"Any tips?" the taller brother/friend asked.

Before you lies a gauntlet that will test your body, your mind, and your soul. Unless you are in the small majority of people who have perfect first marathons, you will encounter waves of crushing pain that will stab you with such force in your legs, your butt, your feet, your toes to bring strong, strapping men and women to their knees. Or at least make them sit on the curb.

"Well, it might hurt. But you'll get there in the end—somehow," I said instead.

They were running slightly faster than I wanted to go. "I have to drop back to save my legs for later in the race," I said. "Good luck! And remember: You will get there!"

"Have a good race!" the taller brother/friend said.

"Yup! You too!"

At mile 3, shadows started to form as the sun pushed away the clouds that had sat over us for the start of the race.

I passed Oceanport's town hall and police station, still empty since Sandy. Because sections of this area of the race were still unsafe, we wound turn after turn through town, and at mile 4.5 I saw streams of runners moving in two different directions, like twin neon ribbons winding through otherwise quiet, empty streets.

Spectators were sparse until mile 5.5, where high-fiving Team in Training coaches were set up at the foot of a bridge to cheer. We turned onto what's become known as Pork Roll Alley. Residents set up smokers and grills and yelled for runners while eating BBQ processed meats and drinking beers and Bloody Marys out of red Solo cups.

"Go, runners, go!" one man in a bathrobe yelled, grill tongs with a sausage stuck on them held up in the air.

"I will, man!" I shouted back. "I will!"

At mile 6.5, I crossed over a concrete bridge on Monmouth Avenue, the only hill in the race. "Hill" is a relative term, since it's barely more than a lip over water in an area where the only other hills are dunes. The flatness of the course is one reason I signed up for this marathon, along with staking a claim back in my home state at my Jersey Shore. As I passed a still-closed school, I saw two runners dressed in black long-sleeved shirts push those sleeves up to their elbows. The sun poked through clouds in chunks, and I knew that the run through Deal—which provided little to no shade and would be run through twice—was going to be worse for them than for me.

It was a pretty start to the race, but a somber one, despite the party at Pork Roll Alley. We ran by houses that were either empty or under construction or being raised to meet new, shifting flood requirements. Driveways held storage units instead of cars. I had written about the Jersey Shore for seven years for magazines and newspapers, plus I'd written two books about the southern part of the coast. Watching Sandy rip apart half of the Jersey Shore was hard, but the slow-motion disaster of recovery was more painful. Already, fights about insurance and recovery funds had broken out, and I knew that it wouldn't get better anytime soon (as of 2015, many of these homes are still empty, as are the Oceanport town hall and police station, and construction on Long Branch's replacement boardwalk started only in June of that year).

I wrote about the race for the *New York Times*, and drove the course six weeks earlier with race director Joe Gigas, gut churning at all of the destruction around us—not just the empty homes but the giant trash piles where people dumped what they couldn't use, the contents of restaurants and beach clubs still out on their lawns.

Still, those towns were determined to put on the races—and Gigas was, too, even though Sandy had bit into his house and swallowed the contents of four rooms. I'd talked to the mayor of Long Branch for my story, too. He was running in the half marathon for the fourth time, and he said that despite the destruction around the course, the race would go on.

"Watching these municipalities deal with this," Gigas told me, a quote I used in the *Times* story, "and then there's me asking, 'Can I run through your town?' No one said no. It's that Jersey can-do attitude."

I came up to mile 7, right before the course turned south for the race's long turn down the coast, and checked my Timex: one hour and ten minutes on the nose. Perfect ten-minute miles. My legs and lungs felt fine. I was running smoothly, my breathing calm.

But it will hurt. It will hurt. It will.

Seven miles had flowed under me as easily as the water under that concrete bridge. Panic and pain held at bay. Just 19.2 to go.

I kept running after that first 5K in Medford, but not in the same way. Training wasn't done to drop my time in a race. It became a tool in my arsenal of staying in shape, in part driven by Stephen.

We met at a networking party at a then-*hot! new! bar!* in Center City, Philadelphia, that has changed hands five times since. When he said hello to me while I waited for a glass of wine—which I ordered in an effort to appear sophisticated despite the women in butt-exposing cocktail dresses and bros in cheap suits ordering shots around me—I almost dropped my wallet. I had been paddling around in the younger end of the dating pool, hooking up with law students and junior associates and assistant project managers who still lived with six of their closest friends and thought defaulting on student loans was funny.

But here was this 100 percent American man in a black leather jacket, snug white shirt pulled across his chest, and faded olive khakis. He had bright white teeth and ruffled black hair that together screamed charm. I would learn soon that he was a grown-up too, with a grown-up job, a house, two dogs. I was twenty-three. He was thirty-five. He was the kind of adult I wanted to be—someone who had seen some shit and lived to tell the tale. He was smart, confident, successful, and as far away from the guys who still went out on Tuesdays for quarter beer night as I was from the moon.

We started spending a lot of time together, first because we kept bumping into each other, then by choice. By the time I left the magazine to try my hand at freelancing, we were calling or texting or emailing every other day, then every day—but just as friends. Very chummy, close friends.

Stephen was sober when I met him. His father had been an abusive alcoholic who went into rehab again while Stephen and I were becoming friends. When we went to his father's condo a year later, Stephen tore apart the place to make sure his father hadn't hidden any booze there.

"I can't stop at one drink," he said to me as we ate lunch at a diner a few days after the rehab phone call. "So I just don't start."

I, of course, was completely in love with him. I had never felt so at ease with someone—man or woman—in my life. I asked him once if he would consider dating, and he said no because he didn't want to ruin our friendship. My choices then were to give up on him or stay friends. I chose the latter. I had watched the despair of my parents' marriage, and I knew I never wanted to be trapped with a person who made me so miserable. I wanted to be with someone I considered a friend, someone who made me feel like Stephen did, and until I either met that person who felt the same way back or I changed Stephen's mind, friends we'd be.

It was during this friend-zone time that I started the boot camp. Stephen took an interest in that too. He was a workout fanatic, and it showed. The more weight I lost, the more he encouraged me to "get on the next level" of fitness. Maybe if I substituted a protein shake for one meal a day, like I'd read in a magazine, I could burn more fat and build more lean muscle. In the weight room, he said, I should stop doing high repetitions with five and ten pound weights and instead switch to lower reps with heavier weights.

"Don't be scared of lifting a lot," he said. "You're stronger than you think."

Swoon.

He told me I should show it off, too, which I did: backless mini dress to a magazine event, low-rise jeans with lace halter crop top to a birthday party. He went with me to each of these, not exactly as my date but more as the older brother, the designated driver.

All that changed on an October night, soon after my twenty-fifth birthday. I was out having dinner with a group of musician friends in Old City in Philadelphia. After dinner at a crummy Mexican restaurant with plastic tablecloths and plastic utensils and terrible food but cheap margaritas, our group crossed over to Plough and the Stars. During the day it was a respectable, quiet, and cozy Irish restaurant that served dishes like Guinness casserole and shepherd's pie, but on weekend nights it became a sweaty-bodies-pressed-together-girls-crying-on-the-phone-in-the-bathroom club. I was standing on the second-story balcony, which shook to the bass of a dance remix of some pop song while a famous violinist tried to stick his tongue down my throat when my cell phone buzzed.

"I fell off the wagon," Stephen yelled over the background noise of whatever bar he was at. "Where are you?"

The Stephen who walked in was not the guy I knew, though. He was bad boy incarnate, his swagger writ large. He wore ripped jeans and a graphic T-shirt and had one cigarette in his mouth with another tucked behind his ear. His movements were exaggerated, his laugh louder, his eyes brighter. He didn't look like the same person, but like a cousin just sprung from jail who was ready to party. The calm, contemplative best friend was gone, and "Steve," as he insisted I call him, stood in his place.

"Scram," he said to the musician, nudging him aside so that we leaned together, hip to hip, against the balcony railing. He lit my cigarette, which I'd bummed off the musician before he scurried away, off his own.

"I don't believe what I'm seeing!" he barked over the music, staring at me. I hadn't smoked since college. I never got the appeal, but I did it there at the Plough and the Stars for the same reason I had done it in college: because I was that boring girl who always listened to the rules, always went to class, always did her job. Everything about smoking was wrong, and I wanted to show that I could be a little bit wrong, too. I had to show Steve that I was a fun girl, someone other than the person he saw as his best friend. "This is not the Jen I know!" he yelled, then licked my earlobe.

When Plough and the Stars closed at 2:00 AM, he took me

to an after-hours club located under a parking garage, pushed me up against a wall, and smashed his mouth against mine while running his fingers up my shirt and under my bra. On the way to his friend's house, where I crashed for the night, I puked out the cab window. I woke up next to him, and puked again, barely making it to the bathroom. After the first time we had sex in a drunken blur a few weeks later, I woke up with bruises on my hips and ribs.

This went on for a year and a half. He liked me. Then he didn't. He didn't want to see me at 7:00 PM on a Saturday night, but he'd call me at midnight saying, "I need you," and I'd get out of bed to meet him at some no-name bar in the middle of the woods, and play Big Buck Hunter until he hailed us a cab and threw me into his bed.

There's no other way to put it: That year and a half of my life sucked. It sucked for a lot of reasons: There's the obvious that being my former best friend's long-term booty call was a time-consuming and soul-draining occupation, but also drinking a lot and smoking a lot didn't make me feel great physically.

Then there was the mental weight. I put a lot of the blame for our half relationship, for the way I couldn't quite make him love me, on myself, a notion that he encouraged. He told me I should highlight my hair (which he offered to pay for), dress sexier, do *something* to make him turn that corner. Alcoholics can be miserable and manipulative, and he knew what he was doing to me, even if—I know, I know—he wasn't entirely in control of his actions.

"You HATE me," he yelled over the phone on one of the nights he made his friend call me back after I hung up twice. "You HAAAAAAATE me." Part of me did. But I went to him anyway. If Steve was going to that much trouble to get a hold of me—if he said he needed me that badly after I told him to leave me alone—maybe we were close to a breakthrough. Maybe if I went this one time, the back-and-forth would finally be over, I'd get my Stephen back, and we would just be together.

"Drink," he'd say as soon as I walked through the door. "Start now. You're behind."

When I was thirteen years old, Avalon, the shore town I've gone to every summer of my life, started a dredging project to widen the beaches. They took sand from the ocean floor and transferred it onto land. It worked, but it also kicked up seaweed. A lot of seaweed. I was determined to swim anyway, but it clung everywhere, catching in the crooks of my elbows, my knees, my hair. I tried to float over it on a boogie board, but it hooked onto the strap that connected the board to my wrist and weighed me down.

That's what dating Steve was like. In David Carr's memoir *The Night of the Gun*, he called this kind of relationship a "minuet of misery." As Stephen dropped deeper into alcoholism, creating and breaking his own rules (it's not a problem if I only drink on weekends, it's not a problem if it doesn't affect my work, it's not a problem if I'm a little hungover at work), and as his calls became later, more frantic, and more frequent, he pulled me down too.

That first 5K in Medford came eight months into this mess. I had managed to eat enough to maintain that training, skating on the edge of eating too little to be too small, but I plunged over the edge soon after. I kept running after that 5K, but it was for him. I wanted to be as small as possible, and I saw running as a path toward that goal. I had a strength training routine down. I was in the weight room four days a week, lifting twenty, twenty-five, thirty, forty, fifty pounds at low reps just like Steve said, but I still didn't look like Jessica Alba from *Sin City*, who he had on a poster in his basement. "You can look like that," he said one night as we played pool, Jessica staring down at me as I tried to sink the eight ball. (I didn't. I scratched.)

If I do that, if I can look like that, I told myself, it'll finally flip that switch in him, turn a relationship held together by spider webs into something solid and real. Running burned more calories an hour than any other cardio I could do in the gym. Running needed to be part of my life then so I could show Steve what I was willing to do for him. I didn't enjoy the miles like I used to. Those days of bounding around Knight Park being serenaded by birds and kids and Little League games were gone. Now I was trapped in the run, like I was trapped with him, trying to use one as the means to an end with the other.

The more I drank, the more I smoked, the less I ate. I vowed to do better with my no-carb, no-fat diet: No more slip-ups. No more carbs at all. And if I did make a mistake—a plate of cheese-covered nachos when out with friends, Saturday sandwiches with Mom—I puked it back up. It wasn't that different from throwing up after a long night of drinking, right? So what was wrong with getting rid of too much food?

On one cool morning six months before the end, when we hadn't called or texted or emailed in nearly a week—a new record!—I went for a run. It was a gorgeous, clear day, the first one after the summer heat had finally broken. The world felt wiped clean. Maybe, I thought, that day could be a new start for me too.

I ran straight for Knight Park on my usual 3-mile route. I started feeling that strength again that I had found in training for the 5K, in moving my body forward, one step at a time. But one minute I was looking at the war memorial on the corner of the park and the next I was staring up at the concerned face of a mom and her two-year-old.

"You okay?" she asked as her toddler yelled "Boo-boo! Boo-boo!" over and over again. "You just went down." I was 115 pounds, a weight I hadn't been since middle school.

"Oh, I'm okay. I didn't drink any water today," I lied, and let her help me stand up. My vision started to fade again, so I held on to her shoulder.

"Let me drive you home," she said.

"No, I'm okay," I said, first to her, then to her son, whose eyes were now wide with terror. I played peek a boo with him until he smiled and offered me his binkie. My vision had stopped graying by then, and I shuffled home.

I spent a lot of late nights on the message boards of Al-Anon, the companion group to Alcoholics Anonymous for family, friends, and children of alcoholics. The group has its own twelve steps, and the first is "We admitted we were powerless over alcohol—that our lives had become unmanageable." It is, word for word, the same first step as Alcoholic Anonymous's twelve steps.

I never went to a meeting because I could never get to that first step. I stopped talking to my friends about it because they were sick of hearing about it. I blamed myself for Steve's problems. I was there on the night he started drinking again, and I told myself he kept drinking because I could not fix him. How could I quit on him now? I didn't want to give up on Stephen even though Steve had become a monster.

"Maybe we should get married," he said one early March day in 2007, after another late-night call, another bottle of pink wine, and drunk sex I sort of remembered. We were lying in bed at about noon, staring at the new paint on his bedroom walls; three different colors of green on three different walls. He had called me at 1:00 AM the night before, and of course I went. My dog was at home and had probably wet her crate. I knew I needed to leave, but I didn't want to break the moment. "We have fun together," he said. "Maybe this is what it's supposed to be like."

Soon after, his Myspace page filled with posts from a gangly woman with an overbite. One late night after we shared a pack of cigarettes, a six-pack of beer for him, and a bottle of wine for me, he broke the news to me that she was his girlfriend, even though he had fucked me a week before. He told me, while holding my hand, that she "did that thing for me that you never could." What that thing was, he didn't say. I'll never know. He thought we could all be friends, he said, lightly stroking the back of my hand. "I'll keep you in the top eight of my Myspace friends."

I yanked my hand from his, knocked the empty bottles off the table, then stormed out, slamming the door behind me. I drove home, drunk and white-knuckled. I emailed him the next day telling him to never contact me again.

For once, he listened. I didn't reach out to him either. I was humiliated. I had wasted a year and a half trying to prove I was enough for someone, again. I hadn't been enough for Dan to at least try dating when we went to different colleges. I hadn't been enough for my college boyfriend. I hadn't built a relationship with any of the men I dated after, because I was not enough for them to try. I opened my body to them, but I wasn't enough of a whole human being for them to want more than that night or string of nights. With Stephen, I thought I was close to finally being enough for someone, and I failed. Again.

The seaweed pulled me under, and I sank even deeper when my grandfather died in May. I was so blinded by grief that I couldn't look further than the week, sometimes the day, ahead. I had a few one-night stands—a bookseller from San Diego, a guy who had once turned me down when I asked him to a dance in eighth grade—but then I took my post-breakup mania a step further and bought a house, a three-bedroom row home in Collingswood, the same town where I'd been renting. My timing was spectacular: I signed the loan papers seven months before the first domino in the Great Recession fell.

My work slowed to a crawl soon after. Editors I loved were fired. Others didn't return my emails. Even the *Jewish Exponent*, my first regular client, stopped assigning at the same frequency. My income halved. Not only was I a sad bundle of bones and skin, but I was an almost-broke one.

That summer I shuttled back and forth between my house and Avalon to write my first book, a travel guide to the Jersey Shore. The advance was meager, but enough to pay for a part-time share in the bottom floor of a bay-side rental with twelve other people. I didn't strut around in a red bikini like I had two summers before. I rarely made it to the beach. Instead I worked during the day, walking these shore towns block by block to take menus, browse gift shops, and write down amusement pier ticket prices. At night I drank, either cocktails made from the makeshift bar in the rental and consumed on the porch until I passed out, or overpriced Miller Lites at the Princeton, a popular bar at the northern end of the island known for its sticky floors, crowds, and unreasonable prices for crappy light beer. I knew no one in Avalon (I found the rental on Craigslist), and I slipped into the background while telling myself I was part of the crowd.

I turned in the manuscript in September. I stopped seeing friends and only showered on days I ran, and they weren't even good runs. They were short, stuttering attempts that maxed out at 2 miles. I found no joy in them. They no longer served a purpose—not even a dark one. They hadn't won me Steve or Stephen, so why bother? Running had failed me, like he did, but I felt a pull toward both, still. I checked my email hoping to see an apology from him, but it never came. I set out on runs hoping I'd feel that soaring feeling from the year before, but it never came. I'd run, then walk. Sometimes I sat down. Once I lay down on a pile of leaves in the park. I didn't care if I scared another toddler or his mother. I was too tired to move on, and stood up only after I was almost run over by a landscaper on a lawn mower bagging leaves.

Five months after the break up, I came out of my hole to help my mom pack up her parents' house since my grandmother was moving into a nursing home. I made it to the top of the stairs on the second floor, then lay down and started sobbing. She sat down next to me, put my head in her lap, and ran her fingers through my hair. I told her everything, and she suggested that maybe I get some help.

I signed up for my first ten-mile race instead.

(I probably should have found a therapist. When I wrote about this seven years later in the *New York Times*, my editor titled the essay, "Running as Therapy." I received a lot of emails from other runners who had also used running to work through break ups, divorce, unemployment, and grief, but an equal number of emails chastised me for suggesting self-care for the depressed. That headline—and piece—was dragged through the mud of the Internet again when Robin Williams, who was a biker and runner, committed suicide. I was told that writing like mine was responsible for people killing themselves. If you have a problem, seek professional help. And maybe try running, too.)

I chose a 10-mile race instead of a half marathon because I thought 13.1 miles was too daunting. A full marathon? Please. I could barely run 2 miles without being killed by a lawn-mower. Ten miles seemed a more reasonable goal. I found out about the Ocean Drive 10-Miler, which was part of the Ocean Drive Marathon, while researching the book. Both races are named after the road it travels, which connects Cape May to five barrier islands of the South Jersey Shore. The 10-Miler started in Cape May in front of Congress Hall, a beautiful hotel I visited often while researching my book, and ended on the boardwalk in North Wildwood.

Cost: $40. I could afford that, but I couldn't afford Lowell without a magazine's budget, so I typed "free 10-mile training plan" into Google and landed squarely on Hal Higdon.

Hal Higdon was one of the leaders of the first running boom. He's been writing for *Runner's World* since 1966, before the magazine was even called that, and he cofounded the Road Runners Club of America, which now has 2,300 chapters.

All I cared about then was that his schedule was free and the training didn't look too difficult. His novice program for a 15K race (which at 9.3 miles was close enough to 10 miles) called for ten weeks of training with four days of running each week, plus one day of cross training and one day for both stretching and weights.

Since I doubted I could run 10 miles in one shot, I planned to get to the finish line by running nine minutes, walking one, and then repeating the process.

Four days a week before lunch, I slipped on my running shoes, plus gloves and a hat since I trained in January, February, and March. Hal had me start at 2 miles, and I worked my way up to 8.

In an interview on the American Public Media radio show *On Being* with Krista Tippett, which airs on our local NPR station, Katharine Jefferts Schori, the twenty-sixth presiding bishop of the Episcopal Church and sub-four-hour marathoner, said, "Runners begin to understand the blessing that comes with putting the body to work and emptying the mind." She was referring to prayer, but I had stopped going to church in college. Those long runs were the closest I came to going back.

Running for long periods of time—an hour, an hour and a half—prepares you to be on your feet for extended periods of time in a race, and those long runs are supposed to be done at a slower pace. This gave me a lot of time with myself. I don't run with music outside, so the only thing I carried with me was my mind. In those first weeks, it was the breakup. It was work. It was the broken washing machine in my new house. It was how I was going to afford the mortgage and the electricity bill and the heating bill that month.

But as my long runs stretched to over an hour, I got sick of myself and my whining. So I started thinking about other things, too, like who lived in that house on the park grounds?

Or how much did it cost to maintain the baseball fields? Who picks up the dog poop in the dog park? Would my dog like it there? These were silly questions for which I didn't have answers, and still don't (except: No, my dog would not like the dog park), even though that same park is still on my regular training route. By filling my head with nonsense, I emptied my mind. The seaweed floated off and hovered over me, as if I'd taken a deep, fast dive. It wasn't gone, but running suspended it, briefly, and released me, letting my arms and legs swing and move and my mind breathe freely, at least for the time I was on the road.

Cold-weather running was a joy I had not known when I trained for that first 5K. Then I ran the most during May and June. I'd start sweating a few steps in, even if I ran at 5:00 AM to beat the sun, because you can't get up early enough to beat the New Jersey humidity. In the winter, though, I breathed deeply and ran in cold, bright air without feeling like my lungs were clogged. I still sweat, but lightly, without that sweat running down the backs of my legs or soaking my shoes. In the winter, I ran with my face turned toward the sun. Running to break up the morning gave my day more of a definition, too: Walk dog, eat, work, run, eat, work, walk dog, eat, sleep.

I focused on running 1 mile at a time because running 1 mile eight times was less terrifying than running 8 miles once, then I applied the same strategy to my work: Find one client to replace the magazine I just lost, get one extra assignment from a client who had kept me on. I became an expert in financial distress, using my own life as material for website articles that paid 50 cents a word. The rate was lower than I was used to, but the editors were so thirsty for content about the recession that they assigned me a raft of short, easy work that I could write quickly. That work kept me afloat.

I still spent a lot of time alone in my house, a house I couldn't afford, but I made an effort to integrate myself back into my old social life. I went to happy hour. I went to the movies. I went to parties. I went to a cousin's wedding shower and did not want to kick a wall. I even went on a few dates. They weren't great dates, and most were fix-ups with unsuitable men, like the forty-two-year-old marketing executive who lived two hours away, the twenty-one-year-old unemployed kid of my uncle's best friend. But having dates meant that I showered, put on an outfit that did not involve an elastic waistband, and smiled through tedious getting-to-know-you questions. I even dated a business analyst for six months without thinking too hard about where the relationship would go. I dated him for the sake of that moment: for company, for sex, for someone to talk to, not as a way to change the course of my life forever and ever amen.

I started to get my body back, too. I no longer tried to manufacture muscles with weights. Instead, I built strength that had purpose. My quads galvanized, my calves strained against my lace-up boots. Training for a long-distance race pulled a hunger out of me that I had fought for two years. So I cooked: recipes from *America's Test Kitchen* and *Runner's World*, a magazine that I also put on my pitching target list. And I ate: beef stir-fry, pasta with mushrooms and broccoli, salads with full-fat feta cheese and olives and olive oil. I re-learned what real food was, and why I needed it. I started to lose the bony look. My cheeks came back. I could no longer see the top of my rib cage pushing up out against my skin. I threw out my scale.

Running became a way for me to take back part of myself, even when I was the one who let others take advantage of me so quickly. I was ashamed that I let Stephen do that to me, and that I had whittled myself down to a matchstick in hopes of changing his mind. The more miles I ran, the stronger I felt, and, though not recovered, at least I made it to a point where I could look for the new road ahead.

Race day was frigid, especially for March. When I woke up, it was 32 degrees with a howling wind. I stayed overnight in Cape May, in the first-floor apartment of a friend who lived across the street from the beach. He decamped to his girlfriend's place so I could terrify myself with every scenario of what could go wrong without anyone watching me. I woke up at midnight, 2:00 AM, 4:00 AM, before finally giving up at 5:00 to get up and try to read away my stress, picking books from his shelf at random and pretending I could find an interest in shipbuilding and 1950s pulp novels, when all I wanted to do was puke. My longest run leading into the race was 8 miles. How was I ever going to do 10? Sure, an extra 2 miles doesn't sound like a lot, but wouldn't they be insurmountable when stacked on top of another 8 miles? What if I didn't make it? What if race officials had to send the tram car that ran up and down the

Wildwood boardwalk in the spring and summer to pick me up? Usually the tram blasted "Watch the tram car, please." Would they change it up just for me? "Watch the passed-out runner, please," and charge me $2 for the ride? I didn't carry any cash on me during races.

An hour before the start, I ate my Cheerios with a banana and whole milk, put on my race gear (long-sleeved top, matching shorts—because I hated running in tights, even in cold weather—plus hat and sunglasses), peed three times, paced inside until fifteen minutes before race time, then walked the quarter mile to the start. I cut through a food and games pavilion, shut down until the summer, and I was stunned by what I saw.

That first 5K was a small community race. This one looked massive to me: Hundreds of runners waited on the lawn of Congress Hall, stretching or talking or laughing. Laughing! Some of these people were about to run a marathon—a marathon!—and they thought something was funny? What could be funny about forcing your body to the absolute limits on a 32-degree morning with a steady eleven-mile-per-hour wind? Who was sick enough to see some kind of humor in that? If I wasn't laughing, maybe I wasn't ready. Maybe I should just get in my car, drive back home, and burn my running shoes in my sink. At least I'd save a couple bucks on my heating bill that way.

But the surge of runners walking toward the starting line carried me forward. I had no time goal, so I drifted toward the back of the crowd lining up on Beach Avenue, the big, grand, nearly two-century-old yellow hotel on our left, and the ocean on our right. Ten-milers wore yellow tags; marathoners wore white.

"First race?" I heard from behind me. This came from an older woman, close to my mom's age. She was short and wearing long tights and long sleeves, a small fanny pack around her waist and sunglasses on top of her head. Her tag: white.

"First ten-miler."

"You'll be fine."

"I don't . . . well . . ." I said.

"Sure you will. This is my twentieth marathon. You get used to it."

Twenty. TWENTY! No. NO. A marathon was a bucket list thing to be done once in a lifetime. No one did twenty. This woman must be a crazy person. She was old. She wore a fanny pack unironically. She could not be trusted.

I would not be fine. I would not . . .

My panic was interrupted by the national anthem. Then the megaphone let off a siren, and the crowd pushed forward. I was on my way, running through spectators that lined both sides of the first quarter mile, then tapered away as we continued down Beach Avenue.

The plan was to run for nine minutes, walk for one minute, then run again. This was a recommended tactic on many running message boards I'd read before the race, and it took a bit of pressure off me to run straight through 10 miles. I felt stupid stopping nine minutes in, right at the point where the Victorian-era core of the beach town gave way to motels and condos. I wasn't alone in doing so, but most run/walk/runners had white tags.

It's okay. Okay. Okay. O.K. Corral? What? No, run. Run.

I had a plan and I was going to stick to it. On this course, right before the mile 3 marker, runners hit the bridge that connects Cape May to the rest of the Jersey Shore. It doesn't look like much when you're driving over it, but it's a long, steady climb on foot, and anyone who went out too fast dropped away when they hit that bridge. I did not, and turned at the foot of the bridge to follow the pack down the Ocean Drive.

The scenery changed here too as I ran on the strip of road that connected Cape May to Wildwood Crest: Gone were buildings and crowds, and in their place reed grass that looked bleached and burnt—but still standing—after being beaten down by salty winter winds. I'd driven over this section of the Ocean Drive dozens of times, but more as a way to avoid traffic on the Garden State Parkway than to look at the scenery. I never stopped to see what I was passing through, which you can't help but do when you're running at a blazing speed of six miles per hour. I read the names of boats dry-docked for the winter (*Chef's Mess, Nuttin' Fancy,* and *Finsanity*). I watched the reed grass blow in that steady eleven-mile-per-hour headwind that gusted up to twenty-three miles per hour that morning. I looked at the sky, a brilliant blue that looked like it'd been dipped in egg whites, a color that can't be replicated in the summer. If I looked at the water, the boats, the sky, the other runners, I told myself, I wouldn't think about how that wind was making my face go numb. The road was closed to spectators, so the only people around were cops, EMTs, and other runners.

I started to forget about not being able to do it by doing it. The walking minutes gave my body a break, especially after mile 5. There, reed grass gave way to shorter, scrubbier cordgrass that grew out of the salt marsh and where fiddler crabs were burrowed until summer. That was about where I felt like those crabs had pinched themselves to my legs. But mile 5 was also where I really started passing other runners, even with my walk breaks. I charged onto the toll bridge (where almost every runner pretended to pay the tolls) and back down the other side, then passed signs for Methodist, Greek Orthodox, and Crest Community summer church service times, which signaled we were almost to Wildwood Crest; then we were in Wildwood Crest, where we hit cottages and motels and—finally—saw some spectators other than emergency services providers. Most looked like they had woken up surprised to find a race outside their front doors but cheered us on with their morning coffee from their decks and porches anyway.

My legs felt like they were sinking toward my shoes by mile 8, and my toes pounded with pain from banging against the fronts of my sneakers, but I was determined to keep on. *Don't stop don't stop don't stop.* I hit the boardwalk in Wildwood at mile 9, running up the ramp to the boardwalk because a group of high school kids screaming at the top told me to. I turned onto the boardwalk and hit the wooden boards, which pushed back up against my feet. I felt like I was bouncing on pogo sticks after pounding the asphalt for 9 miles.

On the boardwalk, we lost those homes that sheltered us from the wind. Here, it slammed into us from the right and rattled the gates covering the closed T-shirt shops and pizza joints on my left. At mile 9.5 the wind ripped off my hat, but I didn't stop to get it, not when I was so close.

The finish line was near Montego Bay, in front of a big yellow building with a motel and water park inside. I moved onto the concrete strip usually used by the tram car at the same time a woman with a toddler started to cross in front of me. I was so close to finishing that I would not have had one qualm about stomping on a toddler or her dumb parent if they stood in my way.

"GET OUT OF MY WAY, LADY!" burst out of my mouth along with my last pained breaths of the race. My mother and sister, who had driven straight to the finish line that morning, started screaming when they saw me.

When I crossed that finish line, a volunteer put a square medal with seagulls wearing running shoes around my neck, and a silver space blanket around my shoulders. I wanted to crawl out of the finishers chute because my knees shook and my quads spasmed, but my mother grabbed me, pulled me out, then held me close in a bear hug. I sobbed into the shoulder of her puffy coat while my sister tried to throw a fleece blanket around my legs. It wasn't just the race, but relief that out of all the crap in my life that I couldn't control, this one thing I set out to do, I did.

My time: 1:36:19. No records. Not even close. But finishing the race was more than enough for me.

That fall, I ran into Steve and his girlfriend in a shoe store. On a whim, I had just accepted an invitation to join the man I was dating in Siena, Italy, where he was working, and I was shopping for a new pair of walking shoes. I saw Steve first: the leather jacket, the bright white teeth. He introduced her as if she were a pageant contestant: this bag of skin and bones with the same sunken eyes I had during my Steve drinking days.

I don't remember what she said. I was focused on trying to say the right things: boyfriend, Italy, boyfriend, Italy (even though he wasn't really my boyfriend). Did I mention I'm shopping for shoes because I'm meeting my boyfriend in Italy? Then I excused myself and my flushed cheeks to the clearance rack at the back of the store where I spent a half hour staring at gladiator sandals, doing the same breathing exercises I used when running intervals.

Seeing him then—for the last time—was like my first trip to Disney World as an adult, when all I could see was manufactured perfection and junk food restaurants and screaming children who were not buying into the happiest-place-on-earth thing, and you know that somewhere in the bowels of the organization is a princess on a smoke break, perhaps next to the in-house jail. Stephen or Steve or whoever he was by then—he wasn't for me. I went home and directed my email program to send anything he sent me into the trash, just in case.

And Italy turned out to be wonderful: six days of cheese and wine and gelato and trying our hand at Italian phrases we mangled with our American accents, and sex and sleeping in until 10:00 AM, and more sex followed by drinking little cups of strong coffee before we repeated it all over again. We broke up soon after, but it was a wonderful trip to take, a time capsule of a perfect week that made me feel wanted and loved again, even if it didn't last when we came back to the U.S.

My only regret was that I didn't pack my running shoes.

chapter 4

PHILADELPHIA HALF MARATHON

NOVEMBER 22, 2009

New Jersey Marathon — Miles 7–12

After turning south, we headed to Long Branch and ran through its downtown–the kind of downtown that tourists never see unless they're driving through. It's not full of cute shops selling flip-flops and sunscreen, but it has a funeral parlor, a hair salon, a locksmith: businesses for people who live there in town, businesses that were inland enough to be largely spared Sandy's wrath, but still in a downtown suffering from blight from failed redevelopment projects.

The half marathoners split off from the marathoners at around mile 11 to complete their miles winding to the boardwalk in Long Branch where we'd all finish under the same banner. Since the half marathoners started before us, I didn't see many, though when I came up to mile 9 I started passing the back of their pack—mostly walkers. Between miles 9 and 10, half marathoners who had finished were crossing back over the course, probably to walk home or to get to their cars.

I tried not to focus on them. *I'm pulling double duty. I'm pulling double duty. Duty. Doodie? No, you don't need to poop. You don't need to poop. You're fine. FINE. You don't need Gatorade. Ever. FUCK GATORADE.*

All cloud coverage had been swiped clear at the exact time that we lost tree-provided shade. Despite temperatures in the high 40s, that sun was still burning at early-summer strength. At the aid station between miles 10 and 11, I took one cup of water to drink and another to dump over my head. I still didn't need to poop, but the pressure on my bladder, which I had ignored over six previous aid stations, pressed. I knew that a Porta-Potty was close to every aid station, and when I saw a kid's bike blocking the one I intended to use, my nerves snapped.

"WHOSE BIKE IS THIS?!" I screamed. *Goddamnsonofabitchkidusingthebathroomthatsforrunnersnotspectators.*

I had so far tamped down my nerves by being consistent in my pace, talking to runners every now and again, and thanking volunteers who blocked roads, handed out cups of water, and directed us through the course. I kicked out perfect ten-minute miles, and any interruption could put my time goal in jeopardy. I didn't want to stop to use the bathroom, but I didn't want to pee myself. Not being able to get right into the Porta-Potty because some kid used it lit a temper I had worked hard to hold down.

That kid—maybe ten years old—popped out from the crowd. He wasn't going to the bathroom, but thought in front of the door of one was a great place to stash his bike. He gave me a look that mixed fear with annoyance. I'm guessing that between my already sweat-covered face and hair frizzing out of the confines of my hair tie, I maybe resembled Medusa. He moved his bike.

I locked the door, pulled down my pants and didn't even bother to take off my gloves, which were by now soaked with sweat.

Go go go go. Stupid kid. Stupid bike. Stupid pee. GOOOOO.

I thought about yanking those gloves off to leave behind, but they were wet with sweat not from my hands, but because I was using them to wipe the sweat from my face like a sweatband.

I wiped, pulled up my pants, stepped out of the Porta-Potty and jumped back into the race, *go go go gooooo,* hustling a few steps faster to get back up to speed. A body at rest tends to stay at rest, and I couldn't afford to lose my groove. A few more half marathoners wandered across the course, now with beers in hand. I sighed as deeply as I could while running. I wasn't going to think about how I could have done a half too and been finished by now. I had too much work to do.

The year 2008 bumped and clicked along. I published that first book in May. I did the grind of local TV and radio appearances, which included sitting on a chair on the Ocean

City boardwalk next to a TV host and shielding a piece of prop pizza from seagulls so they wouldn't dive-bomb at it the exact moment the camera flipped to me. I spent my weekends at book signings, the first of which I sold and signed exactly zero books.

That travel guide, though, saved my freelance career, not through the advance but from what came after it. I used information from the guide to pitch stories about the Jersey Shore to magazines and newspapers, cracking wider the work I'd done already for the *New York Times*, *Philadelphia Inquirer*, and *New Jersey Monthly*. Story by story, bit by bit, client by client, I rebuilt my income. I still stung from what happened with Stephen, but only very late at night when I couldn't sleep, or when I thought I saw his car. I kept burying myself in that work. I replaced the washer that broke three months after I bought my house. I bought a dress that was not on final clearance at the Gap. My dog's collar was no longer the one that came with her from the shelter. And yes, I took that trip to Italy after I ran into Stephen and his girlfriend at the shoe store. I could breathe again.

After the trip, I plotted my next running move: I wanted an easy one. In 2009, I set out once again to run the Ocean Drive 10-Miler and to beat my previous time. After shaking off the shroud of Stephen, running had gone from something I did to escape myself to something I did to reclaim myself. Sure, I still had bad runs, but for the most part running became a joy rather than a chore I did just to keep my head above water. I thought I could run faster, though, if I trained a little bit harder and cut out the walk breaks.

Except for when I worked with Lowell, I never tracked my runs. Instead, I'd cross off each workout with a felt-tip pen on the printout of my Hal Higdon schedule. I never wrote down my times. I never wrote about how the run went either. I didn't think it mattered because *I was doing it*, and getting out the door and running and enjoying running was itself an achievement.

By 2009, doing anything on paper was passé, and a crop of new online logs promised to keep track of your workouts for you. One of those sites, which I still use, is Daily Mile. There, I could input where I ran, how far I ran, my time, the weather, how I felt, and how many miles I put on each pair of running shoes. In return, Daily Mile made charts of my work and told me how many donuts I'd burned and gas saved and how many times I'd run around the world.

Daily Mile is a social media site, too. You can friend your friends, track each other's workouts, and encourage each other by leaving comments on said workouts. You can also search for races and then share that you were running them.

That's how I met Jason. In January, two months before the race, I checked that I was running the 2009 Ocean Drive 10-Miler, and he did too, then he friended me. Most of his photos were from triathlons where he was topless and, in one case, in a Speedo. He looked tall, lean, and tan, with a deep V of abs. (I later learned he was cheap and didn't want to spend money on a triathlon suit until he figured out if he liked doing triathlons. That summer, he'd do a tri in an old surfing wetsuit from the 1990s with a color scheme that made it look like it belonged at a laser tag facility.)

He not only friended me but he also commented on my work-outs. I responded, and then started commenting on his workouts.

And then! He asked if maybe we should meet up for a run because he had never run more than 5 miles and wanted advice from someone who'd been there. He lived in Feasterville, a suburb northeast of Philadelphia, which is a roundabout drive from my house with traffic patterns that made me want to stab kittens. But his parents had a house in Sea Isle City, a town I'd covered in my book. "Why not run down the shore?" he suggested, because he saw a picture from my first Ocean Drive 10 in my profile.

I had a few thoughts. He could be one of the following:

- Hot dude who finds me on the Internet and contacts me because he needs a training partner
- Hot dude who finds me on the Internet and contacts me because he is looking for love
- Hot dude who finds me on the Internet and contacts me so he can lure me into a murder house
- Random dude who steals hot dude's photos and contacts me so he can lure me into a murder house
- Rival freelance writer who wants to embarrass me by making me believe a guy like that would be interested and then maybe lure me into a murder house

The night before our meet-up, I had two tickets to see LL Cool J at the House of Blues in Atlantic City. Why LL Cool J? Why not? And because the tickets were free if I wrote about the show. The casino public relations person offered them on Valentine's Day, when I was halfway into a bottle of pink wine while watching *Scrubs* with my dog, so I had no reason to say no.

In my hotel room, I had one drink, then another. *You can figure out if he's a murderer in a public place,* I told myself, then texted him to see if he wanted to be my guest for the show.

"Yes!" he texted back.

We met in the Fountain Room, a restaurant at the House of Blues. I sat as pretty as I could at the bar in tight boot cut jeans and a black tank top. I had short hair then, a bob that skimmed just below my ears. Every time I turned to the door to see if he had walked in, my hair swung and tickled my ears—at least that's what I told myself was the reason for the little shivers skittering down my neck. I had focused on what clothes I'd wear running, not to the concert. If I'd have known he was coming, maybe I would have opted for something a bit sexier, like a skirt or a boob-focused shirt.

He looked exactly like his picture and not like he was there to turn me into soup. He wore dress pants, a white button-down shirt, and a pinstripe sport coat. His hair wasn't slicked down by water or sweat. Instead it was a sweep of dark, almost black hair across his forehead.

The first thing he did was apologize. "I'm sorry," he said. "I came right from work."

We went to the show, and he later told me he had so much trouble not rapping along because he knew every single word of every single song. Then we went back to my hotel and had a drink at every bar in its casino, after which I grabbed his hand and pulled him to the elevators that went up to my room. We rolled around a bit without most of our clothes, but we didn't have sex because that would have been a bridge too far for me. I still didn't know the guy, after all. I woke up the next morning with the deep V next to me, but instead of diving down into a Speedo, it descended into tighty whities, which looked absurd. I woke him up with my laughing. He went downstairs to get us Gatorade and Advil, and when he came back up to the room, he looked at me, and said, "Let's get breakfast."

We never ran, but we did spend the day together. We started with breakfast at Ozzie's, an old-fashioned diner in Longport with red leather booths and a black-and-white-checkered floor. We took selfies—with a real camera since we both had flip phones—in front of Lucy, a two-story wooden elephant that lived on the beach south of Atlantic City. Then we parked his car in a rest area outside of Sea Isle, and he changed into jeans and a zip-up jacket that he had in the trunk of his car. I drove us to Cape May and gave him the walking tour of places in my book, after which he asked me if I wanted to stop for tea.

"I could go for some fries," I said, and then we feasted on two plates of them with Miller Lites at an old salt bar open that time of year.

The fries, he later said, locked it in for him. He told me he was a goner, and set out to woo me. For our first date—our first real date—he skipped work for a day and took me to a fancy restaurant, one with an actual dress code, for lunch, followed by an afternoon at the Philadelphia Museum of Art for the *Cezanne and Beyond* exhibit. He touched my shoulders, my back, my hip, lightly as we looked at the way Cezanne used blocks of paints to depict landscapes, nudes. Afterward, sipping champagne at the bar on Rittenhouse Square, he told me I dressed well for an athlete, then spent the next half hour trying to explain how that was a compliment. He always opened doors, bought flowers, ordered my food. He said he wouldn't have sex with me until I was his girlfriend, and asked me to be so under Georges Seurat's *Models* painting at the Barnes Foundation Museum. He took me to a black-tie fund-raiser—having bought the tuxedo and a real bow tie that his grandmother taught him how to tie—and I have never before or since felt so golden. Before the event, we had drinks in the basement bar of that same five-star restaurant of our first date, him in his tux, me in a short, gold, shimmering dress. And when the very French and very womanizing chef and owner of the place flirted with me, I shamelessly flirted back while Jason looked on with a half smile that the chef picked *his* date for such flattery.

He had one fantasy sex-wise, he told me one night as we lay in bed, with him tracing his finger up and down my leg. I braced myself for something that would require me to wear leather, a ball gag, or a harness, but then he said, "That we're married." Swoon.

And we finally did run. Jason ran cross-country in college. He was a sleek human being, not just in how he looked but also in how he ran. He was more muscular than the fast male runners I knew, but he glided over the road, almost like an ice skater. His recovery powers were incredible. I stuck to running, but he'd run, swim, bike at lunch at his company's gym, then do a second workout after work. I picked him up one night from a bar in Philadelphia after his friends had run him through the wringer for his birthday. When I arrived, he tried to grab my boob and hit a pole instead, and then fell onto my car when I was trying to get him into the passenger seat. If I had consumed that much alcohol, I'd have spent the next day secluded in a dark hole until past dinner. But he woke up, bright and early and eager to run. I called him Wolverine.

I was slower than him by a lot, but he still wanted to run with me on weekends. That way, he was guaranteed to get in those longer miles by plodding next to me, someone who had done it before and had not collapsed. Our first runs were stutter steps of trying to figure out the best pace for both of us. He ran a little slower than normal, and I ran a little faster. He pulled me along.

We ran the Adrenaline 5K together—"together" meaning he finished more than four minutes ahead of me, which is a large gap in a race as short as a 5K. A week later was the Ocean Drive 10 that brought us together in the first place. We stayed in his parents' shore house. His mother kept trying to feed us plates of bread and pasta throughout the day to carb load, even though what she offered was far beyond what we needed. I was loath to say no and offend the mother of the man I loved. This is a woman who, two weeks later, told Jason she thought I had an eating disorder because I only ate one serving of every dish at her seven-course Easter meal. I didn't want him to know that I'd been there before.

We went to the only two bars open in March for one drink at each, then went to bed, him in his shore bedroom, me down the hall. I couldn't sleep, but not because of the next day. I felt calmer leading into the race than the year before because I knew the course and knew there would be no surprises. I was awake because I knew he was two doors down, just lying there too.

The forecast all week screamed "RAIN! RAIN! RAIN!" I'd run in the rain before, but I'd never raced in it, so in a panic I bought a blue running hat and pumpkin rain jacket from REI. But race morning was also a little bit humid. I stepped in and out of the car three times, with jacket, without jacket, with jacket, before deciding that I should wear the jacket just in case.

"This year it rained," I later wrote in a story about the race for *New Jersey Monthly*. "This year I was cranky. Hundreds of runners were forced to stretch and shake off nerves in the lobby and hallways of Congress Hall. We spilled into the dining areas and even to the Boiler Room, a nightclub with floors still sticky from the night before."

As we filed to the starting line, a woman banged her way through the runners with her bicycle, knocking into Jason's calf and screaming that her thirteen-year-old daughter didn't have her marathon race bib.

"Is this what all races are like?" Jason asked me.

"I haven't run too many, but that's a first for me—both that,"

I said, pointing at the back of the bicycling mother, "and her," I said, meaning a thirteen-year-old running a marathon.

At the starting line, Jason kissed me and told me to pick him up off the road at mile 5. He assumed he'd crash and burn by about then. I drifted further back into the crowd because I knew I wouldn't be anywhere near the lead pack in the race, and as the national anthem played, and we had a moment of silence for fishermen who had been lost at sea the week before, I closed my eyes and breathed deep. I had seen the course before, and had run the course before. My only goal was to beat 1:36:00. I could do it, I told myself. As long as I could deal with the rain.

The start siren went off. A half mile in, I knew I'd made a mistake with the jacket. It created a heat envelope around me. So I stripped it off and stuffed it into the bushes in front of a motel, hoping that it would still be there when I came back. Freed from the jacket, I forged ahead. Mile 1 came, and I stepped over the urge to walk. I paced myself over the first bridge, and by mile 3, runners who went out too fast dropped back, just like they had the year before. I cruised over the marshes of miles 3 through 6, checking my Timex to make sure I was not going too slow. If anything, I thought, I was going too fast, clocking miles at an even eight-minutes-per-mile pace. But my lungs and legs sang in harmony, so I kept pushing ahead. Jason was nowhere to be found.

I started to falter when I crossed from North Wildwood into Wildwood proper. At mile 8, a woman I'd been trailing the entire race stopped and put her hands on her knees. I passed her, singing the lyrics of matt pond PA's "Spring Revives" in my head over and over again to keep my mind off the pain. I turned up onto the boardwalk with volunteers cheering, "Go, runners! Go!" from the ramp, then I found the same concrete strip that I'd hit the year before. Turning around that last bend before Montego Bay was Jason, medal already around his neck. "Go, Jen, go, Jen! You're almost there!" he yelled.

I didn't crumple when I finished this time, but put my hands over my head. The humidity had stuck my shirt to my body, and I was gasping, but I had done it. I beat my goal. I ran a 1:19:55, more than sixteen minutes faster than the year before, and good enough for fourth in my age group.

I was proud of what I had done. Later, my friends at the local running store (we were friends now since I started hanging out there after I bought my shoes and shirts and socks) were shocked at how much I cut off my time.

But Jason had blown both of us away. In his first 10-miler ever, he ran just over an hour, and went home with a trophy.

"I didn't hate it," he said, holding his trophy in hand, then hugged me tight. This was perfection, I thought. He was everything I ever could have wanted.

(I did find my jacket. A kind soul hung it on a parking meter so I would find it.)

This was love, capital *L-O-V-E*, shimmering, bombastic, full-blown love, one that dusted us with rainbows and unicorns and gold foil stars. We went to my brother's wedding that

June, and all of my aunts swore we were next. We'd drive down the shore on Fridays—me going early to get some reporting done, him chasing after me when he left work at 5:00 PM to meet me in Sea Isle. We'd ring around the island— happy hour with half-price appetizers at the Lobster Loft while listening to a terrible duo cover band; then to Dead Dog, which required collared shirts (though you can rent one for a $10 deposit), "609" frozen drinks at Bracas, named after the town's area code. I'd always wear a sundress, because after we'd stroll down the ocean-side promenade back to his house, grab a blanket out of his car, and keep walking down the beach until we found "our" spot, secluded next to a dune on an empty beach, and have sex, slow and deep, while we stared into each other's eyes. After, we'd lie on that blanket, spent and warm and listening to the ocean lapping in front of us, and we'd talk about what our own wedding would be like. My dad, who had become an executive and part owner of the company where he worked and had a lot more money than when my parents split, said he'd pay a set amount of money toward it but nothing else. I wanted to use that money for home improvements because I didn't see the practicality of that money going toward a party when it could be used for something that would last more than one day. But if those were dad's rules, we wanted to use every single penny of it and have a small, lavish wedding.

"Let's rent out Le Bec Fin. Shut the restaurant down just for us."

"Let's fly everyone to Tampa and have a black-tie wedding on the beach of the Don CeSar."

"Let's get married."

"Let's get married."

In August, as a P.S. in a text message, Jason mentioned something about flying to Minneapolis for a few days. That was odd. He'd never been there before that I knew of.

"Why?" I wrote back.

"Job interview."

If there was one thing that had stuck in my craw about Jason, it was money. Not that he was frugal or that he spent too much, but that he was laser-focused on making it. He didn't grow up poor, but when he dropped back to being a part-time college student, his mother told him, over and over again, that he'd never make anything of himself. When he worked as a roofer to pay his way through school, she told him he was lazy and an embarrassment. When he started at the bottom rung at the advertising agency where he worked while still working as a server at a chain restaurant at night, she chided him for taking on an entry-level job.

Even when he moved up the ranks, he couldn't shake this need to prove her wrong. He wanted to be wealthy and successful beyond her—not his—wildest dreams.

Despite hanging on to his job during the recession, which was a miracle given the number of jobs his company shed, he wanted more. A job over a thousand miles away offered it.

Don't panic, I told myself. *It's just an interview. He may not get the job. Even if he does, he may not go. His family is here. His life is here. And I'm here.* I didn't bring up what would happen to us because I was sure—I prayed—that he wouldn't leave, that they'd find a better candidate or offer him too little money or tell him there had to be someone back home who would object to him moving halfway across the country.

"His mother will never let him go," my mom said when I told her why I was sitting in her kitchen on a Friday night and not down the shore with Jason.

"Would you let me go?" I asked.

"Of course. But I'm only a half-Italian mother."

Those last weeks of August took on the quality of a long, sex-fueled good-bye. *Nothing was set in stone*, I thought, looking at him as he slept beside me on weeknights when he stayed at my house, as he dozed on that blanket in our beach spot on weekends. *He would not make this choice.*

He did make that choice. He got the job and was gone by Labor Day.

I broke a little inside. I thought I had found the one, and he had acted like he felt the same about me, and he was just leaving? I didn't tell him that. I was too stunned by his decision, and his nonchalance about it. I should have ranted and raved. I should have grabbed him by his shirt and screamed, "Why are you leaving me? Why are you giving up on us?"

Instead I wept quietly and said that I hoped it would work out, adding that I thought it was giving our relationship a raw deal.

"I can't give up this job," he told me on our last weekend

down the shore. "It's too big an opportunity," he said, careful not to use the word "promotion" because it technically wasn't one. He thought, though, that he'd have a better chance at a promotion after this lateral move. We had run the Captain Bill Gallagher 10 Mile Island Run that Saturday night. I'd had surgery on my shoulder a month before and had barely run since, but I still slogged it out on a hot and humid night, 10 miles over sand, because it was one of the last things I knew I'd do with him.

"But think of what you're giving up," I said that night on the beach, referring of course to me.

"It's not as important." I hoped he wasn't referring to the same.

I tried to talk to Jason about setting up a timeline of where our relationship would progress—like if we made it this many months, I'd move there. If we made it this many months, we'd revisit the marriage question. But he wanted to keep things flexible and see how our relationship worked long distance, if at all. I flew out to Minneapolis in September, and we always had a delirious, almost honeymoon-like time. We ran along the banks of the Mississippi River and marveled at how different it was from the Schuylkill, biked to the Mill City Farmers Market to watch peppers roast in a big metal cage. We went to Nye's Polonaise Room, a polka bar, and bars in former speakeasies, in former banks. On another trip, he took me to a play because it seemed like a sophisticated thing to do. When he worked, I explored that city, and St. Paul, on foot. I found out about a wine stomping event, so we went; we didn't stomp ourselves, but instead watched and tasted wine that had been made that way the year before. I started to think that maybe—maybe—I could fall in love with this place, as long as I was there with him.

Jason never brought up me moving there again, but I thought the concept, as long as we kept trying to hold the relationship together, was inferred. I could see us living in some swanky condo by the river, and then, because our careers were both steamrolling ahead, a lake house. I had stopped taking bottom-feeder jobs and fired clients who mistreated me, delayed payment, failed to pay, or just annoyed me. Instead, I focused on finding quality assignments for quality clients, and my bottom line grew. So by the time we unwound this knot, I thought, we'd also be able to afford a house along one of the state's ten thousand lakes, and settle into the life that I was supposed to live: marriage, babies, and doing what my mother did, which was shipping ourselves out to our vacation spot for the summer while Jason stayed behind during the week and joined us on weekends. Except in this vision, I perfected the situation my mother had been in by continuing to write and work, with maybe a nanny to help, because by then, I pictured, I'd be an in-demand journalist and author, and I'd be able to afford everything I ever wanted. It was a very pretty, sun-dappled, lakefront, golden-sunlight dream—even if it *was* in Minnesota.

When the weather turned colder (oh so much sooner there), we'd challenge ourselves to not walk outside, instead using the skyways that link up buildings in the city, including his apartment building. We'd snuggle deep down into his bed, and I would try not to think about what was coming next. He bought a web cam so we could talk and see each other. But it wasn't the same. He was building a life there, and I tried to get on with mine at home.

We were pulling apart, like taffy. Our two ends stuck together, but the bond between thinned and frayed. I was pulling apart too. To cope, I repeated my process from after the Stephen debacle: I signed up for a race. This time a half marathon.

Today, the half marathon is the second most popular race distance in the U.S., beaten out only by the 5K. From 2000 to 2013, the number of participants in half marathons grew 307 percent, according to Running USA. No, I didn't forget a decimal point there. Three *hundred* and seven percent.

I came in right at the biggest expansion of the race. In both 2009 and 2010, half marathons grew by 24 percent. I ran my first in 2009.

I picked the half for the same reason a lot of people do: It's a good challenge, but it doesn't require the same amount of training, time, dedication, and sheer terror as running a full marathon. After two ten-milers, I was confident that I could cover the extra 3.1 miles.

The Philadelphia Half Marathon stood out for two reasons: First, it was close, and second, it was also in the news every year since it's connected to the Philadelphia Marathon. Another bonus: The race took place the Sunday before Thanksgiving, which meant I didn't need to dedicate my summer weekends to long runs.

Jason pushed my running forward. Buoyed by those once-a-week runs with him, which had forced me to pick up the pace, I started running more and running faster. I posted some of my fastest times in 2009 by not walking during races and by building up race experience. I knew when to press and when to pull back, and how much pain I could take, so I brushed up to that edge. Not only did I blow away my past Ocean Drive 10-Miler time, but I also PRed again in the 10-mile distance that May, running the Broad Street Run ten-miler 34 seconds faster.

I had sworn up and down that I would never run a marathon, but it was on the periphery of my vision as something to maybe do in the future. I knew that if I ran a 1:37:00 in the Philly Half—a 7:24 pace versus my 7:56 pace in the Broad Street Run—I could skip the lottery and earn guaranteed entry into the New York City Marathon, the largest marathon in the world.

I turned back to Hal, but instead of doing the beginner schedule, I bumped up to intermediate, which brought back things like 400-meter repeats, weight workouts, and tempo runs (this is a word with a different meaning for everyone, like pornography—for Hal, it meant a run that builds throughout the workout to a 10K pace).

This was the first time I used running pain as a release. Sure, running 6 or 7 miles at a time was hard in the Stephen recovery, but that was more about standing on my feet and moving for a long time. This was different. I beat myself up through hard workouts. I wanted to hurt.

I tried to push down those feelings of rejection with laps

pounded out on the goose poop-covered Haddon Township track, and pace runs and weights thrown around while dripping sweat onto the weight bench because I'd run on the treadmill just before. Maybe through running, I'd run out the clock on our problems and he'd come to his senses and either move home or have me move there. I didn't need to talk to him about it. I still couldn't talk to him. I didn't want to risk a fight. I never wanted to be that couple, screaming at each other. If I just ran and waited, waited and ran, things would all work out. My punishing schedule lined up with that frustration. I trained well, and I trained hard. My paces in those runs had me optimistic about qualifying for the New York City Marathon.

The Philadelphia Half Marathon was on November 22. On November 5, I was at the Pete Yorn concert at the Electric Factory in Philadelphia. When the show started, Pete ripping into "Can't Hear Anyone," I snapped my head to the right. Something was wrong with the sound system, I thought, because only half of the speakers made any noise. I looked around to see if anyone else would notice—surely someone would notice— but no one did. I had felt cruddy that morning but still went to the show. It turned out to be a nasty head cold, one that curdled into a sinus infection that stuffed up one ear, and then the other.

My younger sister's wedding was two days after the concert. I'm not sure why she asked me to be in it, let alone the maid of honor. We never really clicked in the way that sisters are supposed to. I told her that she was rushing the wedding, which her fiancé took as a sign that I didn't like him (he wasn't wrong). When she asked me if I'd be her maid of honor, I asked, "Are you sure?"

Jason was supposed to go. We swapped flight prices, worked on logistics, talked about what he would wear, and I RSVP'd for a plus-one. Two weeks before the ceremony, he said that he couldn't come because of work—some big proposal for a new client he had to push through.

"I want to be there, but if I leave, I'll be fired," he said.

Before the rehearsal dinner, I saw that his brother posted a selfie of them at Nye's Polonaise. Jason wasn't working. He was barhopping. I called him as soon as I saw his brother's post. He hadn't wanted to tell me the real reason he couldn't come, he said, but his brother had decided to visit that week, and booked the ticket before checking in with him.

"If you can't fucking come to my sister's wedding, then we're done. We. Are. Fucking. Done," I screamed—finally—into the phone.

So on the day of my sister's wedding, I was pumped full of antibiotics and steroids with a nasal spray my doctor said to take only before the wedding and never again because frequent use would lead to addiction. My eyes ringed red from crying. In the pictures, I look like I felt: half-dead, like I had pulled myself into my own grave, purple shadows under my eyes and face bloated by steroids. I had three packs of tissues in my purse and hoped that, if I had to wipe snot from my nose during the ceremony, people would just think I was crying at my profound joy that my sister was marrying some guy I didn't think she knew well enough to make that kind of lifelong commitment.

The ceremony was a blur. I don't remember the procession or the vows, just that I managed to stand upright through the entire ceremony.

Then I got rip-roaring drunk.

I remember watching the groom-bride dance. I remember watching the father-daughter dance. I remember trying to dance and look like I was having fun, and retreating to tables with my family to talk to aunts and uncles and drink red wine. I remember my sister having trouble going to the bathroom because she could not get her dress off. Then I remember her husband telling me, "You're just jealous because no one will kiss you."

I drank more. The next thing I remember is puking into a bush at a gas station while my dad filled up his car.

Then I woke up on the daybed in one of my dad's guest rooms. The combination of hangover, exhaustion, and sickness kept me in that bed until 3:00 PM. Drinking too much and getting sick is one thing. To do so at your sister's wedding and then puke into a bush while your dad is driving you back to his house is another—especially when your grandparents and your new stepmom are in the car.

My dad came to check once to make sure I wasn't dead, and bring me another box of tissues. Then around lunchtime my grandmom came in.

She married young and had my dad when she was nineteen years old. I'd always admired her for what she did: she still worked, became a claims adjuster at a major insurance company in New Jersey, and took no shit from anyone.

She came into my room, sat on the edge of my bed, leaned down and hugged me.

"Jenny, no man should make you feel like that," she said with shaky voice. I had never seen my grandmom cry, ever. I had heard her say "shit" once when I was ten years old, and I still hadn't quite recovered. "He's not worth it. You're so much better than that. If you don't want to get married, don't. You don't need him," she said. I cried harder, and she hugged me harder, then she let me go back to sleep.

As the sun was starting to slide down, I stood up, put on some shoes, and came downstairs.

"Hey hey, she's alive! Let's go for a walk!" my dad said, bundling me into my coat and out the door.

"I'm embarrassed," I said to him and his new wife as we walked down the long driveway to the street.

"Jenny! C'mon! Nothing to be embarrassed about. We're family!" he said. He was peppy for someone who had just dropped a lot of money on a wedding, but he must have still been washed in the afterglow of the wedding and knowing one daughter was finally settled.

"Oh, Jen. Don't worry. I've seen far worse," my dad's wife said. "I'm just glad you could sleep."

We crossed the street to a development of multimillion-dollar houses where they liked to walk. Despite the November date, the sun was warm.

"What's our daughter-father dance going to be?" my dad asked.

"Little Surfer Girl," I said. He had always held my hand as a kid when that Beach Boys song came on.

"Of course. I was thinking the same thing," he said. And I felt a twinge. Of course my father expected me to get married. Everyone did. What if it never happened to me? What if no one picked me? That's what I wanted, right? That's what I was supposed to want, what would make me happy.

Jason had made me feel better than any other man before— had made me feel better than I was by myself. He had betrayed me for the sake of what? Money? To prove a point? I had been so wrong about him—but there had been no warning signs either. Whereas Stephen was cagey, aloof, an addict, Jason had been all in until he wasn't.

Despite that warm, late November walk, the sinus infection and the cold hung on. My training dropped to 10 miles a week. I had two choices going to the starting line of the half marathon: I could hold back and play it conservative given that I wasn't feeling 100 percent, or I could still try to hold that 7:24 pace to qualify for the New York City Marathon.

I am a very stupid person, so I went with option two.

The race started at 7:00 AM, and because I was already a ball of stress and tissues, I didn't want to risk driving. What if I was stuck in traffic? What if I couldn't find a place to park? What if, to get to the starting line on time, I had to abandon my Civic down some alley in Philadelphia, only for it to be scurried away by vandals who broke her up for parts, never to be seen by me again?

I opted to take the PATCO high-speed line, which is two blocks from my house, into Center City and walk to the start. I wanted to leave plenty of time to get to the start, so I chose the 5:10 AM train. That meant getting up at 4:00 AM to make sure I had enough time to eat and poop before the race, which meant setting the alarm at 3:30 AM and then 3:45 AM so I wouldn't oversleep, which meant waking up at 3:00 AM anticipating the alarm going off.

I made my mom come with me, too. I didn't force her to go, but I did plead. I had a bad feeling that the race wasn't going to end well, and I wanted her there at the finish line, even if it meant she'd be standing in the cold for hours waiting for me. She didn't even question why I'd want her there, just showed up at my door at 4:45 AM with a tote bag full of magazines and my grandfather's old flannel jacket, which she threw on top of me.

Temperatures hovered just below 40 degrees at the start of the race. Because I still preferred a deep chill for running, I wore gray capri-length tights, a cotton American Apparel purple tank, and red arm sleeves (which are just what they sound like—tubes of fabric that leave your shoulders and wrists exposed), gloves, and about seventeen sweatshirts.

Normally the only people coming on or off PATCO trains in the 2:00 AM to 5:00 AM block are drunks, but that morning, the platform was full of runners, most quiet and still half asleep. The ride over was silent except for the sound of PowerBar and granola bar wrappers. We filed off the train at the last stop at 16th and Locust. My mom tried to break that silence on the walk over to the start by talking to me about my race strategy and the weather, but I didn't reply. My brain and stomach were both churning, and the crowds didn't help. As soon as I stepped off the train, we were swept up in a flood of people. About eighteen thousand people would finish races that day. I was just a peon in the mix.

This race is put on by the Philadelphia mayor's office, and it's not the most well-organized event. So when I saw locked Porta-Potties at the start, I thought that was normal. When I saw long lines for the open bathrooms, I thought that was normal. I got in line, and despite my cushion of time, the national anthem played before I had a chance to go. I hadn't even seen the starting line yet. I hadn't found my corral.

I stepped out of line and shed one sweatshirt, two, three.

"Give me your tissues," I said to my mom.

"What are you doing?" she asked, transferring the tissues to me as I handed the clothes to her. I hugged her tight.

"I love you," I said.

"But the bathroom . . ."

"C'mon," I said to the three women in line behind me. I found a bush about 20 feet from the Porta-Potties, dropped my tights, and let it go. They did the same, trying not to look at each other but giggling. I passed the tissues around.

"Hey!" a cop said as we were wiping.

"What are you going to do?" I asked. "Chase us?"

We flung down our tissues like football penalty flags and then sprinted out to the Benjamin Franklin Parkway to join our corrals.

Given my aggressive plans and estimated finish time, I was put in the green corral, the third group out of seven (not including the elite runners). This meant I was standing next to a bunch of very skinny people who were absolutely not wearing cotton.

The Philadelphia Half Marathon shares its course with the first half of the Philadelphia Marathon, and both races start at the same time in front of the Philadelphia Museum of Art, heads down the Benjamin Franklin Parkway toward city hall, then shoots down with a few twists and turns to Columbus Boulevard, home to panhandlers and strip clubs. After that, we turned west along South Street, made famous by an old doo-wop song but now a lane of sex toy and T-shirt and "tobacco" shops, then up to Chestnut Street. This was the longest straight shot in the race, about 2 miles long, and when it ended, we were about halfway to the finish. It's also where the most crowds are because it's in Center City and easy to get to by public transit.

I held my pace through those first 7½ miles. I remember feeling cold, then hot, and the strain of running at that pace broiled my lungs—but I thought that was how I should feel. I was holding steady 7:30 miles, and if I was going to hit my time goal I needed to feel it through the entire race, even if the head cold still clung to my nose, my throat, and my lungs. I stared at my feet all through Chestnut Street (and missed a half dozen people looking for me). One of my editors was at mile 7.3 because his son was visiting Drexel University that weekend and they decided to stay to watch the race. The turn off Chestnut is at the Drexel campus. I wanted to pass the school with my head held high. And I did, until the course turned into the residential area around Drexel, where stately old brick homes had been turned into frat houses. Bros blared rap music and did keg stands to celebrate the race.

That's when my body gave out. My legs shook and I took one step, another, then stopped and walked, the 7:30s draining out of me. I had never had a bad race before. I had only ever walked because I planned to walk. I planned to destroy this race. Instead, I hobbled along 34th Street thinking how I could get a cab or take a bus or train back to my mom. But I didn't have any money, and good luck getting a cab through a half marathon and marathon start/finish setup, even if I did have cash. I didn't bring my phone, either, and there was no Uber then.

The only way *to* was *through*. So I started running again, but slowly, and I continued to shuffle past the Philadelphia Zoo and Fairmount Park until the turn at mile 10.5 that brought me down Martin Luther King Jr. Drive. By then the sun was up, and I was glad I had worn a tank top because we ran into that full sun. The most I remember about that stretch was the whoosh of the cars on the Schuylkill Expressway, which parallels the Drive, and trailing a woman running in a bra with thin straps, her muscled shoulders sparkling with sweat.

And I turned my focus on getting back to my mom, hoping it would distract me from an all-body ache. *She's been standing out here in the cold for you. You are not going to quit. You are not going to give up.* At mile 12, the air turned giddy—not for me because I was gulping it—but around me. Pairs of friends running together shouted, "We're there! We're there!" Two college boys in Penn shirts hugged each other. And, oh, did the marathoners throw us the stink eye, because they still had half a race to go. I said nothing and did nothing but put one foot in front of the other, and when we made the final turn around Eakins Oval with the finish line in sight, I did not throw my hands in the air in victory for that perfect finish line photo. I crumpled, stepping out of the way of other finishers, and put my hands on my knees to suck in air and dry heave.

So much had gone wrong in the last three months—and especially in the last three weeks. If I could have pulled off that win, if I could have made running love me when Jason could not, I would have felt like I had accomplished something— SOMETHING—in the last full year of my twenties. Instead, I was just another runner in gray pants and a purple shirt who finished that day—barely.

I stood back up because I started to feel cold, and let a volunteer drape both a medal and a silver space blanket around my shoulders. "Congratulations!" she said. "You did it!" Maybe she thought they were tears of joy.

I walked through the finisher's chute and grabbed water but no food. Mom was waiting for me at the exit, my grandfather's big flannel coat open and ready for me.

"Don't talk to me," I stammered through my tears. "Just . . . don't talk to me."

It was a rude thing to do, especially because she was the only reason I had continued through to the finish line. But my lungs and throat were stuffed, both from the cold and crying. Then I pitched forward to lean on my knees again. She removed my space blanket and put on the flannel jacket, pushing my arms into the sleeves like she had put my snow coat on as a kid.

"I didn't make it," I sobbed. "I wasn't even close."

I had not told my mom my final goal. I never tell anyone in case I miss. When people ask me what I want to run, I usually say "I want to finish and not require immediate medical attention." Then I'll give what I consider my highest offer of a time. The goal was to run that 1:37, but worst case 1:40. I told my mom I wouldn't take any longer than two hours. I ran 1:53:06, more than sixteen minutes over my goal time, more than a minute per mile over my goal pace.

"Jenny, you finished exactly when you said you would," and patted me on the back. "You did it. You ran a half marathon!"

I looked up and wiped my tears on the jacket sleeve, leaving a trail of snot on the wrist.

"I'd give you tissues but you peed on them," she said.

We made the long, slow walk back to the 16th and Locust PATCO station. I swatted away the idea of a cab because I wanted to keep my legs moving and ward off the pain that I knew was coming, and I figured we'd stop at a bar on the way home. I wanted a drink, but because the race starts early no bars were open.

As we walked down Chestnut, I noted the timing mats in the street.

"I wonder what other race is today," I said.

"That was for your race. You ran here."

I needed to eat something. Post-race hunger clawed at my stomach. We stopped at Little Pete's, a corner diner with a cigarette machine in the vestibule, linoleum counters, and unbreakable beige coffee cups. The chill had caught up to me by then, and I started to shake.

This is a place known to be a haven for all walks of life, but even the waitress gave me the eye.

"She's not homeless," my mom said, "but a half marathoner," and pulled my medal out from under my coat.

They gave me my coffee for free.

The Ballad of Jason and Jen would have a few more stanzas. He came home for Christmas and apologized, taking me to dinners and on long walks through Collingswood to try to win me back. I flew out to Minneapolis to see him for Valentine's Day, and when his grandmother died in March I was at the funeral. But in the end, the center did not hold. We drifted, and even when he moved to New York City I didn't pursue him, because why? Why would I let him pick me back up again just to throw me off a cliff again?

The last time I saw him was on my thirtieth birthday in July of 2010. He was home to spend time in Sea Isle, and my family had rented a shore house for that week. We had a drink at the Carousel Inn, which is neither an inn nor has a carousel, but it is an outdoor bar. It was about 1,000 degrees, and he was late. He skipped my birthday party that night (I didn't want him there, and I lied to my family about meeting him after the party, saying instead that I had some more friends who wanted to see me that night), but we bar-crawled around Sea Isle, visiting all the places we'd gone before when he still lived here and we were still loopy with love (drinks at the Lobster Loft back bar, Dead Dog, Bracas, and then made out on the floor of Ocean Drive, where we'd gone before the Ocean Drive 10 in what felt like an eon ago, when the clock struck midnight). We then talked on a lifeguard chair and he grabbed at me to make out again, but I pushed him away. I don't know what I said, but it was far from those post-sex beach musings. My tolerance for words that didn't match action had run out.

Besides, I had another man coming to see me later that morning. The Nick era had begun.

Chapter 5

BIRD-IN-HAND HALF MARATHON

NOVEMBER 6, 2010

New Jersey Marathon — Miles 12–13

At mile 12, we left downtown Long Branch and turned onto Ocean Avenue to enter the southern part of town, the wealthier section. More homes here are used only seasonally. Some are large, severe, and guarded by long driveways, hedges, and, in one case, a griffin. Ocean Avenue is wider here, but its fault for racing is a big one: Here and in Deal, the next town south, the only shade provided would be the shadows of streetlights that curled overhead, and we'd run that strip twice.

Before we crossed into Deal, though, we turned off Ocean Avenue to run around Whale Pond Brook, a 0.7-mile jaunt off the

main road. Because the course had to be rerouted off boardwalks in
Asbury Park and Ocean Grove, it made up distance with a few turns
away from the shore and into the respective towns. One of these was
at mile 12.

I started passing people here, a little earlier than I'd anticipated,
even though I kept my pace—in spite of the Porta-Potty stop.

*Keep your speed. Don't go too fast. Keep your speed. Just
keep your speed. Just keep swimming? Just keep swimming. Just
keep swimming.*

Back at mile 11, I had fallen into step with a blond woman
about my age. She told me she was three months pregnant and
running this race after having run the Boston Marathon three weeks
before. She had finished just before the bombs went off. This was her
redemption race.

"I just want to run and feel safe again," she said. She ran strong
next to me with a tiny little belly protruding from under her race bib.
If she hadn't told me she was pregnant, I would have assumed it was
from an overexuberant carb load the night before.

Between miles 11 and 12, we closed in on a couple running the
marathon together. For the last half mile she had been futzing with
the arm band that held what I assumed was an MP3 player.

"Do you want me to stop and fix it?" her partner asked. He
looked older than me, face slick with sweat, and strained.

"No!" she snapped back, ripping off the arm band, the sound
of the Velcro detaching like a shot that echoed off a redbrick church
on our right. I turned to my temporary running friend. My eyebrows
zipped up, as did hers.

"I told you that this wasn't going to work," she said, trying to rewrap and attach it while running, and slowing down. "And now my neck hurts!" she yelled.

Her partner took the MP3 player from her. "I'll fix it," he said. Their pace slowed, and they fell back closer to me and my temporary running friend.

"NO!" she said, and grabbed it back, then stopped in front of me. I sidestepped around her.

"Do you want me to fix your neck?" he asked, pleading now. Runners and a few spectators stared too.

""NO!" she yelled. "I don't know why I'm doing this with you!"

Watching them fight made ugly memories try to jump into my brain.

My temporary running friend broke away. Her fiancé and his mother—who didn't know my friend was pregnant—were up ahead. Her shirt had +1 printed on it, and that's how they were telling her soon-to-be-mother-in-law that she was also a soon-to-be-grandmother.

I pushed ahead without her. The words of the "Cell Block Tango," from the musical *Chicago* shoved my memories out of the way. *"He only had himself to blame . . . "*

Picturing those women of the cell block kept flashes of my past running fights from clogging up the gears, which I didn't need when I was still dropping ten-minute miles despite the blip at the Porta-Potty. My legs and lungs and hips felt fine. I needed my brain to stay calm and clear if I was going to drop-kick the second half of the race and cross the line with my head held high.

After Jason and I reached our inevitable, slow-motion car crash of a conclusion, three options presented themselves, running-wise:

1. Stay the course. Despite bottoming out at the end of the race, I was still in the best running shape of my life. The Philadelphia Half Marathon is at the far end of the fall racing season, bumping up against the start of spring's training season. I could roll that training over into setting another PR in the Ocean Drive 10, and try the half again at one of the dozen spring races in the area.

2. Take a break, at least from distance training, just like I planned to do with dating.

3. Run harder. A lot harder—and farther too.

I went with number three, and set this goal: Run a marathon, and run it fast enough to reach what is considered a mark of excellence for the amateur runner, which is to qualify for the Boston Marathon. I saw no reason why I could not do this. I had been posting faster times, and I didn't see any reason why I couldn't set a high bar and reach it, especially when my state of mind wasn't so much *La la la, I love running, so I should do more of it and be good!* but more grim determination.

Running harder hadn't helped me get over Jason the first time around, but I didn't blame the running or the training. I blamed getting sick, my sister's wedding, for me being wrong—

about everything. This time, I told myself, I would do better, and it would work.

In 2009, a twenty-nine-year-old woman needed to run 3:40:00 to qualify for Boston. That meant covering 26.2 miles at a pace of 8:23. Yes, that was hard, but it was still about a minute slower per mile than what I had needed in the half marathon, and I held that pace for 7.5 miles. *Don't get sick and you can do it*, I told myself. *Simple.*

I printed out Hal's Advanced 2 marathon schedule, the most difficult one he offered. No matter that I'd never done a full marathon before. In addition to 400-meter repeats and tempo runs, this schedule added 800-meter repeats, hill training, and pace runs, with only one running day off per week instead of two.

I targeted the New Jersey Marathon on May 2, which meant eighteen weeks of training starting the first week of January.

As I took a running lunge forward, the sport did too. From 2000 to 2009, the number of finishers in U.S. road races increased 37 percent across all distances, according to Running USA. In 2010, the organization produced its first-ever half marathon report because of what it labeled the "astounding growth" in the number of finishers of the half. Marathons saw 10 percent more finishers in 2010, the largest one-year percentage increase in any of the previous twenty-five years. Marathoning, Running USA reported, had become a "mania." In 2009, women surpassed men in races: 53 percent of race finishers were women that year (5.4 million), compared to just 23 percent of finishers in 1989 (908,000).

"Training for and running a marathon is something that one can control unlike the stock market or the economy," Running USA wrote in its 2010 marathon report. And, for me, a way to tighten control over my emotions, find some sort of solace in the wake of being dropped—again.

I was going to take running, which had failed me at a crucial part in my life, and pin it to the ground. With hard training, I could crush it, dominate it, make it my bitch. If I wanted it enough, tried hard enough, trained hard enough, I could control running and center at least part of my life. I would not let the breakup with Jason remind me that I was a failure, that no one would love me, that I would die alone. If I ran hard enough— even if I ran alone with my podcasts again instead of with a glorious, gorgeous human being who proclaimed that he loved me—I could win.

Another mania took hold in 2009: barefoot running. Christopher McDougall's *Born to Run*, which is about the Tarahumara Indian tribe, was published in 2009 and hung on to the *New York Times* bestseller list for more than four months. Part memoir, part reportage, the book championed barefoot runners (like the Tarahumara) and outlined how once McDougall gave up bulky, overly padded running shoes, his running injuries disappeared. The Mizuno Wave Riders 9—my first pair of running shoes, bought in 2006—clocked in at nine ounces. I ran the 2009 Broad Street Run in Asics that looked like they carried their own flotation devices.

After *Born to Run*, running shoes shrank. Vibram FiveFingers, those funny toe shoes, showed up in my running store, in races, and, as a marker of quick-flash fashion, on hipsters, who wore them on their fixies on their way to the PATCO train. (By 2010, hipsters discovered Collingswood, fleeing here from Philadelphia to get their kids into our schools without feeling like they were giving up and moving to the suburbs—we had row homes and a train. I could deal with that, though their proclamations that they "discovered" Collingswood were grating.) In the 2009 Broad Street Run, I ran next to two guys who skipped shoes entirely. Minimalist shoes made up the fastest-growing segment in running for 2010 and 2011, according to the *Wall Street Journal*. Companies like Merrell, New Balance, and Fila got in on the act too.

Jason and I both read the book during his first fall away. We both bought Nike Free shoes, too. They weren't much different from Jason's regular shoes. He preferred to run in racing flats, something he kept with him from college. Running in flats was a big change for me, though, and I stuck with it even when he didn't stick with me.

I felt lighter and faster in those shoes. They made me feel like a real runner. Those tiny white and yellow shoes looked more like slippers with laces than running shoes. Like those other real runners, I rounded the track on an 800-meter repeat once, twice, then did 400 meters of recovery running in between, and repeat, repeat, repeat again. Instead of putting my head down when I passed those other runners, I smiled and nodded (track etiquette: Run counterclockwise on the sprint, then clockwise on the rest lap in between). Sometimes if the runner looked friendly, I'd offer a high-five, and they'd slap back, our gloves muffling the noise.

But by mid-February, a prick of pain settled into my right hip. As I progressed through the month, charging up and down Haddonfield's steep Centre Street hill, surging through pace runs at a speed that pushed my lungs to bursting, that prick became a stab. I pressed on, grinding through tempo runs before lunch and pace runs on Saturdays, then I'd down Advil and take a long, hot shower, after which I'd still be soaked in pain.

I stopped lifting, too. I didn't want free weights to get in the way of my devotion to the sport. I turned over the keys to my body to running on the promise that it would save me. I could not give up. I would not allow myself to quit like Stephen and Jason had quit on me.

On my first 19-mile run, I made it out 1.5 miles before turning back home, pain radiating from my hip. I changed into my old Asics. I made it a half mile again before I quit. I walked back home and threw my shoes across the living room. I slunk upstairs, crawled into bed—still in my running clothes—and pulled the covers up over my head while my dog tried to lick my sweaty face.

All that running and I think, to some extent, running in the wrong shoes, had killed my butt. The real name of the injury is gluteus medius tendinosis, but my doctor called it Dead Butt Syndrome. When he told me, I laughed.

"I know," he said. "But you can recover."

The injury is the inflammation of the tendons in the gluteus medius, one of the three large muscles that make up the butt. It was my first running injury.

As much as it hurt, that dead butt led to my first big break in writing about running. When I wrote about the injury in the *New York Times* later that year, I described the injury as so: "If you think of the pelvis as a cup, the muscles that attach to it, including three gluteal muscles and the lower abdominals, interact in an intricate choreography to keep the cup upright when you run or walk. If these muscles are strong, the cup stays in place with no pain. If one or more of those muscles is weak, the smaller muscles around the hip take on pressure they weren't designed to bear."

My body struggled to keep the cup upright, and those muscles tore. Scar tissue set in, which sent the injury into a feedback loop that had me walking back to my house instead of running 19 miles.

This wasn't my first piece for the *New York Times*, but it was my first about running, and the first that drew a lot of attention—warranted and not. When I first had meetings at the offices of *Runner's World*, one editor called me Dead Butt Girl. A guy who blogged anonymously under the name Angry White Dude called me a "yuppie libtard running freak" and wrote over and over again, in a mocking way, that I'm a Starbucks coffee drinker. Well, sorry, Angry White Dude. I'm a Dunkin' Donuts kind of gal—though yes, you do seem very angry.

To recover, I was ordered to stop running, break up that

scar tissue through sports massage (a.k.a. agony), and rebuild the muscles in my abs, back, and legs to keep the cup upright—the same muscles I had kept tight through weight lifting but ignored while on my Boston Marathon qualifying-time quest. This would take time, though. I would be out for four months.

I still made it out to the Ocean Drive 10 that year, turning in a 1:22:46 performance, which wasn't terrible, but it wasn't close to what I wanted, in either distance or time, and the pain was shattering. I waffled at the expo about whether or not to bump up to the Ocean Drive Marathon. I had run 17 miles in one shot. What's 9.2 more? What's a little more grinding pain when I already felt so flat and dull, like a winter sky tamped down by fat gray clouds? Just as I reached out for a pen to make a change on my registration, my mom took me by the shoulders and steered me to the 10-Miler packet pickup table.

Only after the Ocean Drive 10 did I take my running break. I felt like a fish flopping around on the sand, grit lodged in my gills and eyes. I retreated to the stationary bike and stared longingly at runners on the treadmills, even though I hated the treadmill. I felt floppy too, like all the work and training and muscles I'd built from running were melting away. I was afraid to eat too much but afraid to eat too little. I did not want to turn back into the 115-pound waif I was with Stephen. I didn't want to inflate into a heifer, either.

In May, the New Jersey Marathon came and went. I'd booked a room along the race course—nonrefundable—so I went anyway and picked up my race packet. I thought I'd scoop out a few coupons, but I was so angry at being there yet not really being there that I threw the bag in the trash, free race T-shirt and all. The night before the marathon, I went to a Kentucky Derby party in a red strapless dress and floppy hat, then lay on the beach the next day while the race went ahead without me, afraid to look up toward the Ocean Grove boardwalk in case I saw runners passing on their way to the marathon's turnaround point. I kept telling friends who asked how I was doing that I was fine. I told myself that I was fine. See? How could I be sad in this floppy hat? Sipping this mint julep? Lying on this beach in this tiny string bikini on top of this fun Superman towel? I *was* super. How could someone like this have a sad thought in her mind?

Through that early summer, after the dull gray clouds wiped away, I bloomed—not in a flower-buds-and-soft-green-grass sort of way, but in anger. I drove too fast, cut through lanes too close. I stayed out too late, partied too hard, and snapped too quickly at people around me. I didn't have that time running on the road to myself, that place to work out problems and aggression, even if it was just burning a little extra energy charging up a hill. I turned back to the weight room, sometimes spending an hour pounding out reps listening to hard-core rap music, dubstep, death metal. It didn't have the same calming effect, though. I stayed mad.

I was mad, at Stephen, at Jason, even at Dan, for rejecting me. Anger was better than acknowledging the desperate, weepy voice in my head that cried they were right to reject me, and that I'd end up a sad, lonely spinster with a dozen cats even though I'm allergic to cats. Anger was better than that.

So when I walked into a bar in South Philly and sat next to a tall guy with shaggy hair, the first thing I thought was *Ugh, get a haircut, hippie. And stay away from me.*

That night, I was In a Mood. When I'm In a Mood, I stomp around a lot and lose my verbal filter. I put on a short, black dress and three-inch heels and stomped to catch the train to Center City to attend a Thursday night fund-raiser at a swanky hotel. But my friend Adam, whom I had met while working on a story, texted me and said I should come down to the South Philly Bar and Grill to watch the final game of the Stanley Cup.

South Philly was often a no-go to me. I couldn't easily walk there from PATCO, and when I did go—for work, to meet friends who lived there and wanted to convince me it was a hip new neighborhood where all the cool twenty-somethings moved—what I saw was all garish neon slapped onto cheesesteak places, and no grass. No thanks. I didn't like cheesesteak, so I had no reason to go there regularly.

The fund-raiser was boring, but I didn't want to go to this bar either (see: In a Mood). But I told Adam that *FINE*, if I could catch a cab in the rain, I'd come. I stepped out of the Bellevue, and there was a cab.

FINE, I thought as I stomped into the car. The driver took

me out of Center City, past the run-down buildings and homes
along South Broad Street, and turned down what looked like an
alleyway with cars parked on both sides and bikes whizzing by
close enough to touch their handlebars on the cab's side mirrors.
The driver stopped in front of a neon-lit bar that matched the
cheesesteak places. Outside guys with no necks and gold chains
smoked cigarettes and took breaks from yelling into their cell
phones to yell things at the pretty girls going by. And next to
them were Adam and Derrick, Adam in a black T shirt and
Derrick in an old Flyers T-shirt.

The hostess, in a tube of black that pushed up her tits and
pushed out her ass, which made my little black dress look like
a caftan, told us that she couldn't seat us until our entire party
arrived, despite a still-empty bar behind her. I huffed. All I
wanted was a goddamn drink.

And who's the late one in our party? In strolls this big guy
built like an oak tree with reddish hair that came below his ears,
T-shirt, ragged shorts, and flip-flops.

"FINE. Let's go," I said, turning on one heel and stomping
behind the hostess to a back table.

This was game six of the Stanley Cup, do or die for the
Flyers. I wasn't much of a hockey fan and neither were Adam
and Nick—that long-haired guy—but Derrick was. He flipped
and flopped and stood and jumped and ended the game with
his head in his hands when the Flyers lost in overtime. The rest
of us talked around him.

As the drinks continued, the conversation turned to how

we lost our virginity, then how long you should wait before having sex with someone.

I, being In a Mood, countered everything they said.

"What if she wants to go?" Adam asked.

"Then fuck her," I said. "She's an adult. She knows what she's doing."

"But don't girls worry we'll lose respect for them?" asked Nick.

"Are you kidding me? Did I miss us stepping back into the 1950s? And by the way, we're women, not girls," I replied.

Adam and I debated how many dates you should go on before having sex. He said three. I said it depends. "Maybe she just wants some dick. And we can lose respect for you too."

I took a gulp of my Miller Lite, rolled my neck, and told this story:

"I was dating this guy Jason. We met at a concert, and I woke up next to him the morning after—but no sex. Not on that date, not on a date where he took me to Le Bec Fin . . . ("Hoooa" from the group).

"For his birthday, I booked us a room at the Rittenhouse Hotel. We were going to a black-tie that night. Everything was perfect. He was gorgeous. I wore a little gold dress that stopped just inches short of my snatch. We were lying in bed. He's on top of me. I can feel his dick pressing into my hip, and I'm like 'Yes! Finally!' Then he breathes into my ear 'I don't want to have sex until you're my girlfriend.' All I could think of was, 'I just want to get fucked!'"

Nick and Adam laughed so loud they broke Derrick from his hockey bubble. I sipped my drink, pleased with myself.

I gave Nick my card because his company was hiring and I thought my friend Jen might fit the bill.

On what we would later call our first "date," he met Jen and me at a corner wine bar in Center City on a soft summer night. They talked shop for a bit, but then the conversation was between the two of us as Jen watched. I felt something there, and he did too: He asked me to dinner a few days later.

As we talked, a van ran a red light and smashed into a black sedan. We watched as the medics came, and as tow trucks haggled over who would the haul away the wreckage. No one was killed or even taken away in an ambulance, but it was a big mess that left people limping as they walked away.

Nick was married when we met, but separated. She had moved out while their lawyers hashed out a divorce settlement. At first I didn't mind his situation. I still wasn't over Jason, and I didn't want a boyfriend. I didn't want to get hurt like that again, and I figured a fling before trying to seriously date again would be a good idea, like releasing a steam valve. I had no interest in anything long-term, and what I saw as Nick's semi-unavailability was a perk. He encouraged me to date other people—which, hey, why not. I had been out a few times with a runner I met in a group run, Nate, a redhead with a sub-three-hour marathon PR, but he had just split from his fiancée and said that he didn't want to start something with me that he couldn't finish.

Where Nate was quiet and shy, Nick was a bullhorn. He told me up front that he was "kind of an asshole." On one of our first dates, right before my thirtieth birthday, he pointed to a parking meter and said, "That's you. After your birthday, you expire," a joke he'd keep making for the next two and a half years. He said what he thought, did what he wanted. He loved to debate because he went in knowing he was never wrong. I liked his confidence, his assertiveness. He was a good temporary match.

Our first real date, he bent down to kiss me before I caught my train home and while grabbing my hip accidentally pulled down my strapless dress. My boob popped out, which sent us into gales of laughter—and I hadn't laughed like that in a long time. We had sex for the first time on the Fourth of July on a futon mattress on the floor of his bedroom, because he still hadn't replaced the furniture she took. He let me bring my dog too. No guy I had dated before had ever invited both of us over. The three of us watched the fireworks from his roof deck, us sipping wine, my dog—who isn't bothered by fireworks—zipping from plant to plant sniffing away, then sitting on a bench between us as the colors boomed.

It wasn't supposed to last. I was very conscious of being the one after the wife, and I had not given up on Jason just yet (that last encounter on the lifeguard stand was the month after I met Nick). But he stuck. We dated through the summer and into fall. I met his sister, his mom. On a warm September day that straddled the seasons, Nick came with me to Ocean City to keep me company and make funny faces at me while I had my head shot taken for the second edition of my Jersey Shore book. After, we ate greasy pizza at Mack & Mancos, then strolled down that boardwalk, our arms linked, my heart thrumming. *Oh shit*, I thought. *I may want him to stay.*

Finally—*finally!*—my doctor cleared me to run again that fall. I danced the first time I took my first few steps into a run, and even though I felt almost as unsteady as in those first workouts in training for my first 5K, I knew I could do it—and I did. My body remembered the motions. I welcomed that time back into my life, one that didn't require a gym membership or headphones to drown out other people. My body and brain were free.

I didn't feel the same pressure to control running anymore, either—breaking your butt does that to you—and my life was on a more even keel. I was getting laid on a regular basis. My hip wasn't screaming at me anymore. Work was booming too. Since I started freelancing, I'd occasionally done work for the company where I'd spent the summer before my first year of college, where my dad was now part-owner. We didn't work together, but when I'd come into the office to write newsletter copy or help with big proposals, he'd take me out to lunch at the Manayunk Diner, which wasn't very good, but Dad lived in the Pennsylvania-side suburbs of Philadelphia and missed New Jersey diners. This was as close as he could get, and it was a short drive from work.

That year, they needed emergency help after their marketing person quit with $1 billion of proposals to write, so I had a steady stream of income again on top of my regular freelancing work. By fall, I had finally said goodbye to Jason, and while the cloud of "what was wrong with me to make these men leave" still hung—I was sure Nick would figure out whatever my big, giant flaw was and cut me off too—now I could push that cloud away without rage smashing it.

I settled on the Bird-in-Hand Half Marathon, a race near Lancaster, Pennsylvania, as my comeback run, and I had help training. Nick ran the Broad Street Run 10-miler that year, and despite not really training for it, being sick, and running on a day where temperatures brushed 90, he ran ten-minute miles from start to end. He offered to train with me for the half marathon for the first few long weekend runs until the distance became too much for him. He showed up at my house in old running shoes with an MP3 player, but he never turned on the music as we finished a five-mile loop around my town. We ran 6, then 7 miles, then 8, until he signed up for the race, too. He took me on my first go-round of the Fairmount Park loop, which is just over 8 miles along Kelly and Martin Luther King Jr. Drives. It includes the final stretch of the Philadelphia Half Marathon and is also where flocks of runners go to log their weekend miles among walkers and bikers (I know of one running team called "On Your Left"—after our first run through I understood why). I was used to training on wide, quiet suburban streets and empty park paths. There, I ran into a half dozen people I knew.

On those long runs, Nick and I talked about life. He talked

more about why his marriage ended (she didn't get him, she spent too much money, he should have broken it off when her mother demanded he buy her an expensive wedding dress). I talked about my past, too, not just about Jason but about Stephen and my books and how I clawed my way through the recession. Because I didn't need to look at him, I could talk about things that would have been hard to say face-to-face. Unlike running with Jason, there was no negotiating the pace because we were at the same one: slow enough to keep talking but fast enough to still be a challenge. I started to miss his banter when I ran by myself on weekdays. Podcasts were far less interesting than unwinding another person's life while on a run.

After working off-site for a month, the marketing director of the company where my dad worked asked me to come into the office on a full-time basis—temporarily—until they found a replacement for their marketing person. Dad was thrilled. He had encouraged my writing career, but this meant I'd be around more often. I bought a bunch of boring black slacks, shells, and cardigans, hired a dog walker to take Emily out at lunchtime, and commuted five days a week to Bala Cynwyd, Pennsylvania. I'd come into work an hour early to work on my freelance projects, sneak in interviews and calls between the gaps in proposal due dates, and then finish those stories on nights and weekends.

Nick's ex-wife was connected to that industry, and a proposal with her name came across my desk. With his last name. I almost texted him that he had a relative he didn't know of, then I realized who it was. This woman with a smiling face and professional head shot and smart bob and pretty smile was her. The evil one. Who, Nick said, on their August wedding anniversary, texted him asking if they could make up and make babies, who started wearing her rings again when she found out he was dating someone, and then used me as the foil to try to heal their relationship even though she had moved out months before we met.

It was a very confusing time. And we talked about it while running, Nick sharing his life story, and me deciding how far and where we'd run.

We ran a tune-up 5K in October, two loops around Knight Park to raise money for the Collingswood Public Library. Nick trailed me for the race until the last 100 meters, then beat me by five strides. I still finished first female in the race—the one and only time I won a race—and in return was given a trophy as long as my arm and a pair of Vibram FiveFingers.

I wore them to run on the beach a few times, which is the only place I ran barefoot anyway, then donated them to Goodwill. I went back to the Mizuno Wave Riders, too, and apologized to the shoes that I ever strayed to hop on the barefoot bandwagon. The Nike Frees were banished to dog-walk duties. I last wore them in a mud run I finished with Nick, after which I threw them out. Goodbye, shoes Jason loved. And goodbye, Jason.

(I know a lot of runners who are still Vibram devotees, but the bubble has burst. By 2013, sales of minimalist shoes fell through the floor. In 2014, sales dropped by 50 percent just through the first half of the year, according to SportsOneSource, which tracks the sporting goods industry. In 2014, Vibram settled a class action lawsuit brought by customers who felt they were deceived by advertising that the shoes could prevent foot injuries—claims that they alleged were not based on scientific evidence.)

I chose the Bird-in-Hand Half Marathon, because it was a small, first-year race. I didn't want to do a big-city race again in case I collapsed again. If I flopped, the only people who would see it would be those running and the Amish, whose fields were the scenery for the race. Then I could safely retreat to my ten-milers with no one knowing that I couldn't tack on an extra 3.1 miles without the wheels coming off.

Nick and I stayed at a Best Western in Lancaster. He didn't seem nervous as we dressed. I was. My hip had held up through the training, but I hadn't pressured it with any kind of speed work. What if it snapped? What if the pain returned? What if I failed again and tipped the balance I had finally found?

Compared to the Philadelphia Half Marathon, the size of this crowd was a speck, our cars just filling the parking lot across the street from the starting line. After the national anthem, we set out over rolling hills on roads that were only partially shut down. Cars whizzed by. Buggies, their wheels grinding along the side of the road, passed us too. I learned that cows could run when one saw me at one end of her pen and then kept up with me for the length of the farm.

Nick stuck behind me the entire time, but I sensed he wanted to go faster.

"Just go," I said at mile 10. My hip was holding up, but I felt the first stirrings of that familiar end-of-race breakdown in my legs and uncomfortable burn in my lungs, and we still had 3 miles to go.

"No, I'm not leaving you. I'm not doing that like he did," he said, a reference to Jason.

He pulled even with me at mile 12, and told me to push. We turned toward the finish on a field—a field that was wet at the start of the race and turned into a mud slick by the time we crossed through.

"I can't keep it up," I said to Nick.

"Yes, you can," he said, and jumped in front of me.

I turned onto the field, splatting my feet down into a slick of mud, and fought to keep upright. I crossed under the finish banner, and put my hands on my knees as Nick walked through to grab a bagel and water. I finished in 1:55:43. He finished just ahead.

"See?" he said and hugged me. "You could do it. And that wasn't so bad."

We ached and creaked around that night, collapsing into his bed at 8:30 PM. As I was about to turn out the light, my dog in his lap, he said, "How's your hip?"

"Fine," I said.

"Good. Now you're ready for a marathon."

I liked Nick. I liked hanging out with him and being attached to someone who was so smart and savvy and who seemed to like me and my dog. He walked Emily and played with her and carried her around his house, bought her toys to keep there, and let her lick his legs after a run. I fluttered on the edge of scared and excited. I was getting too close. His divorce was finalized that fall, and instead of being relieved at his relationship status, I had started to worry both that I had rushed into another relationship and that it would collapse around me as soon as gave in to what I knew I felt. I reminded myself that he was honest about that relationship, and he liked to point out how I was "better:" that I was "petite" (I laughed when he said that, but he said that in comparison I was a compact person), that I was better with my money, more mature, smarter, and, as he said, I could "take" his personality. I could roll with his sometimes off-color jokes, even when I was the butt of them, and that I really understood him where she didn't.

By New Year's Eve, I knew I was sunk. We cohosted a party at his house that was planned as small get-together and ended up a rager. That's not why it was a less-than-ideal event, though. Nick played a horrible prank on me earlier that day by convincing his friends through texts and Twitter to make me think that you needed to wear costumes to the Mummers Parade, a Philadelphia New Year's Day parade with roots in blackface. I didn't want to go because, well, who wants to be associated with that? Especially when the race's supporters see no problem with some comics and musicians still including red face and yellow face in their acts, or doing routines with references to minstrel shows?

Of course no one attends the parade dressed in costume, but I didn't know that, and because Nick and his friends posted about picking up their (fictional) costumes on Twitter, and I asked them on that public platform what they meant, I looked like a fool. "You're too sensitive," Nick told me. I didn't think I was too sensitive, not when this man orchestrated a group effort to embarrass me—all online where everyone we knew would see. I told him to go fuck himself and that I wasn't coming over that night.

But after apologies and promises of how much fun the party would be, I showed up at his house with my dog, my face still puffy and red from crying. I ignored him until the party started to fall apart, first with a girl in hippie jeans who dropped a beer on the floor then tried to rub the beer into the wood floor "because no one will notice." I kicked her out, and order was restored. Nick and I still went upstairs for a midnight toast on his roof deck with a bottle of champagne, where he kissed me and told me he loved me and that he wanted to spend the rest of his life with me. And I went to the parade the next day, pushing down my squeamishness about supporting such an event because I wanted to be a good girlfriend.

I even wrote about him in my second *New York Times* running column, a piece titled "Fitness Goals: Run. Race. Beat the Boyfriend," about how I started dating someone who hadn't been a runner yet he ran more race miles than I did throughout that year. "Before I met him, I craved the solitude of those long, lonely runs. Now I want his wry companionship next to me for every mile," I wrote.

The essay ran early in the new year. I proclaimed to the world: "He is mine." I was still worried he'd drop me like the others had done before, but I was having fun with him. I was conscious of being thirty—Nick reminded me of that. My third sibling was on his way toward marriage. I decided to hold on and hope that the same would happen for me

Chapter 6

PHILADELPHIA MARATHON

NOVEMBER 20, 2011

New Jersey Marathon — Miles 13–16

The halfway point rolled under me the same way my hips and legs rolled together over the asphalt into Deal: smoothly. Legs: check. Hips: check: Lungs: check. Bowels: empty. Brain: nearly so.

Before the race, I broke the course up into a five-part checklist: Oceanport/Monmouth/Long Branch; Deal Part 1; Asbury Park/Ocean Grove; Deal Part 2; and the finish. I made the first part the longest on purpose so that every section I knocked off after that would be short, leaving me multiple victories leading up to the finish line.

Four? FOUR more segments left? I thought as I passed the Deal

Casino, a summer beach club with a big, lush lawn facing the street, but whose contents had been tossed out by Sandy.

You are fine. FINE. You're halfway done with the race and you feel good. You probably don't look good, but that doesn't matter. Doesn't matter doesn't matter. Fluffy matter? Is that a dog over there? Do not stop to pet the dog!

The only shade offered along this stretch of Deal Part 1 came from streetlights curling overhead. I dreaded this segment, knowing the sun would beat down on me just as I was reaching the race's halfway point.

And who knows how you'll feel when you come back through here. No, stop it. STOP it.

Despite temperatures in the 50s with a cool ocean wind winding its way a block inland to where we ran on Ocean Avenue, the sun still screamed May. I dumped another cup of water on my head at the next water stop. Right before the mile 15 marker, I passed butt cheeks girl. Her shoulders and the bottoms of those cheeks were burned.

The course was wide here: a big boulevard with shoulders on each side, separated in the middle by three vertical strips of brick. By then, Oz Pearlman, the leader in the race who had won twice before (and would win that day) passed by on his way back to Long Branch, followed by a trickle of fast runners that turned into a creek, then a river coming from where I still needed to run.

You're fine. You're fine. You're not trying to beat them. Stick to the plan. Stick. To. The. Plan.

I don't remember much about those miles because they were

boring. The tough women of Murderess Row from Chicago hung
around my head, dancing in their strips of black costume, all legs and
abs and swinging hair, red flags in their hands to indicate that, yes,
they were guilty. *"He took a flower in its prime / And then he used it!
And he abused it!"*

The only real noise was the *phat-phat* of sneakers on road and
the distant crash of the ocean, both sounds playing over each other,
over and over and over again. *"It was a murder but not a crime!"*

Murderesses were fine. Boring was fine. Boring was more
than fine because I had no distractions to throw off my balance: No
encounters with any fighting couples or cars stopped at barricades,
drivers mad that they couldn't use the road over which we traveled.
I wasn't talking to anyone by then, not because of pain, but because
my mind was done running around its own hamster wheel. It
blanked, which is exactly what I wanted.

I passed mile 16–the farthest I'd gone in training–without a blip
in my body and only a small thought that what lay ahead was, at least
for this training cycle, uncharted territory.

I hadn't completely given up on the marathon after hurting
myself in 2010. It still scared me, though, carrying with it a
big fat fear of bleeding nipples, runners breaking against The
Wall, and making otherwise sensible people poop their pants.

The marathon, like every other race distance, became more
popular through the '00s and beyond, though that growth was
still modest compared to that of the half marathon, according

to Running USA. I saw why. Training for a half marathon is like eating chicken nuggets, while preparing for the marathon is like starting out with the whole bird—unplucked. It's not simply doubling mileage. It's dedicating a sizeable chunk of your life to the training: the running, the preparing for the running, the recovering from the running, the eating and sleeping right to continue to do all the running.

In 2008, as I was training for my first Ocean Drive 10-Miler, I read the book *First Marathons*, a collection of essays from runners retelling their first marathon attempts. In it, everyone from a nun to a husband-and-wife team to recovering addicts to legends of the sport share how they started running and their first marathon experiences, whether they were great races or disasters.

I had watched marathoners, too. In 2010, I ran the Asbury Park Relay Marathon on a two-person relay team. I did ten miles after my ultrarunner friend Sam ran the first 16.2. The race included eight laps around Asbury Park, and while I ran my part, Sam helped pace his friend Chris, who was doing his first marathon. Chris hoped to qualify for Boston through it.

Except Chris bonked, big time. On my last lap, I found them both sitting on the curb. Chris's calf had seized, and Sam was feeding him salt pills to get electrolytes into his body to loosen up the cramps. When they came in through the finisher's chute everyone started cheering, thinking they were done. Sam held his finger up and said, "One more! One more!" as embarrassment flushed across Chris's already red face.

I didn't want to be that guy, banging on my calf at mile 20 of a marathon. I didn't want to be the runner who pooped herself, or who hit that wall, or who broke her butt in training—again. But I also didn't want to be the writer who wrote about running without ever finishing a marathon.

As Nick started to toss around possible marathon options, I went back to *First Marathons* and reminded myself that if an obese, chain-smoking nun could start running at fifty-four and then run fast enough to qualify for the Olympic Marathon Trials, I could finish just one marathon without shitting my pants.

After I ran the Bird-in-Hand Half Marathon and did not break myself, I tried to get over the still-present fear of breaking myself through volume. Nick and I ran seven races in eleven weeks that spring (another Adrenaline 5K, another Ocean Drive 10-Miler, and Broad Street, plus the Cherry Blossom Ten Mile Run, Asbury Park Half Marathon, the first Phillies 5K, and the Virginia Wine Country Half Marathon). "Jamming all those races into such a short time took the competition out of it," I wrote in the *New York Times*. "I wasn't running for medals or gift certificates or free shoes. I ran because the courses were there, friends were there, the finish line was there."

Nick was all in. I introduced him to my local running store friends, bought him a GPS watch, and stocked up on Shot Bloks for two instead of one. By June, a year after we met, we talked about that first marathon almost as much as the possibility of me moving into his house.

Nick presented this as a practical move. We were doing a constant shuttle between our two places, usually ending with me and Emily sleeping at his house, then I'd shuffle to work, bumping and pushing my way through South Philly traffic, to bump and push my way back through one-way streets and four-way stop signs to pick up my dog and go home, adding about a half hour to my already long commute.

Plus, Collingswood became that place hipsters went to breed. I could rent out my house for more than the mortgage, taxes, and insurance cost per month and turn a small profit.

Nick kept talking about marriage and kids, and that the only way to figure out whether our relationship would work was to live together. I agreed, but hesitated—not for any religious or traditional reasons about living together before marriage, but because it felt rushed. I felt as if he wanted to push us ahead with a shove instead of a nudge, as if his life timeline hadn't changed since his divorce. He just stuck another woman in that role.

Then there was his house. It was a lovely three-story house with finished basement and roof deck, but it was in the wrong place. It was also one his ex-wife picked out. On Google Maps, the photo of the front door features a blue wreath, one she put there.

I had not, as he predicted, fallen in love with South Philadelphia. To me, it was still claustrophobia-inducing, harried, and dirty with trash everywhere—on the streets and sidewalks and overflowing out of trash cans. It wasn't what

I wanted and what I already had: a nice house with a small lawn in a small town, where trees draped over every street. I had been groped four times already in South Philadelphia, and once while walking my dog at night, a man in a truck told me exactly what he would to do to me when he bent me over the hood of that truck. Of course these kinds of things happen in nice towns because jerks live everywhere, but these incidents were concentrated where Nick lived. I understood why people wanted to live in the city. I got their rationale. For a lot of people, the clustered convenience of having so many things at their fingertips, of living without a car, makes them happy. And I liked visiting and enjoying the bars and restaurants and people and culture, but I also liked going home to sleep in my own bed where the only real noise at night were the sounds of leaves slapping against each other in the wind and the train passing by.

Nick assuaged my worries about living in South Philly by saying that it would be temporary until repairs were done on his house. He asked me to call my realtor, and we spent our Saturday afternoons walking in and out of three- and four-bedroom Collingswood houses, debating whether we'd buy a fixer-upper or pay the extra money for a house that was already updated. My dog's new phobia of my car sealed the deal. I started throwing stuff out, putting my furniture on Craigslist, packing boxes, writing the listing for my house.

Before meeting with the realtor, we'd run the Fairmount Park loop. We still talked, but the tenor had changed. It wasn't discussion about our lives and who we were, but how we would move forward together. Nick was taking the lead in our pace—ramping it up ever so slightly to where I was just a bit uncomfortable—and in mapping out how our future would go. That left me a bit uncomfortable too, because it was made up of his vision, not mine.

"I don't want to do Philly for my first," I said about that marathon. It wasn't so much that I'd done poorly on the half there before, but I didn't like the course, and my unease with the city was growing. It seemed silly to give it my first marathon.

Nick's only response: "I like this city. You live here now, so you better learn to like it. That's the marathon we're going to do."

Here's how we trained: On Tuesday, Wednesday, and Thursday the alarm went off at 5:30 AM and I rolled out of bed to take Emily for a walk, after which I'd shove Nick to get up. When he finally did, we walked a block and a half to a gym, a three-story building with Rocky-wannabes throwing weights around on two different weight-room floors, with one room on one level dedicated to cardio machines. The ceilings were low, with two rows of treadmills close to the televisions hanging from those low ceilings. Behind was a walkway, then two rows of elliptical machines. I tried to be as far away as possible from the woman who set herself up on an elliptical and talked on a Bluetooth the entire time she pedaled away, yakking loud enough that I heard her over my music. Who she was talking to so ecstatically at 6:00 AM, I have no idea, but by the end of marathon training I wanted to shove the Bluetooth down her throat.

We'd run mile after boring mile to nowhere, staring at the closed captioned broadcast of *SportsCenter* or local news, which always reported on the weather, the traffic, one scary medical story about how I was going to die at the hands of some common household product, and then something about cute animals. Nick taught me the trick of laying a Phillies rally towel over the treadmill monitor to keep myself from staring at the numbers tick slowly by. I challenged myself to not move the towel for as long as possible, because when I did, I was never as far along as I wanted to be.

Wednesdays were the longest treadmill days, with runs stretching to 5, 6, 7, 8 miles, one step after another into the boring abyss.

By the time we worked up to 7 miles on a Wednesday, I learned that the treadmills threw you into automatic cool-down after sixty minutes. I kept pushing the pace up only to be slowed down again. I was so frustrated—and so close to being done after an hour of boring running into nothingness—that I smacked the display.

Then it was a hustle back home to shovel down granola and milk, shower, and then drive to the office with the windows rolled down, still sweating but hoping the air would blast my hair dry and cool me down. In the parking lot, I'd coil my hair into a bun, hoping the look came off as slick and chic instead of a frizz-balled mess.

It was a boring job, but it was a steady one and a temporary one that allowed me to work on freelance projects when office work was slow, and occasionally have lunch with Dad, who in his new life seemed a changed man from the last time he lived at home. He loosened up, smiled more, was happy. I liked seeing him like that.

I obliterated all debt still hanging around from the recession by collecting that full-time salary and letting someone else pay for my health insurance while freelancing at the same pace I had before. I cracked *Runner's World* that spring, and did my first interview for them over the phone with my office door closed in the hopes that no one would walk in while I was asking Michael Palin of *Monty Python*—Michael Palin! of *Monty Python*!— about his running experiences over the last thirty-plus years.

"I have never come back from a run feeling worse than when I set out," he said in that lilting British accent as I quietly freaked out on my end of the phone. "It is terrific in a sense that I clear my mind. I come back from my runs with more energy and concentration."

Then I'd go home, bump and push my way through the South Philadelphia four-way stop sign gauntlet to push and shove for a parking space somewhere close to the house, hopefully between cars that would not treat my bumpers like suggestions rather than stop signs, walk the dog, and then wait until Nick came home and figure out what we'd eat to satiate a new, never-ending hunger that ate at our stomachs.

We were doing Hal's Novice 1 schedule, which called for

four days of running per week with one day of cross training and two days of rest. Wednesdays were pace runs. Saturdays were long runs. It was lighter than what I did when I had tried for the New Jersey Marathon, but more exhausting to complete since I balanced running with a job for which I needed to shower and the needs of Nick, which proved to be monumental.

In the run-up to moving in together, Nick had been devoted, loving. Despite his opinion that he was never wrong, he seemed committed to building a life that would work for us both. One reason he wanted to run a marathon that fall was so I could get one in before I had our first child. After Jason, I stopped trying to think about *those* things like weddings and babies, but when Nick held my hand and said that Josephine, my mother's middle name, would be a wonderful name for a daughter, I melted just a bit inside.

When I moved in, though, something shifted, and I found myself trying to change myself into what he kept telling me would be the best version of me.

These comments were harmless at first. Maybe I should dress a little nicer, so I met with a stylist at Nordstrom. Maybe I should spend a little more time with his friends versus going to New Jersey to see mine, since his were close by. Harmless, right? But these criticisms grew in frequency and vigor. My music tastes weren't just different from his anymore. They were unsophisticated. Of course I should put my freelance work aside if he needed me to do something for him, like go to the dry cleaner near his hometown, a forty-five-minute drive each way.

He really needed that tie for his meeting, and I had all that spare time with my less-taxing profession. When someone egged the house, I was the one who cleaned it up because he had something important to do. I scrubbed at yolk and whites that had frozen on the stairs while the neighborhood walked by and stared on their way to church.

But I did these things and rarely complained, because to complain would start a fight. Maybe that's what would make a relationship finally work for me. Nick was so masculine, with a personality turned to eleven, and I assumed a slightly submissive role, thinking it wouldn't be so bad to let someone else drive the car for a little while. When the balance tipped too far, I didn't say anything, just went uncomfortably along.

The Saturday long run became a flash point. Where before he gently pushed the pace to slightly uncomfortable, now he ran too fast for me, and I spent most of these long runs trying to catch up.

"Just go ahead," I'd say as I trailed him, trying to keep the pace. On most training plans, especially for beginners, long runs were supposed to be done at an easy pace, and the one he set was not easy. I knew where the car was. I knew how long we had to run. I didn't care if he finished ahead of me.

"No. You need to keep up. It'll make you faster."

Then there was the timing of our runs. I wanted to at least start before sunrise so I didn't roast the entire way (later, when I trained for the New York City Marathon in 2014, I started long runs at 4:30 AM). Part of that was preference. I hated running in the heat. Another was practical: I've had eczema since I was eight, and it's triggered by stress, heat, and humidity. Nick brushed aside my concerns. My eczema would be under control if I could just relax, he said, and running in the heat more often would make running in the heat less painful.

I tried to grind through a 9-mile run with Nick before Hurricane Irene hit that August. An eczema outbreak had already been stirring, setting up residence on my eyelids and in the crooks of my arms, but it lit on fire as I tried to run in coupy air down Columbus Boulevard.

"Nick, I need to stop," I said.

"Why?"

"It hurts."

"How can a skin problem hurt? It's a rash."

"I am telling you, Nick, it hurts," I said, and stopped.

"This wouldn't be such a problem if you'd just relax," he said, stalking back to me. "You wouldn't have these breakouts if you could control your emotions." He's taller than me by half a foot, and he stared down at me as I ran my nails over the patches of eczema on my arms that by then were weeping pus. "Now come on. You're going to finish this run."

I let him go ahead of me, dragging myself to keep up, him occasionally looking behind me to make sure I was still there.

Once we turned off Delaware Avenue to run the mile back to the house, he picked up the pace because he liked to end on a sprint. "Come ON," he yelled back at me.

I stopped with a half mile to go and walked home, slammed

down some Gatorade, and stomped up into my office where I scratched the patches on the insides of my arms raw. Three days later, my doctor declared that my eczema was infected and he put me on heavy dose of antibiotics and steroid cream. When I told Nick, he still insisted that I could control it if I really tried.

In this relationship I shoved myself aside, and by the time I realized what I'd done, it was too late. When I questioned him or raised a concern, I was either wrong or burdening him, so I just stopped and tried to change myself, my habits, my everything, to not be that burden.

After most of our long runs—if we didn't need to meet with the realtor—I'd shower while Nick let Emily lick his legs, then I'd nap. After his shower, we'd go out and gorge ourselves on cheeseburgers and fries and craft beers. I'd smile again, laugh again, touch my still-hot face and wonder what the fuss had been about. I was too sensitive, just like Nick said. Everything was fine. As the fall progressed, we stopped meeting with the realtor. Nick said it was because our running schedule was too heavy, and I was interviewing for a job at *Runner's World*, which would mean a move to Emmaus, Pennsylvania, about an hour from Philadelphia.

"Why move so soon if you're going to have to move again?" he said. When I didn't get the job and wanted to set up more viewings with the realtor, Nick said to wait until the marathon was over.

As summer rolled into fall, and the nights cooled, I thought things would get better. I quit the full-time work for my client after it became clear that they didn't think the job was temporary. Dad was disappointed. "I thought you found a home here," he said, but he wasn't my boss, and he knew me well enough to let me go. That cut out the horrible commute, though I still woke up early to run on treadmills with Nick because he said he wouldn't do it if I didn't, and that if he wasn't ready for the race, it would be my fault.

But that also meant that I was stuck in that house, in a neighborhood I was slowly starting to hate, all day. Fall didn't make me want to put on a sweater and explore the city. It made me want to go home and run around Knight Park.

"Why do you keep telling me this?" he'd say when I brought up that the contractor—the one who was supposed to be finishing the repairs that would let Nick list the house so we could finally move—had not shown up that day. Again.

"Because it's unprofessional of him. I was trapped in this house all day waiting for him, and he couldn't even call?"

"I have enough to worry about without you pushing this onto me. Why don't you support me. And what's with this 'trapped'? This is a beautiful house. You should love it here."

On repeat.

On the day of our twenty-miler, Philadelphia was hit with a freak October snowstorm, and we stopped 6 miles in. We were supposed to go to a Halloween party that night in costumes Nick had picked out: cow for me, farmer for him, that whole cow/farmer/milk-for-free joke. I hated the idea, but I didn't tell him that, and Nick had a way of presenting things he wanted without making me think I had a choice. "It'll be funny!" he said. But the party was snowed out. Still, that cow costume hung on my side of the closet for months after.

I tried to fit into this new life, even if it chafed. At first, I thought it was because I hadn't lived with someone else since graduate school, and of course there would be a transition period. I could make it fit, I told myself: because it was time for me to grow up, get married, have kids. I had already walked a different line than the rest of my family. Chucking your job out the window to be a *writer*—twice—was almost as foreign to them as me suddenly becoming a *runner*, an activity that my father was assured would lead to my early death. That person, the one who was the independent, home-owning entrepreneur, knew that she could forge ahead on any path that she so chose.

But then there was another plane of existence running under me, like the belt of a treadmill, about what I should be doing with my life. That was a hard path to avoid when it was what everyone else in my family was doing. It's what kept me chasing after Stephen and Jason long after they deserved my attention. By the time I lived with Nick, my baby brother was about to get married. My older brother and his wife had their first son. My sister had hers two weeks later, and was cooking baby number two.

"Wouldn't it be nice if they had another cousin?" my dad asked me when I was visiting one day. We were in the kitchen, and Nick was out in the yard playing with my dad's dog. My dad didn't say much about Nick to me—"I trust you," he said multiple times. But he wanted to know when we would take that next step.

"You have enough grandkids, Dad," I said to him on a visit I made to his house on my own. I didn't let my father know that Nick didn't really like him and didn't make that drive with me unless he had to.

"You guys would make some great athletic grandchildren. I'm counting on your genes to give me a superstar," he said.

"Dad, he's just divorced."

"But it's done. You know I have money set aside for a wedding. Just say the word."

I don't think my dad was conscious of the pressure he put on me to move in a direction I didn't know if I wanted to go. To him, marriage equaled happiness, and being complete, and he wanted me to be happy.

No one in my family had drawn outside the lines. They all got married, had kids. Sure, college, a job, and career were important, but in the early twenties only. My late twenties were supposed to be dedicated to motherhood and family. Already in my thirties? I was behind. My sister had quit her job as soon as she had her first son. The Miller kids were expected to march along in the same direction, and I had thrown us out of step.

And here was someone with a good job, who didn't have two heads, who seemed to like me though I had flaws. We talked about weddings and babies and rings. What woman in her right mind would turn that deal down? I told myself to be content—relieved even—that someone had finally seen something in me that was enough to want to live with me and seriously talk about a future together. He wasn't a drunk like Steve. He wasn't going to up and move without me like Jason. And even if the little digs and comments grated me, I wanted to try to make it work. Nick's go-to joke was that given my age no one else would want me, so I was stuck with him.

After the fiftieth, hundredth, two hundredth time I heard it, I started to believe him.

I woke up on marathon morning at 4:00 AM, then 4:30 AM, and then, when the alarm finally went off at 5:00, shoved myself into sweatpants and a jacket to walk the dog, and stepped outside into warmth. November 20, and the pre-sunrise temperature was already 50 degrees and spiked with humidity. I took Emily far enough for her to poop and pee, then slammed back into the house.

I woke Nick up. "It's HOT," I said, swapping out the short-sleeve shirt I had planned to wear for a blue tank.

"It won't be so bad."

While he went through his pre-race rituals, which included taking a shower, I stomped to Dunkin' Donuts to get us both coffees, which was supposed to make us poop. He took the upstairs bathroom and I the downstairs, checking the weather on my phone again as if, at my insistence, the forecast would flip to cold. I switched between sips of Gatorade and coffee until the coffee worked. *At least that's done.*

I should have been prepared for race nerves by now, but this pressure was enormous, made worse by worrying about another person. We also hadn't agreed on how to get to the race, a big mistake for someone like me who likes to plan ahead.

"Call a cab," he yelled down the stairs.

I did, and was told the wait was forty-five minutes. So we walked twenty minutes to the Broad Street subway line, and took that to city hall to join in with other runners who convened in that spot to walk to the start line.

The marathon hadn't changed much since I ran the half in 2009, except officials crammed more runners onto the course by allowing more half marathon runners in, so again I was stuck in line for a Porta-Potty, and again I peed by a tree, this time with Nick shielding me with my hoodie. He had bought a bib from a faster but injured runner, so he gave me a quick kiss and set off for the first corral behind the elites. For my first marathon, my only goals were to finish and not require immediate medical attention, so I set a conservative projected pace, which slotted me into the gray corral, three corrals behind Nick.

I planned to use my first Ocean Drive 10 strategy: Run nine minutes, walk one minute, run nine, and repeat. I was nervous about the distance, especially since we hadn't done that twenty-miler. When the race started and we shifted forward to the start line, one corral after another, that was still the plan.

Except race organizers never changed the course to accommodate that larger size of the half marathon field, which jammed the road through those first narrow streets, some of which still had cars parked on the side of the road. I started dumping water on my head at the first water stop. I came up on a water stop at mile 5 at the same time I was taken over by a pace group, made worse by the water stop being positioned on the turn off 6th Street onto the long chute of Chestnut Street. There was no way to stop at that moment without tripping or falling on someone, so I kept going, no walks allowed.

Since I'd run the first half of the course when I did the half marathon in 2009, I knew the dips and valleys and climbs, slight as they are. I stopped to pee at mile 7. By then the crowds had loosened up on wider streets, and I could start to run/walk/run. My hips protested at mile 9, and I told them to shut up. At Memorial Hall in Fairmount Park, right before mile 11, I tried to rip open my package of Shot Bloks, but my fingers fumbled and a spectator did it for me. By the time we hit the stretch along Martin Luther King Jr. Drive, the half marathoners started celebrating, and I knew why marathoners had given half runners the stink eye here in 2009. To hear their relief at being nearly done, knowing you must double up, is deflating, especially when you enter that second half on shaky ground. I told myself I was fine—I was FINE—and that I'd do better without so many people around. Good riddance.

In the 2015 Los Angeles Marathon, Japanese runner Mao Kuroda kept with the lead pack through most of the race before falling back and finishing fourth. It was her first marathon, which Olympian and broadcast commentator Tim Hutchings called "taking her giant steps into the dark."

That's what it felt like when I reached the second half of my first marathon. I was going where I hadn't gone in a race before, but instead of taking giant strides into the dark, I tripped.

I turned in front of the Philadelphia Museum of Art to the second half of the course, which is an out-and-back to Manayunk along Kelly Drive—the road opposite Martin Luther King Jr. Drive—and that's when my intestines felt like they were trying to drop out of my body.

I stopped to use the bathroom again at mile 15, and watched people whoosh by in both directions, the faster runners coming in to the finish, the rest of the pack heading out into the second half in the other direction.

That's when the race really fell apart. I waited ten minutes for the Porta-Potty, then lost more time trying to push my bowels clear. I'm not sure what happened. Many runners don't in these situations. The most likely culprit was all that Gatorade I had before the race (I no longer drink it because of its sugar content). When I finally made it back onto Kelly Drive, my legs had started to stiffen, and I never quite shook them out again. When I hit mile 17 and the first hill of the second half, my hips went from protesting to screaming, and I again told them to shut the *fuck* up. At mile 18, we turned to Manayunk, a Philadelphia neighborhood of hills and bars lined with people partying and cheering, a shock after the quiet of Kelly Drive. There I remembered that it was a rolling hill, and that this was not the flat course the organizers advertised. At mile 19, I passed a woman who had not made it to the Porta-Potty in time. At mile 21, on the way out of Manayunk, I hit the beer stop set up by the Philadelphia Hash House Harriers, a local chapter of a worldwide organization dedicated to beer and running. A friend had pretzel M&Ms waiting for me there, which I scarfed down, followed by a small pour of beer. The booze didn't faze me. I felt so hot—burning really—that I sweat it out by the next mile marker. Then it was back on Kelly Drive to finish the race.

This part of the marathon is a dead zone, much quieter than the same trip on the way out because there were fewer runners on the course then. It's away from Center City, and it's not easy for spectators to get there when they don't have the option of driving. There was virtually no support (a local running store has been working to get more people out there, to some success). The sun pushed temps toward 60 degrees. At water stops, I walked, drank, and poured two cups of water over my head, hoping that at that point it would soak my braid to lie on my neck and cool me down. I went back to run/walk/run, stopping once every nine minutes, and then, by mile 22, running eight minutes and then walking for two.

Step step step. Bang bang bang. This didn't feel like running. It felt like hurling myself across nails, pain rocketing through my body with every motion. My hips gave up screaming. They wept quietly, along with my thighs and my shoulders and my back and my toes. Between miles 23 and 24, I saw two people taken off the course on stretchers.

I didn't quite hit the wall. I wasn't running strong enough to crash into it. Instead, I crumbled. My legs stopped wanting to move. Just before mile 25, I saw two people I knew—the first ones aside from my M&M mule that I'd spotted in the entire race. They screamed and yelled and I gave back a weak wave. At the 25-mile marker, I stopped to walk again. I thought I'd run the rest of the way, but my legs seized up and stopped me short. At mile 26, I stopped again.

"Go go go! You're almost there!" a spectator yelled at me. I wasn't. Those last 0.2 miles stretched ahead like an unending spool of road, growing longer the more I looked at it. I got mad. I didn't need to be shamed by spectators for walking. What were they doing that morning other than ringing cowbells and drinking coffee and enjoying what to them must have felt like a nice warm day, not hellfire?

At the last 0.1 mile, I heard Nick, his mom, and sister screaming for me. He had finished and changed already. I didn't stop then, even though my body revolted at being pressed to move forward, and came across the finish with a lunge of relief.

I wasn't triumphant, but just glad the whole thing was done and over. I ran a marathon, and I never had to run one again

Finishing time: 4:34:01. Nick beat me by forty minutes.

Post-marathon was a blur. Nick and his sister walked ahead to an Irish pub. His mother accompanied to get me into dry clothes while I moved myself forward with a series of lurches.

No one in my family came to the race. My nephew was being

christened that day. I called my mother to tell her that I didn't die. I thought it would be a joke, but then learned that two people had died on the course that day, one person at the finish of the half marathon, and another right before the finish in the full marathon, right behind Nick.

At the bar, I ordered nachos and a bloody mary, eating a few chips and the olive from the drink. We took pictures. I look stoned. The hoodie I threw on after the race was soaked from my braid and my shirt. In that picture, my shoulders are slumped, my smile both sleepy and forced. I couldn't sit down. I couldn't stand up. I shifted from bar stool to standing and back again. I couldn't get comfortable because pain radiated from muscle, bone, tendon, ligament, from every pore in my body.

The food helped a bit, and I could soon remember my name and at least talk about the race.

Nick and I walked back to the subway, blinking like moles in the sun. I hadn't packed sunglasses. Philadelphia teemed around us, shoppers and walkers taking advantage of the late November sun. Nick had finished strong, but he wasn't exempt from the post-marathon pain. We hobbled our way down to the subway, both taking each stair one at a time, one foot, two foot, one foot, two foot.

That night, when my hunger finally caught up to me, I shuffled to the nearby Acme wearing black pajama bottoms, my marathon finisher shirt, an old pair of running shoes, and picked up a tub of Party Mix for me and Hot Pockets for Nick. I swore to the cashier that I was not stoned, but she looked at my food and glazed face, and nodded back with a look that said she thought I was full of shit. I ate half the tub and passed out, my hand still coated with orange grime and pretzel salt.

My first marathon was done. And I'd never do it again, I told myself.

A few weeks later, Nick and I spent the weekend in Cape May. Our hotel included a shop that sold antique jewelry. On the morning we left, he told me to go in and try on some rings. I tried on a few that looked nice, and landed on a square-cut diamond with . . . some other diamonds around it. I really don't remember except that it was from the 1920s and very sparkly. Even when Jason and I talked about getting married, I didn't envision the perfect ring or even perfect ceremony aside from those late-night musings. Instead, I envisioned the life we'd live together, which I saw as grand. Here, with Nick, that vision was a blank.

"How much?" Nick asked.

"This one is $15,000. A real value for that kind of cut, which you can't get in a modern diamond," the salesperson said.

I'm glad I was still holding the ring or I might have dropped it on the counter.

"No, that's too much," I said, sliding it off my finger and putting it back on the velvet mat on the counter. I didn't want to have that much money on my finger, let alone ask someone to spend what was close to my house's down payment on a piece of jewelry.

"No, it's not," Nick said, and asked for the appraisal information.

He didn't buy it, but took home a card with its information. I got into his car for the ride home with the same post-marathon glaze on my face. I told myself to stop being uncomfortable with the idea that a man wanted to buy me a $15,000 engagement ring. Discomfort soon turned to terror. I still wasn't sure about Nick, and our first months of living together didn't inspire confidence.

So instead of talking about it, or asking Nick to not play the stupid folk album that I hated, I fell asleep, waking up as we crossed the Walt Whitman Bridge out of New Jersey and back into Philadelphia, hoping that it'd all sort itself out before I had that ring on my finger.

chapter 7

CHICAGO MARATHON

OCTOBER 7, 2012

New Jersey Marathon — Miles 16–18

Hot. It's hot. So very hot.

Two cups of water for my mouth, two for my head. At the water stop just before mile 16, the volunteer in heavy hooded sweatshirt and gloves who handed me water that I promptly threw on myself looked at me as if I had asked her to cut off my ear.

It's only 50. In August, you ran a half in 75 degrees. This is better. This is better.

Two for my head, two for my mouth.

The Murderesses took a break as we crossed out of Deal at mile 16.5 then ran briefly through the towns of Loch Arbour

(population 193) and Allenhurst (population 493), popping out on
the other side at Deal Lake. We ran over a flat bridge to plunge into
Asbury Park, Bruce Springsteen's muse that had finally pulled itself
away from being that place that ripped the bones from your back and
being both a death trap and a suicide rap.

Born to run. Barefoot run? No, not for you. Not for you. Blue?
Blue water? Could I jump in the ocean after the race? Would I ruin
these shoes? I could. I could. Hot. So very hot.

We ran past the hotel I slept in the night before, then past
the Stone Pony, which is still an active concert venue and a musical
pilgrimage site, and a new condo project. I had thought of moving here
after leaving Nick: new city, new start, a beach and boardwalk to see and
use every day, and the chance to plant my flag in a town on the rise.

"Runners! Runners! Runners!" a woman with a cowbell on
Kingsley Avenue yelled as she *clanged clanged clanged* along. I gave
her a thumbs-up, that thumb still encased in a sweat-soaked glove, as
we turned toward that bridge into Ocean Grove.

Runners runners runners. Running. Running. You are running.
You are fine.

And there it was: mile marker 18, where I'd started walking in a
marathon six months before.

———

Nick and I had reached an agreement about the dog. I walked
Emily at whatever time she woke up in the morning. He
walked her before bed and at any time in the middle of the night,
because, a year in, I still did not feel safe in our neighborhood.

Somehow on the way down the stairs once at some ungodly hour, the summer after the Philadelphia Marathon, Emily got underfoot. Nick tripped and fell.

Before I called out to see if he was okay, this thought flashed through my mind, like a beam from a lighthouse: "If he's dead, I'll have my way out of here without hurting anyone's feelings." And then the beam turned off.

Things had not, as I hoped, gotten better as we settled into our new lives together. As fall turned to winter, then spring, Nick's criticisms became more frequent (that I didn't like football, card games, his favorite band) and even bizarre (that he was reconsidering having kids with me because I was allergic to eggs). He also nixed the plan to move to Collingswood and insisted we were staying in the city.

"I'm not ready to leave, so we're not moving," he said from his lounge chair in the basement. I sat on the couch, *Tosh 2.0* playing on TV.

"I don't want to stay where we're at, Nick. That was not the plan," I said without looking at him.

"Get over it. People love it here. You need to see that," he said, twisting his wrist in a way that cracked all the joints of that wrist and his hand, a habit he knew I hated, but continued to do anyway. "What's wrong with you?"

What *was* wrong with me, I wondered. My discomfort with the neighborhood, with Nick, had turned from frustration to despair.

I know I was not the perfect girlfriend. A pallor falls on me every winter, sending me to the couch and books with no desire to socialize, but my bigger flaw, Nick later said to me, was that I didn't tell him what was wrong, or I'd stop right before we dug into the problem because I didn't like raised voices. But this situation went beyond those bad winter days or being disgusted every time I went to take the recycling can in and found some asshole peed in it ("If you'd take it in right after it's emptied, that wouldn't happen," Nick said).

When I did bring something up, I did so quietly and calmly and didn't fight back when he protested against my protest, or accused me of being too sensitive, of not being able to get the joke. *Well of course I'm wrong. I should be able to get that joke.*

When he did listen, another problem sprung up in its place. It was like cutting off the head of a hydra: One was gone, but others popped up to replace it. When I asked him to stop making stupid blond jokes, he instead focused on me being from New Jersey. When I told him to stop making fun of our shared home state, it was that I wasn't from Collingswood but Camden. I couldn't win with him, so instead of screaming and yelling and telling him he was making me despondent, I stopped bothering. I had vowed to never get in screaming matches like my parents had, and I refused to engage in them here. This was my fate, I told myself. And like he said: I better get used to it.

This life, one that looked so good on paper, didn't suit, and I couldn't figure a way out. I realized I'd made a mistake soon after I moved in, but I didn't want to be a quitter. I already felt like a disappointment and a failure, and I didn't want to add another notch to my belt of dead relationships. So I stayed.

We split up in running before we did as a couple. I told him that it was because he was too fast for me, but I also didn't want the push/pull of fights about where and when to run. I skipped a possible battle about our running incompatibility by deciding to run solo.

That first post-marathon spring, we ran another series of shorter races and eyed another fall marathon. The Chicago Marathon appealed for a few reasons. We had both run half marathons fast enough to qualify for seeding in front corrals. Chicago is a World Marathon Majors and would carry with it all the razzle-dazzle of a top-notch race. It also didn't have a half marathon on the course at the same time.

I wanted payback for Philadelphia, and to outrun whatever was nagging at me about this situation in which I found myself. I later wrote about training for Chicago on a blog that I'd started about being a freelance writer: "I bought a sub-four hour schedule, figuring if I could skip the GI issues and long port a potty lines, I'd be able to drop 30+ minutes from my time. . . . Six workouts a week? I got it. Nine miles of hill repeats on a Wednesday morning. Sure, why not. Workouts on Saturday AND Sunday? Bring. It. On."

Plus, I reasoned, I knew what to expect. I wasn't taking great strides into the dark. I knew what lay ahead.

When I signed us up for the race, I dimly registered that Chicago, being an October race, would mean a full summer of training. That training lined up with one of the hottest years on record in Philadelphia. In June, temperatures routinely brushed the 100-degree mark.

For the first weeks of long runs, I'd wake up at 5:00 AM, try to poop, then feed and water myself before stepping out into an already creeping sauna with a running water bottle that wrapped around my hand and $5 in my pocket. I'd start out down 9th Street past Pat's and Geno's, neon still blazing, each with drunks waiting for cheesesteaks. I continued down 9th, through the Italian Market and past more drunks stumbling out of an after-hours club, then turned up Pine Street, where cabs were the only cars swooshing by. Along the way, I passed brownstones with manicured flower beds hanging out of their windows. Then a turn on 23rd Street and take that to Fairmount Park. Anytime I saw a person, I played a game of Still Up/Just Up? to keep myself amused and my mind off the heat. What has she been up to for the last six hours? Is that person he's with his lover or friend? Or, maybe that person in body glitter just likes to walk down the street early in the morning.

Once in Fairmount Park, I ran down Martin Luther King Jr. Drive, hoping that my water would last until I reached a fountain. On one 12-mile run in July, my route crossed that of the 20 in 24 Ultramarathon (now called in24), where, along with shorter races and relays, runners tried to run around the Martin Luther King Jr. Drive/Kelly Drive Loop as many times as possible in twenty-four hours. It was a hazy day, but the park was bursting with summer lushness, the paved trail along the river passing under an archway of big fat green leaves that would have shaded the course if there had been sun. Still, the air was a mucky mess, and a light breeze off the river didn't make much of a difference.

"Sweat rolled down my legs and pooled in my shoes, making them squish with each step," I wrote in an essay in *Runner's World* about that run. A race volunteer kept offering me water, but at first I declined because I didn't feel I deserved it. In the essay, I wrote that I felt that way because I wasn't as dedicated as those trying to run for twenty-four hours straight, but that feeling of being less-than had washed through the rest of me too. Free water? No thanks. I was meant to suffer (though I did take the water when I passed him on the way back, and later knocked back a second bottle that I bought with my cash at a gas station on the way back to South Philadelphia).

On most weekdays, I'd shake Nick awake so he could go to the gym. Sometimes I'd go with him. Sometimes, I'd head out on my own runs, pounding out miles on endless sidewalks festooned by trash and grime, trying to start before heat clamped down.

But that didn't even work. Running there offered no solace or mental break. I was harassed and chased and grabbed. Once a group of men smacked me on the ass as I passed. A guy working at a seafood place near the Italian Market grabbed my breast as I ran by. I'd hustle my way out of South Philly, but even that wasn't a help. While on Front Street in Old City, part of the

Philadelphia Marathon course, a man stepped into my way and tried to block me. I dodged around him, but he chased me, calling me a filthy whore. These all happened after the sun had come up. No one did a thing. Even when nothing happened, I was always on guard, waiting for that next hand or body to reach out to me. When I told Nick and his city friends what happened, they just nodded and said that it was the price I paid for living in that part of the city, as if it were the only drawback, a small thing that I endured in exchange for living in their gentrified utopia. So I'd join Nick again on the treadmill (with the same woman still talking on her Bluetooth to who knows who), or drive to New Jersey to check my P.O. Box, park the car somewhere, and run.

In July, a bug bite on my leg became infected, and my doctor put me on antibiotics that made running nearly impossible. At the same time I was diagnosed with ovarian cysts, and another doctor was adjusting my birth control to see if medication would stop them from forming. One side effect was that I sweat uncontrollably at night. Most mornings I woke up on soaked sheets. Getting up to run and sweat some more didn't work so well.

By August, the heat in the city was too much to bear, so instead I'd drive to New Jersey, set up my water and Nuun—an electrolyte tablet that's dropped into water to create a sports drink without sugar—on my mom's porch and run a 4-mile loop over and over again around the shaded park and lake near her house.

Whenever she woke up, she'd drape a towel over the arm of a porch chair so I could wipe myself down.

She always had chocolate milk for me in her fridge, which I'd chug after the run. I never wanted to eat anything right after finishing on those hot days, but I could get that down. Then I'd either lie on and sweat all over the pale green carpet the previous owner had left in the house or shower so we could go to Club Diner for BLTs and fries and coffee.

Sometimes I'd bring up Nick, sometimes not. She didn't put any pressure on us to get married, but was curious about our plans the same way she wanted to know what my next book would be.

"You don't sound too excited about this," she said one morning after we ordered and I mentioned we were still thinking of a winter wedding—though which winter, I didn't know. I never looked at the menu because I ordered the same sandwich every time, even if it was 10:00 AM.

"I am. But there's so much we need to sort out first," I said.

My heart wasn't in anything—not in Nick, not in running. I still wrote, of course, because I couldn't pay my bills otherwise. But these pieces were impersonal and standard, like a feature on how to not be a jerk in a race, or the differences between being an introverted and extroverted runner. Of course those stories were necessary, but they didn't take a lot of creative thinking. I spent most of my time writing profiles about the work of faculty at a Philadelphia research university for that school's public relations office. It paid well, and I was grateful for the work— and I liked getting out of that damn house to spend a chunk of my workday somewhere else. That year was a blockbuster one for me, at least financially. But the writing didn't require the same kind of elasticity of the mind as, say, a deep dive into why Catholic schools in New Jersey were closing.

My training suffered too. I cut back my mileage, and on the day of my 20-mile run, I quit after 8. My brother and his wife and son were at my mom's that weekend, and my nephew, round and cute and stubby at two years old, stood on a couch by the window as I came in after my second lap, waving. So I stopped, cleaned myself up, and went to breakfast with them instead. On the way back, I blasted "Sloop John B" by the Beach Boys on my car radio, first singing and then screaming, "Let me go home / Why don't they let me go home."

Training never clicked. Partly because of the heat, partly because I was struggling to reclaim my running from inside this dark pit of warping myself to try to please another person who didn't act like he loved me very much, which we both blamed on me. I was so tired of trying not to make Nick angry. I wasn't myself anymore. My father later described those last months as if someone had turned off my light. I was a shell, doubting and re-doubting my every move, hoping that I wouldn't upset the delicate, shifting balance that I didn't know how to maintain. Because this was what I was supposed to do, the expired parking meter: Get into whatever car was still parked in my spot.

I did leave once, briefly. It was another fight over where we lived, but it was really about everything, about me feeling trapped in that house, in the ball I'd turned myself into trying not to bounce and annoy him, and his claim that I didn't do enough to "get better" after I'd been diagnosed with the cysts—whatever that meant, given that I'd spent nearly $2,000 on diagnosis and treatment, on top of expensive health insurance premiums. I packed a bag and drove to Cape May. I booked myself into the same hotel where we'd stayed before, with the antique store that had my ring. I paid too much for a room facing the ocean and cried for two days straight between looking at Craigslist ads for rooms to rent in Cape May and Asbury Park, eating lavish room service meals, and running, pounding out miles again along the promenade in that old town, and then crying some more. I peeked into the store with the ring. It was still there. I was relieved.

I knew I had to go back and sort things out, but when I did, Nick apologized, telling me that he was wrong, that he would do better, that we'd find a solution, he'd find another contractor to replace the one who kept not showing up, that he'd try to be the man I needed him to be. He told me again that he wanted to marry me, and asked me if I wanted to marry him too. I said yes. I don't know if I could have said no in that crux of an emotional moment, or if I wanted to.

I wanted to believe him, that it wasn't so bad. I really did. I had moved into this man's house for some reason, and we had what could be a bright future together, as the grown-up, sophisticated couple I wanted us to be and that so many other people saw.

By the time we ran Chicago, that incident had turned from

a sweet reunion and new start into another example of how I had abandoned him, and how I couldn't be trusted.

If we hadn't already booked a trip to Chicago for the marathon, I'd like to think that I would have ended things sooner. I kept telling myself "after this trip," because how weird would it be for him if we were on the same flight? I didn't want to upset "people," and by "people" I mean everyone in our lives—me, him, our friends, the dog, our families. My mind still ran on those two planes: the one that knew everything about this relationship was wrong and that I could not continue this way without ruining my life, and the one motored by tradition telling me that I was taking steps toward the life every woman should have, whether those steps made me happy or not. If I left the relationship, I'd become a stereotype: a disappointment, a failure, the single thirty-something woman who was too picky and couldn't just settle for the one she had, who was unable to walk the traditional path in life to marriage—even an unhappy marriage—and motherhood, just like my mother had. *Look at the ring he wants to give you!*

I also blamed myself. Nick had told me what he was like when we met, and I thought I could handle it. I could—but only part-time. Full-time was too much. Was that his fault? No. I told myself it was mine.

Running blanked on me, too. I struggled even in the taper, slogging through three- and four-mile runs—with dead legs.

I boarded the plane to Chicago, despondent and praying for a miracle—any kind of miracle.

Here's what I remember about the Chicago Marathon: Cold at the start line. Very organized corrals. Bruce Springsteen's "Born to Run" blaring as we went off. Finding a friend at mile 3. Dancing drag queens in Boystown. A surprise bridge with a hill at mile marker 26. Spotters up on wooden platforms past the finish to catch anyone who collapsed at or beyond the finish line. A medal and space blanket placed over my shoulders, a sticker to make sure the top of the space blanket stayed closed. A beer shoved at my hands, which triggered not a feeling of celebration that the damn thing was over, but vomit. Staggering out of Millennium Park— an exit that, cruelly, included stairs. Wind howling down State Street as I tried to remember the way back to my hotel room. I don't even remember crossing the finish line. I finished in 4:56:17, a disappointment.

Everything leading into this marathon had predicted that result. I even brought my phone and music with me, which I only do when I know a race is going to go poorly. My hips started aching at mile 8. I walked at mile 18. By mile 20, I knew I was sunk, the pain far worse than it had been in Philadelphia. I ran/walked/ran without even a plan for how long each walk and run segment should be.

"It was slow and agonizing, but I kept moving forward. I did not stop," I wrote in a post-race recap. More than just bad training welled up in me on those lonely last 6.2 miles. The nights of sweating to soak the sheets. The frost covering my relationship with Nick. "Sloop John B." I took all of that into the race with me. This thing that had been so important and wonderful and life giving had turned its back on me when I needed it the most.

When I finally staggered into our hotel room, Nick was already showered and changed. He finished nearly an hour before me and waited for me, but I was too slow, and he was too cold, so he went back to the hotel.

"I want to watch the Eagles game," he said. I wanted to lie on the bed and cry my face off and punch my legs until I couldn't feel them anymore. But I got into the shower, and hustled through a short, hot one when I wanted to lie on the shower floor and let the water run over me until my skin pruned. I knew Nick was waiting and hungry and impatient, so I shut off the water, shoved my screaming legs into tights, put on soft loafers, and lurched and lunged after him to a sports bar showing every NFL game that day. I sat across from him, medal around my neck, and ate the olives out of bloody marys and picked at the nachos in front of me.

"Free shots for marathoners! Free shots for marathoners!" a waitress called to us and the people at the table next to us, who also wore marathon medals. I almost threw up again. I barely touched the tasting menu dinner Nick had planned at Mercat a la Planxa that night—lovely restaurant, but it's on the second floor, which required walking down stairs both to go to the bathroom and to leave. "No," he said quietly when we saw the stairs leading up to the restaurant. When we left, I was tempted to walk backward down those stairs. I wouldn't want to eat until lunch the next day, when I ate my way through Portillo's: hot dog, fries, and steak sandwich washed down with chalice of beer, then capped off with a milkshake.

Despite the bad race and my rush to get past the bad race, we didn't have a terrible time. There were flashes of why I had moved in with him, and why I still had a lingering hope. The day after the race we had drinks at the top of the John Hancock Center, smiling goofily that we had done a second marathon. That night, we found two seats at the bar of a steakhouse next to someone who had appeared to have ordered up a hooker for the night. But those moments were just that: flashes. By the time we flew home to Philadelphia, we settled back into our lives of mutual misery.

Three weeks after the marathon, Superstorm Sandy made landfall in Brigantine, New Jersey. The week leading up to the storm had been calm. We figured it would hit somewhere else, or weaken, or turn, like so many hurricanes had done before. That feeling turned to rising panic as Sandy moved as if she would hit New Jersey dead on. Then came the grim watching and waiting as people boarded up their homes and fled inland right before Sandy smacked into the middle of the coast. I watched it happen in real time through social media accounts and live webcams, horrified as I stood at my desk trying to sort through tweets and posts to determine what was real (that a roller coaster was in the ocean in Seaside Heights) and what was not (that the Ferris wheel at Morey's Piers in Wildwood had fallen over). While the South Jersey Shore was largely spared, the North Jersey Shore was pummeled, with roads upended, boardwalks destroyed, entire blocks wiped out, homes flooded and tossed into the ocean. Nick kept telling me I needed to let it go, forget about it until the next day, but I couldn't. I knew too many people whose homes and lives were being destroyed.

When he finally pulled me out of my office to get something to eat, I followed him in a daze to a corner bar. A group of his city friends had gathered there, laughing and joking as if a chunk of my home state wasn't drowning. They worried about whether the homes they rented for vacation would be okay without showing even a hint of concern for the people whose lives were being destroyed. As they laughed and drank and joked about how maybe they'd have the next day off because of all the rain in Philadelphia, I tamped down my urge to grab them by their flannel shirts for being so goddamned self-centered and not seeing outside of the bubble they created around themselves in this hellhole of a city. Other people were suffering, dying, losing their livelihoods and their homes. *And you sit here and drink and laugh and hope the rain keeps you out of work tomorrow so you can drink more tonight? You can be so myopic? What about your souls?* I'd have rather have been standing in the storm than sitting in that bar in that moment with those people—Nick included.

I play the "shoulda" game a lot, even now. I shoulda been more assertive. I shoulda been more vocal. I shoulda left sooner, had one of those screaming matches. Maybe things wouldn't have ended so badly.

But when two people are locked in the spiral of a disintegrating relationship, it's hard to see outside the tornado, and it's easy to keep doing what created it in the first place. First I blamed me, then him. Over time it changed both of us, two people trying to stick out a bad deal, and it made us both different people from the two who had met in a shitty bar in South Philadelphia that day in June. Maybe we could go back to being those two people again, but we wouldn't be able to do it together. Someone just had to make the first move to get out.

The rest of October, then November, then December, I thought about leaving. My tenants' yearlong lease was up in November. They bought a house and switched to a month-to-month lease until they closed on their new home, so I could, in theory, move home. On the worst days, in that hour between when I could write no more and when Nick came home from work, I'd close my eyes and imagine life without him. Sometimes I saw clouds and sunshine and me floating above our misery. Others, it was me and Emily walking down the beach into a sunset in brilliant shades of pinks and oranges and purples, with Guster, my favorite band (which Nick hated), following behind me, softly playing "Jesus on the Radio," a song that says "Don't look back, there ain't nothing there to see," while the waves lapped at my toes. Both shared the same things: freedom. Release.

But I couldn't do it. I didn't want to yank everyone into

chaos. I knew that ungluing us would mean wrenching not just my life apart but another person's too—and even if I slumped over when I heard the three beeps on the security system followed by the click of my dog's nails on the hardwood floor signaling that he was home from work, he was still a person who at one point I had loved very much and who was obviously unhappy too.

I started writing a weekly running column for the *Philadelphia Inquirer* that November, and my editor and his wife asked me and Nick out to dinner. Nick refused, saying it was in New Jersey and he didn't want to cross the bridge, so I went without him, making excuses and smiling stiffly until the topic of conversation turned to something else.

We went to Key West before Christmas, a disaster of a trip that started with us trying to run through town, me leading because I'd been there before, with Nick questioning every turn I took us on, and ended with me sobbing in our hotel room after he spent the day telling me how much he loved brunettes— which I was not. But again I didn't fight and tell him to stop. I just sat there and stewed until I exploded in tears.

Of course it wasn't just that fight that upset me—it was everything. This relationship had broken me down to my smallest parts, a slow, steady erosion of myself that finally stripped me bare. The last time I'd been to Key West was with Jason, soon before he moved, and even though that relationship had ended, it never made me feel so small. The idea of being a failure if this relationship went bust was still running through my mind, but the alternative—a failure, but a free one—started to look like the better option.

I knew that I was going to leave him when we got back—which I did, though I waited until after New Year's Eve. I drank too much white wine at a friend's party, which I threw up for hours, white-hot up my throat.

In January, I sat down with my friend Kristen, whom I hadn't seen much since I moved to South Philadelphia, at a diner near Collingswood, and talked around the edges of my decision to move out. Then I drove to my mom's house and told her I was leaving.

She looked me straight in the eye and said, "Okay. I'll change the sheets."

The break up moment was anticlimactic. While he was out with his sister, I packed as much as I thought I'd need for a week. I waited, nervous. I almost unpacked the bag, but I knew if I didn't leave then, I never would have gone, and ahead I only saw a life weighted down by a $15,000 ring—of children and obligations, of being his wife with his name, which he insisted I would take—with me shunted to the side.

When he came back in, he looked at me. I looked at him and said, "I can't do this anymore."

We sat on the futon in my soon-to-be-former office and hugged. I felt awful. For me, for him, for what I perceived as me ruining our lives.

We hashed briefly through what would go next: Who

would keep the dog? (Me, but he'd hold on to her for a few days.) When would I pack and move out? (When he left for a ski trip in Vermont that I was supposed to take too). Then I left, driving right to my mom's, screaming "Why won't they let me go home" the entire way.

chapter 8

NEW JERSEY MARATHON

MAY 5, 2013

New Jersey Marathon — Miles 18–20

We crossed a concrete footbridge over another lake, but this time we headed into Ocean Grove. This bridge has a gate smack in the middle that is locked every night from midnight until 5:00 AM. The gates were added in 1995 to–in theory–keep thieves from Asbury Park coming into a town that bills itself as God's One Square Mile.

The gates are still there, open, and runners teamed through them at different levels of distress. After crossing the bridge, we ran down a sidewalk parallel to the lake before turning into the heart of Ocean Grove.

Oh, there she is.

Waiting at that turn was Mom in a beige puffy coat, pale blue jeans, sneakers, turquoise hat with COACH embroidered across the front, with both camera and Clif Bar at the ready. *Thank God.* Not just because I was hungry, but because seeing that familiar face, which had been at so many races before but never a marathon, was a relief. I bought her that hat the first time she came to a race and I couldn't find her after. Now she's impossible to miss.

Oh, there she is. There she is!

I waved so she could see me as I came down the sidewalk as I passed her, I yelled, "Open it! I'll get it on the way back." She snapped a photo at the exact moment I opened my mouth. It's a lovely commemorative shot.

Our mileage in Ocean Grove was short, just over a mile run past Victorian and Victorian-inspired homes. I passed the nineteenth mile marker, then turned back toward the lake and another footbridge into Asbury Park, and back toward Mom.

She took strides with me to hand me the Clif Bar. "So many people tried to eat this before you," she said. Mom would run her first 5K the next weekend, and was more than capable of running with me for that short of a clip. I took two big, sticky bites before handing it back to her.

Mom knew that, around this point in previous marathons, the wheels had started to come off. But here they weren't. My legs started to show signs of weakness—a pang here and a pain there and a bolt of something in my left foot that had died back down to a dull ache—but I didn't feel like a wreck, not even close. I felt like the previous 19 miles were just another run like any of the hundreds of runs that had come before.

"I'll see you in an hour," I said to her. Finishing in an hour meant that I'd be running faster than a ten-minute-mile pace for the rest of the race. I should, according to my plan and training, be able to do that without falling apart.

I crossed back into Asbury, ready and prepared to meet mile 20–and what lay after.

———

As Mom promised, she changed the sheets.

I could have gone to a lot of places other than her spare room. I could have rented an apartment in Cape May or Asbury Park like I dreamed of when I left Nick briefly. I could have bought another house. I even looked at a few, including one around the corner from the one I owned in Collingswood—a steal except that it had ivy growing into the basement and a kitchen that needed to be replaced.

But after living in someone else's house, renting didn't appeal to me. Neither did laying out a lot of cash to buy a new place that needed major upgrades. My tenants scheduled a closing date, so I decided to move back in and live with Mom until then.

While Nick was in Vermont, Kristen, Mom, and Jen, who had been with me at the wine bar on my first half-date with Nick, helped pack me up and had me ready to move out in three hours. I didn't have much: books, clothes, no furniture except a chair and a bookcase. It was a warm January day, and we all sweat as we worked.

"Can you turn down the heat?" Jen asked.

"I don't touch the thermostat," I replied.

"I'm so glad you're leaving," she said.

I put two boxes and two duffel bags in my mom's spare room, which held the bed that I had given up when I moved in with Nick. He kept sending me emails about how I was a terrible girlfriend but he'd still take me back if I worked on my issues. I ignored most of them, and tried to start again.

When I lived with Mom after college, we didn't see too much of each other. I was at school most nights and working three days a week with lots of library time in between. Then, we shared a big house with a living room, family room, half-finished basement, five bedrooms, and two and a half baths. Except for holidays and in the summer when my younger siblings came home, we were the only two people there, and could glide through our daily lives without running into each other. We didn't even need to watch the same TV show since we had two TVs.

But she'd since sold that house and moved into a two-bedroom, one-and-a-half-bath, one-thousand-square-foot house. It was cozy and the right size for her, but tight for people who did not share a room. My old bed barely fit into the second bedroom, which was also her office.

I was a mess. In those first weeks I veered from dizzying happiness to have left Nick and South Philadelphia, to paralyzing fear that I was going to be alone for the rest of my life, so unlovable that even the dog didn't want me. I could tell she missed Nick. She sat on the loveseat around the time he came home, as if he'd changed houses too. She lay at my feet during the day, staring up at me with her big brown eyes. I apologized to her over and over again.

Nick had made noise about keeping Emily. On that I would not budge, even when I caved on everything else. I didn't fight him to get back all the money I paid toward the new bedroom set we bought when I moved in. I complied when he demanded I refund him his half of the $500 he paid toward Emily's last heart exam. If he had kept Emily, I might as well have lain across the sewer drain on Mom's street and let the rain and chemicals and runoff from all the pesticide-laden lawns in the neighborhood do their job.

Mom and I weren't quite Oscar and Felix, but it was the first time I lived with a parent as an adult (and no, a recent college grad doesn't count as an adult). During the day, I plucked at my keyboard hoping to find the inspiration to work, watched *Law & Order* reruns, and tried to not look at Nick's Twitter account to see if he was subtweeting me. I'd text Mom about dinner and make something either from her bottomless freezer or from the groceries I insisted on buying for the both of us (Mom laughed at the suggestion that I pay rent, so that was the least I could do).

We spent most nights across from each other at the dining room table, shying away from talking about the one thing that was on my mind. Mom had rebuilt her life after the divorce, but I hadn't had a chance to really see the woman she'd become until that time we lived together. While she still owned the big family house, she'd worked nights and weekends at a grocery store to pay that mortgage and the taxes on the house while also saving for retirement. She never quite caught up in her career after taking so much time off to raise her kids, and not having a college degree gave her a ceiling, she thought. But brushing close to sixty, she still kept studying for and taking tests and getting clearances that would help her advance her career.

"I don't regret it," she said one night over salad and steaks. "I have you kids, and I love you all. But things could have been different."

In a lot of ways. If she'd gone to college, maybe she wouldn't have gotten married, or she'd have kept working after she had my older brother. She had been seven months shy of qualifying for a pension at her job when she quit. Or maybe my parents would have gotten divorced earlier. I don't know. It was hard sometimes to look at the parents I know now—who get along, who cohosted events for my siblings' weddings and babies, who posed for pictures with their kids and laughed with each other— and see the same people I had lived with before. In some ways, it gave me hope that I could get past a situation that had been much shorter and less fraught than the end of their marriage, and that I would laugh again soon.

My parents had their faults, especially when they were still married, but together they had given me the tools to get out of that relationship: college, a drive to succeed, independence. I was able to leave Nick because, while I felt pressure to get married, I didn't depend on him financially. I was able to control if and when I had children, so I wasn't latched into a situation for them. I had my career, my own savings, my own retirement funds. I owned property. I could leave a bad situation.

Another result of Mom and I living together then: She started running too. Mom was a teenager when Kathrine Switzer officially became the first woman to run the Boston Marathon. Switzer registered under the name KV Switzer, and even after a race official tried to rip off her bib and pull her off the course she finished and then went on a worldwide mission to start women's marathons with hopes that women could run the marathon in the Olympics too. "We knew if someone were not recognized at the highest level of the sport, nobody would take them seriously," she said to me for a story I wrote for RunnersWorld.com about women's-only races. I freaked out over talking to her about running the same way I had when I interviewed Michael Palin.

Switzer was one of many women who opened the doors for us to claim the marathon as our race too. When people have asked me why women lag behind men in marathon participation (in 2013 and 2014, women were 43 percent of finishers in U.S. marathons and 61 percent of finishers in U.S. half marathons, according to Running USA), I don't think it's so much that women feel they have less time because of their quest to "have it all," but that we're still playing catch-up. When Mom was in high school, girls in her class could practice with the cross-country team but they couldn't compete. She graduated in 1976. Title IX had just been enacted in 1972.

As an adult, Mom found biking, first with a kid strapped into a seat on the back and then in long rides with an outdoor club. She started running by including little "pick-ups" while walking, and when she wanted to run more she asked me if I'd take her to the local running store to buy shoes.

"Why didn't you tell me you were running?" I asked when we walked through downtown Haddonfield on the way to what I referred to as "the store." I spent enough time there that it had become Cheers. "Jen!" they'd yell when I walked in, and I walked in a lot more since I moved back to South Jersey.

"What if I don't like it?" she said (she did like it—over the next two years she would hire a running coach, finish a dozen 5Ks, a 10-miler, and two triathlons).

While I encouraged her running, she pressed me to go out more. But to where? To what friends? My only friends I had while living with Nick were Nick's friends. In talking to Jen and Kristen as they helped me move out, I realized how long it had been since I'd spent any time with either because Nick didn't like them. Once I moved out of the neighborhood, most of the people who I thought were our mutual friends receded. I couldn't trust them with the wailing going on inside of me. How did I know they wouldn't tell him?

I was also going broke. I had $10,000 saved, but I burned through that money quickly. I didn't want to work. I forced myself to write my newspaper column, and punched out a story and a pitch here and there, but some days the only thing I could do was walk the dog. At night, Mom caught up on *Downton*

Abbey, her in an old IKEA chair, me curled up with my dog and a fuzzy blanket on the loveseat that had been my grandmother's.

I blamed myself for what happened with Nick, and while I wound and rewound everything I did wrong—from being a bad girlfriend to staying too long—I did irrational things. Despite my waning savings, I had every room in my house repainted, the carpets ripped out, and the hardwood floors refinished. I bought a $900 purse. I hopped on a flight to Las Vegas, giving the cover that I was there to write a profile for my college's alumni magazine, though I failed to mention in my pitch that I had dated the subject of this profile, and he said he missed me. I let him and booze and sunshine wash away my pain for a little while. I booked a flight to Alaska for Memorial Day, and then a trip to Florida for the end of February.

And I ran. Mom lived a half mile from Haddon Lake Park and Audubon Lake, which made up that 4-mile loop I used to train for the Chicago Marathon. I had played at that playground and hopped over that creek and fished at that lake as a child. In the summer, having access to a clean bathroom and endless water at Mom's is what made the loop most attractive. I didn't need that endless water in the winter, but I needed the pattern, a familiar one: I wanted to run the same thing over and over again until my feet bled.

The idea of running another marathon had played at the fringes of my mind even before I left Nick. Between Thanksgiving and New Year's Day, I ran at least a mile a day as part of the Runner's World #RWRunStreak winter challenge.

That forced me to start running again after Chicago when I
wanted to punch running in its face. Spring, I thought, would
be easier for me. I hated running in the summer under the
power of those ten thousand suns. A spring marathon meant
winter training.

One book I brought with me to Mom's was *Hansons Marathon
Method: A Renegade Path to Your Fastest Marathon*. For the first
time in book form, brothers Keith and Kevin Hanson, along with
Luke Humphrey, shared the training philosophy they used for
their Hansons-Brooks Distance Project, a professional running
group that produced Desiree Linden, an Olympic marathoner
who nearly won the Boston Marathon in 2011—a feat that had
eluded Americans from 1985 until Meb Keflezighi won in 2014.

I liked the idea of being a renegade. I also liked the idea of
running a marathon and not diving in the last 6 to 8 miles. I
wanted to train hard, and this guaranteed it.

Eighteen weeks. Six days of running a week. The longest
run on the schedule was 16 miles, but those miles wouldn't be
easy, nor would the workouts around it. That's because weekends
stacked mileage on Saturday and Sunday with no rest day or
cross training day on Monday. With Hansons you run another
4 to 7 miles on Mondays, and after *that* comes your speed or
strength work, like 400-meter or 800-meter or mile repeats.
Then you get a day off on Wednesday before you jump into
what for me was the worst workout of the bunch: the tempo
run, which to them means running at marathon pace, starting
at 5 miles in week six and ending at 10 miles in week seventeen.

No build-up to that pace through the workout. No shortcuts. Just run what you're going to run in the marathon, with a warm-up before and cool-down after.

The most I'd done in training in one week was 40 miles. Hansons maxes you out—on the beginner program—at 57. That may be half the weekly mileage of a professional, but they are also doing their easy runs at a pace that's faster than I run per mile in a 5K. Not only would the training be hard, but it would also be time-consuming.

"I can't possibly do this," I said, then drove to the library and photocopied the schedule. I wanted to do better. I needed to do better.

Hansons looked impossible, and I needed the impossible, and I needed something to make me screw my courage to the sticking place so I wouldn't quit when the mileage built. So I pitched a story to the *New York Times* and offered to be the guinea pig in testing out this method. The 2013 spring marathon season would be the first where people could buy the book and have the time to train with the method. I guessed—and hoped—that I'd be the first journalist to do so.

I wanted to beat myself up. I wanted to serve my penance, for a lot of things: for failing in the relationship, for failing to get engaged, for failing Nick, but most of all for failing myself. I had let myself get trapped, and for that I must atone. It didn't occur to me at the time that Nick might deserve some of the blame, too. At the time I hoisted that cross onto my shoulders, and ran with it.

"We take a straight-talk approach when it comes to teaching you about marathon training; we won't sugarcoat, offer any supposed shortcuts, or treat you with condescension," they wrote in the first chapter. "Indeed, the marathon wouldn't be big deal if it didn't require a little blood, a lot of sweat, and perhaps a few tears."

I had a lot of all three, especially the last one.

In honor of leaving Philadelphia and coming back to New Jersey, I chose the New Jersey Marathon—again—which is on the first Sunday in May. It shared the same date as the Broad Street Run. I was so twisted up by the last year that I saw this as a defiant move, turning my back on the race and the city that I had grown to hate. Fuck you, Philadelphia. You all do your little 10-mile race while I go out and put on my big-boy pants and run a fucking marathon along New Jersey's beautiful but broken beaches.

In rejecting that boyfriend, that house, that engagement ring, that situation that brought my wretchedness, I was picking up something that was home to me—a race in my state, at my Jersey Shore. I turned my back on everything that I was supposed to have loved, and set out on my own.

Over those eighteen weeks, I became a machine. I pushed everything else aside and focused on two things: work and running. When my weekly mileage pushed past 45 miles a week, I added napping and eating.

My tenants moved out in February, and while contractors

took to my house, I skedaddled to Florida for two weeks, parking myself at the Don CeSar Hotel in St. Pete Beach. My first night there, I sat at the lobby bar and made friends with the bartenders, who invited me to play in their Oscar pool—and I won. The next morning, I ran 4 miles in a dank fog and waved at pelicans along the way. The morning after that, when I woke up to 95 percent humidity, I took to the gym treadmill to do 600-meter repeats on the treadmill—the only time I'd hit a treadmill during the entire course of training.

By the time I crossed the state to spend four days with my grandparents in Sebastian, the humidity evaporated and temperatures topped out in the 60s—a cold snap for them, but beauty for me. I woke up early and ran laps around their retirement community. The early morning walkers in their winter coats and hats and gloves were concerned about me running around in shorts and a tank top.

"Aren't you cold?!"

"You'll make yourself sick!"

"Where are you from, Alaska?"

The first morning out, my grandfather left his house right after I did, and followed me in his Cadillac from 20 feet behind to make sure I was okay. Grandmom always had coffee and bacon ready for me when I returned.

We didn't talk much about what happened, except that I would be okay.

"Men, what are they good for? Nothing," Grandmom said over her one glass of wine at their very-early dinner.

"You want to get married? Great. Don't? Great too. You want to have a baby? That's fine. You don't need a man for that."

On another night, she said all men are schmucks. When women on a talk show asked the male guest why men acted like that, he laughed and said, "Because we can get away with it."

"Bums!" she cried.

Bums.

When I came home, I walked into a familiar front door, but a different house, like running into an old high school friend who grew up into a stone-cold fox. No longer was I going to be living with the choices of the previous owners, like thin green carpet and a living room painted the color of cornhusks. The hardwood floors shone, paired with a living and dining room painted warm but different shades of beige. I ran upstairs to see the seashore turquoise room that would be my office again, the pale blue that helped add to the sanctuary feel of my bedroom. I didn't want to share this—any of this. I was home. One of those first nights back, when I'd had two glasses of wine but no place to sit, I hugged the wall between the dining room and galley kitchen. Mine. All mine. Again.

Except of course I had almost no furniture, linens, kitchen utensils, plates, cups, or knives. "Why don't we have breakup registries?" I asked Mom as I raided her kitchen and linen closet. She gave me two plates, a bowl, butter knife, fork, spoon, paring knife, one pot, one laundry basket, and one set of sheets. I moved in with that, my two duffel bags and two boxes, my dog, and an air mattress, since my aunts were in town for the Philadelphia Flower Show and needed my bed. The first night the air mattress broke, and I woke up on the floor.

I ordered a $2,300 couch from Pottery Barn, a giant L-shaped thing that would take up the entire wall of my living room. I found the plates I wanted in HomeGoods, then ordered the entire set from eBay. After a Saturday run, Mom and I went to whole house auctions, and from there I bought a vanity for my bedroom, silverware, cups. A new bed frame came from a furniture dealer in Pennsylvania whose warehouse stank of cigarettes. I bought an octagon-shaped dining room table from a guy in Camden, and for months I sat at that table on a paint-splattered folding chair.

As the house progressed, and the running progressed—to twenty-four, thirty-nine, forty-one miles per week—I progressed too. I didn't stare at the ceiling at 3:00 AM anymore. Whether that was because I had quieted my mind or because I was too tired from running, I don't know. I didn't care how I got there, but I did.

I went out. I dated, too, an older man named Alan who liked exclusive clubs, good wine, good food, cigars, and me. We met at a running event even though he wasn't a runner anymore. It was a half relationship, one I rolled with for nine months. When we ran into Nick on a date with one of my former South Philadelphia friends, Alan looked at me, looked at Nick, and said, "I'll do whatever you want me to do." It was perfect for that time in my life. We never lay on the couch and watched movies, or spent weekends in bed or doing annoying shopping errands together or even talked about a future together. He was a good distraction (and fantastic lover). I saw him maybe once or twice a week. He was there, but I didn't really let him into the life I was re-creating.

Through it all, though, I was a little shaky, like a baby deer trying to stand on her feet for the first time. One wrong step and I'd fall over again. I was so tired and worn from running that I didn't know if I was doing it right, or just beating myself up.

I faltered most on tempo runs, which were every Thursday. I always went out too fast and then stopped to walk, or I'd go too slow, panic that I was going too slow, then go too fast and stop again.

In the middle of March, I flew to Seattle for a conference and was scheduled to run an 8-mile tempo when I landed.

I had every excuse in the world to not attempt a tempo run, let alone an 8-mile run. I had woken up at 4:00 AM to make the first flight, then sprinted through Dulles International Airport to catch my connection for a six-hour jaunt to the West Coast. I had forgotten to bring my own food on the flight and relied on what I could pick off the overpriced menu. Once I landed and found my hotel, I parked myself at the best-reviewed restaurant near my hotel (thanks, Yelp) and tucked into a sandwich and coffee, which tasted like rocket fuel compared to the Wegmans brand I brewed at home.

Then I walked to what I thought was a running store to buy Shot Bloks because of course I'd forgotten them too. I asked the guy working there where to run. "Uh, we're more of a biking store," he said, and handed me a free tourism map with my Shot Bloks.

I had bonked on my previous tempo run, which was supposed to be an eight-miler that I had cut at the knees at four. I could have curled up on my hotel bed and taken a nap. I could have gone sightseeing, drank more rocket fuel, and watched fish being flung around Pike Place Fish Market. I could have gone to the top of the Space Needle. I could have brooded. Damp and drizzly Seattle is good for that.

Instead, I lay out my running clothes and stared at the map. Then I put on my running clothes and sat on the toilet playing with my phone for fifteen minutes. Then I turned on my iPad and Googled local running routes. Then I went to the bathroom again. I don't usually run with my phone unless it's a weekend long run and I'm listening to podcasts, but given that the chance of me getting lost was 1270 percent, I tucked it into the back zip pocket of my shorts, cradling a sleeve of Shot Bloks.

The best bet seemed to be a path named the Elliott Bay Trail, which I could get to by running from my hotel, crossing under the Viaduct to the water. Water. Wouldn't that be nice! I ran to the water, turned south and next to the water...and shipping containers and boats and that elevated highway. Every time I thought I lost the path, I'd see a sign pointing me forward, or a dude on a bike with a couple of kids in a coupe on the back, and then knew I was at least not going to be taken, *Taken*-style.

It wasn't a pretty run, and I hate running on concrete since it's harder on your legs and knees and feet than asphalt is. I got turned around a few times, including into a rail yard, where I had to figure out how to run around the tracks or cross over in places I wouldn't be hit by a train.

But in all the worry and fretting and thinking, *Am I really running next to a container field?* and, *Why is there a Home Depot right next to the Starbucks headquarters? Do coffee people like DIY home projects?*—I just did it.

My mind was on things other than *OMG HOW AM I GOING TO HOLD THIS PACE for 26.2 miles?!* I didn't go out too fast. I held the pace. I got lost, but when I found the Viaduct again, I knew I would at least be guided back to the street that led up to my hotel. I breathed easy and deep, and when my pace ticked up faster, I didn't do anything about it.

When I finished, I put my hands above my head and yelled "YAHOO!" which echoed off the Viaduct, but I didn't care if someone turned around to stare. I had done it.

That was a turning point. It was the first time I thought that maybe all this would work out, if I could keep training, not get hurt, eat the right thing the night before the marathon, and not end up in the Porta-Potty multiple times along the way. That maybe I could run faster than 4:35 and be triumphant at the finish line. And that maybe, just maybe, I'd get through this. Not just the run, but all of it.

The day after I landed back in New Jersey, my couch arrived. After I wrestled the slipcovers onto the cushions, I lay down on the couch, my dog hopped on top of me, and we both took a nap.

March flipped into April, and I mowed down more miles, surpassing 50 per week, then 54, 55. I was tired and nervous, always thinking about the race even when I wasn't supposed to be thinking about it, like when walking my dog or interviewing running coaches for my *Inquirer* column. I toured the course with the race director, and I wrote a *New York Times* piece about the race going on after Sandy. Then I worked on the essay about training using the Hansons Marathon Method. I interviewed the Hansons, too. My editor—and every other marathoner who knew what I was doing—focused on the fact that I would not run 20 miles at any one time in training.

"Everyone asks, 'Why a sixteen-miler?' My question is, why a twenty-miler?" Kevin Hanson said over the phone. "I'll tell you why. Because you've been brainwashed. Because every program out there has a twenty-miler, so it must be right?" When the story ran, my editor zeroed in on that twenty-miler too, and titled it "Marathon training—minus the long run." I cringed. The training was the hardest physical thing I had done in my life—twenty-mile run or not.

On April 15, running became a target. I wasn't at the Boston Marathon. I watched the professional race on my iPad in my dining room, and then, buoyed by a feeling of "yeah running! RUNNING!" I went out on a 7-mile run on a warm, sunny day. I didn't carry my phone. When I returned,

I expected to check the marathon website for the times of all the people I knew who were running the race. I had about a dozen text messages asking me if I was okay, if I was home, and sorry to hear what happened.

The rest of the day was a rush to find people. I checked the Boston Marathon website for their results and saw those for friends who had finished around when the bombs went off, or 5K splits that stopped updating after the 40K mark. Where are they? Where *are* they? Some were in hotels in lockdown. Others wandered around Boston. No one had cell phone service or any real idea what was going on. One friend who saw both bombs go off but was far enough away to not be hurt ran to her hotel room and left Boston as fast as she could, post-9/11 New York City fresh in her mind.

I sat at my dining room table, bumping from computer to phone, trying to find these people and not destroy TV producers and reporters from rival papers calling and emailing me for information on people that I hadn't even found yet. I never liked writing straight news and that morning confirmed this for me, as people I didn't know kept emailing and calling, telling me I needed to give them the phone number of someone who just survived a terrorist attack. I met Alan that night and drank too much red wine while watching a woman who had just lost her job do shots and yell along with every song she chose for the jukebox, and spent the next day on the couch watching updates on finding the people who did this, who killed those people and

JEN A. MILLER 213

maimed so many more. I called Mom and told her she wasn't allowed to come to my race.

"I can't let you take that chance," I said with a half-sob.

"Of course I'm coming," she said.

"Then you can't stand at the finish line."

"I'm getting as close as I can. You can't stop me."

I wrote about her that week in the *Philadelphia Inquirer:* "I know there will be a hitch in my heart, and that the images of a bomb going off in a crowd of people, who on Monday were doing the same thing she's going to do, will play over top of the reality of what I'll see in front of me as I near the finish line. But she'll be there. She always is. She's the reason I'll run hard toward that finish line. I can't picture it otherwise."

I booked my room. I stalked the weather forecast, fretting about the possibility of full sun but relieved at the forecast temperature. One week away. I tweaked my ankle, and panicked. I went to New York for a writing conference, and a bike messenger going the wrong way down a one-way street clipped my shoulder.

I'm doomed! I wailed into my pillow at night. The Hansons don't believe in a long taper, but I cut back mileage anyway to give my still wonky ankle and weirdly clicking knee time to heal *please God heal* for the race.

May 1 came and went. I picked out my race clothes—almost exactly what I'd worn in the Ocean Drive 10-Miler that March except I changed the visor to yellow for Boston. While everyone

else in the Philadelphia region fretted about Broad Street and
10 miles, I stared down 26.2. I started to carb load. I packed
my Shot Bloks and Body Glide and sunscreen. And then, that
Saturday morning, Mom drove me to the race expo to pick up
my packet, then to our hotel in Asbury Park, and deposited me
in our hotel room. I ordered room service and watched *Chicago*
on a local TV station on a grainy old television. And then, after
half of a Miller Lite, earplugs in place because Mom snores, I
fell asleep.

chapter 9

NEW JERSEY MARATHON

Miles 20–26.2

I crossed the 20-mile marker, and my body held together. All I had left was a 10K–a lousy 6.2 miles. I passed the Wonder Bar, from which Tilie loomed over us with his Cheshire cat grin. Instead of crossing a bridge over Deal Lake, like we had on our way into Asbury Park, we left on a road that wound around the east end of the lake. It had been upended by Sandy and couldn't be repaved in time for the race, so we ran over gravel the marathon had put down. We passed a home where Sandy had gouged out the garage but left a car–still parked inside–behind.

If I thought I had been running on a warm summer day the first time I came through Deal, I was broiling now, grabbing two waters for my mouth, two for my head, and one for my face.

All I saw around me was pain in the movements of the runners who slowed or walked around me. I passed them by the dozen.

Just keep swimming. Just keep swimming.

Mile 21. Mile 22. I didn't stop, but hurt laced through me. My hips ached, my shoulders burned, my left foot cried. My legs started to knock on my brain and say, "Hello! We are displeased!"

9:55 mile, 9:50 mile. From my legs: *Please can we walk now, just for a moment?* From me: *Shut the* fuck *up.*

Mile 23. Just a 5K now.

Just a 5K. Just a 5K.

Just keep swimming. Just keep swimming.

Mile 24. A hop and a skip to the end. At 24.5 miles, we turned toward the street that had once run parallel to Long Branch's boardwalk. Crowds started to gather here, not a sprinkle but in clumps. Pain bloomed now, everywhere, but I was so close, so close. I was not going to stop.

Mile 25. I looked at my watch and tried to do mental gymnastics to see if I could beat my time goal. I would PR, that was for sure, but the number that popped into my mind could not possibly be true. I could not possibly have run that fast.

We came off that road and through Pier Village, where the streets in front were usually jammed with cars, but open to runners and, today, wall-to-wall crowds.

If you'd have been there
If you'd have seen it
I betcha you would have done the same.

Mile 26. I could see the finish line ahead. I saw my friend Erin and stopped briefly to kiss her baby. And then, up onto the pavers next to the railings that were still bent from the storm.

And finally, oh my God finally, there is the finish line, there is Mom in her Coach hat with her camera, behind a barricade, as close as she could get to the finish line. I put whatever power I had left into my legs to cross that line. In the pictures Mom took of that moment, my eyes are closed, a bright smile of relief across my face.

I had done it. I had fucking done it. My time was 4:19:07, fifteen minutes faster than Philadelphia, nearly forty minutes faster than Chicago. I had set out to slay the marathon, and on that chilly, sunny, brilliant Jersey Shore day, I did it.

Of course I cried a little at the end, but happy tears. I staggered, punch-drunk, grasping that medal that had been placed around my neck, a pewter-colored circle with a spinning New Jersey in the middle. I pushed my way out of the guarded finish area, found Mom, and wrapped myself around her, burying my head into the soft folds of her winter coat, and heaved a sob. Not in anger or in pain (though that was surely coming), but because it was over. And I won. I beat the marathon.

"Oh my God, Jen. Jen. Jen. You did it. Look at you. You did it."

The time would break no records. It wouldn't even get me close to qualifying for the Boston Marathon. I finished in the middle of the pack. But none of that mattered. In running, the only markers you try to beat are you own, and I had done it.

I wish I could say that everything about my running life after that race was perfect, but running is rarely a perfect sport. After the marathon, Mom and I did a tour around Asbury Park: I had fries and a bloody mary at the Wonder Bar, then a shower (because I smelled so bad at the Wonder Bar I was worried about offending the other patrons) and a nap (because I couldn't keep my eyes open after one drink), then a greasy cheeseburger at Tim McLoone's, and then I was still up and able to play games at Silverball Pin Ball and eat a big fudge sundae topped with crème de menthe before falling into bed at 8:00 PM. Two days later, though, I could barely walk. My foot had screamed at me during the race because I had nearly broken it—probably when I hit hard, freshly poured concrete late in the race in Ocean Grove in those shoes. While I had trained in them on my long runs, I hadn't run on concrete in them, and either the underlying problem was already there and that jolt caused the injury, or the jolt did it on its own. I was in an air cast for most of the summer. The angst over not being able to run didn't register with me, though, not like it had when I'd hurt my hip. The joy of having conquered the marathon hugged me until I could run again that fall.

Since I started running in 2006, the sport has changed— for the better, I'd say. It's more inclusive now. Race sizes have swelled (the Broad Street Run added a lottery in 2013), but that's because the concept of a stereotypical runner has been broken down. When Mom ran her first 5K at fifty-eight years old, no one told her she didn't belong there. The sport is no longer an exclusive club for the young, skinny, lithe, and male. In 2014, U.S. 5Ks had 8.3 million finishers, according to Running USA. Women rule the sport. More and more people are jumping onto this bandwagon, and that's not a bad thing.

After the New Jersey Marathon, I ran two more: Charlottesville, to see how I'd do on a hilly course (not well) and the New York City Marathon because, well, it's New York, the largest marathon in the world.

But my running is different now. I'm not running away from anything, or toward anything. I run because I like it. I'm not trying to beat my body into a specific shape, or trying to run out my problems. Running is part of my life now, like writing and dog hair on my couch and clothes. It's an important part of that life, but I'm not trying to break any personal records or even set new PRs every time I race. I just want to be out there, and be.

That's because my life now is calm and flat, like I am floating on that bay. I live a small life in a small town with a small house and a small dog, and I am content. I don't know if I would have reached this point without running, but I'd rather not know. It's a cleanser for my mind, body, and soul. I'll often be out running around Knight Park and think about all the times I ran it before, from the first time I changed the time I ran to lap those Little League games to when I passed out because I wasn't eating enough to when I lay down in the leaves and waited for something to come and save me. But now I know that I didn't need something to save me. I had it in myself. Running gave me a little push.

For so long, I thought that running was a Sisyphean task. With that race, on that day, when the medal of a spinning New Jersey was placed around my neck, I realized I was wrong. Through running, I am the phoenix, reborn. And I will keep turning to running, and being reborn, until I can run no more.

REFERENCES, RESOURCES, AND NOTES

Bowerman, William J. *Jogging*. New York: Putnam Pub Group, 1977.

Carr, David. *The Night of the Gun*. New York: Simon & Schuster, 2008.

Germano, Sara. " 'Barefoot' Running Heads Into the Sunset," *Wall Street Journal*, May 8, 2014.

Humphrcy, Luke, and Hanson, Keith. *Hansons Marathon Method: A Renegade Path to Your Fastest Marathon*. Boulder: Velo Press, 2012.

Kislevitz, Gail Waesche, *First Marathons: Personal Encounters with the 26.2-Mile Monster*. Halcottsville, NY: 2006.

McDougall, Christopher. *Born to Run: A Hidden Tribe,*

Superathletes, and the Greatest Race the World Has Never Seen.
New York: Vintage Books, 2011.

"Running USA Annual Marathon Report." Running USA,
March 23, 2014. www.runningusa.org/marathon-report-
2014?returnTo=annual-reports.

ACKNOWLEDGMENTS

It seems like a cliché, but it's true: I could not have written this book alone. I'd never have done it without a supporting cast.

Thanks to my agent Mackenzie Brady who looked at a two-page pitch and saw this book inside, and then tirelessly fought for that book to come to fruition. Thanks to my editor, Stephanie Knapp, for helping me see what I wanted to say and pushing when she needed to get a better book out of me. Your guidance has been invaluable. Kudos, too, to the whole Seal Press team for shepherding this through to become the beautiful book that you hold today. You ladies rock.

To my editors at the *New York Times, Philadelphia Inquirer, Runner's World, Running Times, RunnersWorld.com* and *Zelle. com*: Toby Bilanow, Tish Hamilton, Meghan Loftus, Scott Douglas, Sarah Lorge Butler, Erin Strout, Elizabeth Comeau, and especially John Quinn, who I'm sure would have come up with a better title for this book if I'd asked. The work you guys have given me not only fueled and funded my running habit, but it also funded my life, especially while I wrote this book. Thanks for keeping the dog in fancy kibble and me in new running shoes.

To Erin Graves, who read the first essays that formed the bones of what this book would be. To my readers Brian Eastwood and Amy Hill Hearth. You read the early drafts of this book in exchange for nothing but my gratitude, and you will have it forever. The book is better because of you both. To Andy Cliver, Dan McQuade, and Liz Yaeger, who let me read parts of the book out loud to make sure I got the wording and pacing right. To everyone who answered tiny little questions to make sure the book is as accurate as possible: Jen DeDecker, Glenn Fleishman, Kristen Graham, Gretchen Williams and Jack Wright. To my support crew of Nathan Baker, Caren Chesler, Jen Gertel, Garrick Goh, Leah Ingram, Gerard and Jill Pescatore, Amy Z. Quinn, Marc Steiner and William Stokes, who let me talk about this book far more than what must have been interesting or tolerable. To the women of the Atomic Engineers, who told me not to give up on this idea. I am so thankful to you all.

To New Jersey Marathon race director Joe Gigas, who drove me over the 2013 marathon course while in the home stretch of getting ready for the 2015 marathon. Any errors along the way through those Jersey Shore towns are mine. You'll be back on the boardwalks soon, Joe. I know it.

To the South Jersey running community, especially Dave

Welsh of the Running Companies of South Jersey, and the members of the South Jersey Athletic Club. You guys not only helped me feel like a real runner when I was starting out, but have been supportive of my writing career, and of this book.

To my family, for putting up with this very weird thing that I do. To Dad especially, who is my biggest fan and loudest cheerleader. Thank you so much for being there for me, not only now, but for telling me I wasn't crazy when I quit my job in 2005 to chase a dream. And to Mom, who, while I wrote this book, let me come over her house and yell, "I don't want to do this anymore!" after which she'd hug me, tell me it would be fine, and suggest going to Club Diner. BLT on wheat toast with mayo, a side of fries, and a side of ranch dressing. Hold the coleslaw.

© MARC STEINER

ABOUT THE AUTHOR

Jen A. Miller is a veteran freelance journalist whose work has appeared in the New York Times, Runner's World, Running Times, Salon, and The Guardian. *She also writes a weekly running column for the* Philadelphia Inquirer. *She lives in Collingswood, New Jersey.*

Selected Titles from Seal Press

For more than thirty years, Seal Press has published groundbreaking books. By women. For women.

Run Like A Girl: How Strong Women Make Happy Lives, by Mina Samuels. $16.95, 978-1-58005-345-7. *Run Like A Girl* explores how the confidence and strength that sports help to build makes women stronger and better prepared for life's many challenges. In this inspiring book, Mina Samuels uses the personal stories of women and girls of all ages and backgrounds—as well as her own—to take a broad look at the power sports have to help us overcome obstacles in all arenas of life.

Super You: Release Your Inner Superhero, by Emily V. Gordon. $16.00, 978-1-58005-575-8. *Super You* is a fun, friendly, and unabashedly geeky guide to becoming the superhero of your own extraordinary life. With activities in every chapter to help identify each person's superpowers and personal kryptonite—and weapons against it—*Super You* is the perfect sidekick for every growing hero, empowering everyday people to transform into the most kick-ass versions of themselves.

Fast Girl: Don't Brake Until You See the Face of God and Other Good Advice from the Racetrack, by Ingrid Steffensen. $17.00, 978-1-58005-412-6. Fast-paced and fun, *Fast Girl* is the quirky, real-life chronicle of how one woman stepped outside her comfort zone, shrugged off the shackles of suburban conformity, and changed her entire perspective on life through the unlikeliest of means: racecar driving.

Gorge: My Journey Up Kilimanjaro at 300 Pounds, by Kara Richardson Whitely. $17.00, 978-1-58005-559-8. Kara's difficult but inspiring trek speaks to every woman who has struggled with her self-image or felt that food was controlling her life. Honest and unforgettable, Kara's journey is one of intense passion, endurance, and self-acceptance. In *Gorge*, Kara shows that big women can do big things.

What You Can When You Can: Healthy Living On Your Terms, by Carla Birberb and Roni Noone, $16, 978-1-58005-573-4. What You Can When You Can (#wycwyc) is a book, a movement, a mindset, and a lifestyle—one that harnesses the power of small steps to let you achieve your health and fitness goals on YOUR terms. The #wycwyc (pronounced "wickwick") philosophy applies to anything and everything that contributes to a healthy, happy life: nutrition, exercise, physical and mental rejuvenation, and so much more.

The Nonrunner's Marathon Guide for Women: Get off Your Butt and On with Your Training, by Dawn Dais. $17.00, 978-1-58005-431-7. *The Nonrunner's Marathon Guide for Women* is a fun training manual for women who don't believe that running is their biological destiny but who dream of crossing the finish line nonetheless.

Find Seal Press Online
www.SealPress.com
www.Facebook.com/SealPress
Twitter: @SealPress

MAY - - 2016

ULTIMATELY RESPONSIBLE

ULTIMATELY RESPONSIBLE

WHEN YOU'RE IN CHARGE OF IGNITING A MINISTRY

Sue Nilson Kibbey

Abingdon Press
Nashville

ULTIMATELY RESPONSIBLE:
WHEN YOU'RE IN CHARGE OF IGNITING A MINISTRY

This book is printed on recycled, acid-free paper.

Library of Congress Cataloging-in-Publication Data

Kibbey, Sue Nilson.
  Ultimately responsible : when you're in charge of igniting a ministry / Sue Nilson Kibbey.
    p. cm.
  ISBN-13: 978-0-687-33492-6 (alk. paper)
  ISBN-10: 0-687-33492-6 (alk. paper)
  1. Christian leadership. 2. Church work. I. Title.

  BV652.1.K53 2006
  253—dc22

                                                2006022108

06 07 08 09 10 11 12 13 14 15—10 09 08 07 06 05 04 03 02 01

MANUFACTURED IN THE UNITED STATES OF AMERICA

I'm grateful...

for paid and unpaid leaders both at Ginghamsburg
Church and beyond, whose stories of courageous
ministry have taught and inspired me

for colleagues Michele White, Michael Pollard, and
designer Brad Wise, whose creative teamwork helped
important details of this project come together

and for my husband Chuck and daughter Amy, whose
loving encouragement provides a launching pad for
the fulfillment of my own calling

CONTENTS

FOREWORD

I first met Sue in the early summer months of 1999. Ginghamsburg Church had begun to reach a place of plateau, and nothing I tried seemed to make a difference. We had all the dimensions of dynamic worship with strong contemporary music, media, drama, and teaching. But our discipleship structures were no longer adequate to assimilate the three thousand people who were coming to the five weekend worship celebrations each week. As a matter of fact, the children's ministry was struggling to hold its own, and the teen ministry was going backwards. The prophetic DNA that had taken the church from ninety people to three thousand people was no longer being effectively transmitted.

There are two dimensions of leadership that are absolutely essential to every growing movement: visionary leadership and strategic management. These critical dimensions are very rarely found in one person. This is why God teamed Moses' visionary leadership with Aaron's strategic management. Most churches fail to grow because they are over managed and under led. Ginghamsburg began to plateau because my visionary leadership exceeded the day-to-day strategic management structures that were in place to ensure the implementation of the vision. I am a much stronger visionary leader than I am a strategic arranger of daily systems that are essential for the implementation of the vision.

Sue's strategic management as executive pastor combined with my visionary leadership as lead pastor has moved Ginghamsburg Church off plateau to awe-inspiring places of mission and ministry. Sue's field tested principles found in this book are practical and applicable for every size church. This book is a much-needed strategic tool for any leader who is ultimately responsible.

Mike Slaughter
Ginghamsburg Church
Summer 2006

"The local church is the hope
of the world, and its future rests primarily
in the hands of its leaders."
-Bill Hybels

CHAPTER

1

THE INTENTIONAL LEADER

A short distance from my house sits a small cemetery. Situated only yards off the heavily-trafficked main street of town, it encompasses a few dozen secluded gravestones that are inscribed with lifespan dates of various lengths. This small collection is split by a central sidewalk down the middle, which is part of my daily walking route. Though I didn't know a single one of the departed while they were alive, their names have now become familiar. I wonder what each one was like. If they could speak today, what would they say? Did they spend their time living for what really mattered? Did their heartfelt priorities match their actual outcomes? Did they spend years worried and distracted by that which was temporary and trivial? Or did they bring courageous influence and inspiration to others that left a legacy?

The small deceased company resting next to the cemetery path perpetually reminds me of the amazing, urgent gift of this day. Today. This is the time and now is my chance to make it count, to live for what really matters. To seize leadership. To understand it. To practice it and pursue it. To craft my participation in the challenges, crises, tragedies, and triumphs of this particular day, so that it provides a foundation, upon which another chunk of God's legacy can be effectively built into others' lives. This is the pressing challenge you face as one whom God has called to be a servant leader.

It's not your own noteworthy, public accomplishments that imbue those around you with inspiration and encouragement to run the race with excellence. It's the downright practical, daily, moment-to-moment choices you make as their servant leader that God uses on behalf of their spiritual growth and ministry deployment. Great leaders in Kingdom work are willing to sacrifice ego, self-significance, and self-imagined importance of position in order to live downward into increasing effectiveness, no matter what it takes. They are afraid to die—until they have maximized the elusive combination of godly leadership, management, and contagious vision that fuels the body of Christ. It is the passionate, relentless commitment to learning this art that God uses to transform an ordinary person like you into the intentional leader.

I've called this book *Ultimately Responsible* because that's the extent to which true leaders in the making take ownership of their call to lead and manage ministry. Being ultimately responsible doesn't mean that you ought to—or should—take care of every detail by yourself. It does mean that you are ultimately responsible to provide the spiritual inspiration, the masterminding, the choreography of direction in simple and motivating terms so that those around you not only get in touch with their desire to serve God but also rise up and get rolling on what must happen.

Use the "Intentional Leader" printable worksheet on the *Ultimately Responsible* DVD, chapter 1 as you and your team work through the concepts in this chapter together. Study the scriptural underpinnings through the "Intentional Leader" printable Bible study found there, too.

You and I have observed that leaders come and go in every church. Paid or unpaid, certain leaders gain momentum as they go while others sputter and fade out. Some are likeable, some are highly organized, and some are deeply mature in their faith. Most feel the weight of the responsibility they have assumed. Yet few leave a lasting imprint on the ministry they serve or in the lives of those they lead. If you have ever wondered if your efforts made a difference, or felt discouraged that your leadership isn't fully effective, take heart. It's possible to learn the art of ultimate responsibility so you can become a powerfully intentional leader.

What Paradigm Do You Mirror?

I met Anna during an intensive training seminar for church pastors and ministry leaders who desired to identify and maximize their unique strengths and skills for ministry. At the beginning of the day I asked each of them to jot down his or her greatest personal challenge in church leadership. A young, articulate woman, Anna shared openly about her struggles: "I've always felt criticized for my ability to take charge and make things happen. It feels like the members of my church probably think I am too bossy and outspoken, though I do get the job done!" Anna paused, and then added, "People probably think I'm not really cut out to be a minister."

Later in the day, I asked the leaders to respond to another reflective question. "Remember back. Who was your first role model of ministry leadership, the first one you can remember? Effective or not, what do you most strongly remember about that person as a leader?" I then pointed to a bottom-line reality. "The imprinted impression of that first role model, even if it was a poor one, will serve as your primary (albeit unconscious) paradigm of what ministry leadership is supposed to look like. Even if it negates or conflicts with your own God-given talents, until you take the time to extricate yourself and learn a new healthy ministry leadership paradigm, you will struggle in your growth and maturity as a leader of God's people."

Anna began weeping openly. "I see it now!" she said. "The first pastor of our church I remember from when I was young was a soft-spoken, godly man whose mission was to keep the peace at all costs in the congregation. The church didn't grow or change much, but he was loved for his sweet spirit and his ability to be a pastor to persons in a crisis. I'm suddenly realizing that my own struggles to accept myself as a ministry leader have to do with how different my own 'git 'er done' approach is from what I've always thought a 'pastor' is supposed to be like—my childhood example. I think that deep inside I've assumed there's something inadequate about me, because I'm so different than that [first pastor]. Are you saying it's okay to give myself permission to embrace who I am, not that old paradigm? Or maybe learn the best of all worlds?"

Whether your most influential role model was imprinted in your memory by a terrific, talented individual whose gifts have made you feel pale in comparison, or whether his or her example left much to be desired, I challenge you to clarify your unconscious paradigm for leadership. Your next task is to re-define it to make room for what is yet to be in you, built around realizing your potential through learning and practice. That second task is what the coming pages are about. Like Anna, you will experience a breakthrough toward becoming an intentional leader the moment that you let go of attempting to mirror another's model, and start fresh by building upon your own unique foundation. Begin now—don't wait until you are many years into serving God's people, wondering why your impact has been indiscernible.

Three Primary Components

Ministry leadership with lasting impact—whether in a whole church, a ministry area, a committee, or a team—incorporates a *dynamic blend of three potent components*. None of these stands alone; each enhances the other two, and you must intentionally choose to keep learning and practicing all three—every single day. This advice is not only for pastors. If God has allowed you any type of leadership role, you must be in the business of proactively maturing in these areas.

Through work and consultation with hundreds of pastors, church staff, and unpaid ministry leaders, I've seen that most persons have some natural proclivity for one or two of these components—and a few individuals naturally embody all three. As you read the description of each, see where you recognize yourself.

For further help in identifying which of these attributes may be your primary "default" ministry leadership component, take the "Primary Components Assessment" found in chapter 1 on the *Ultimately Responsible* DVD.

1. Spiritual Shepherd

A great ministry leader must have an ever-deepening love for God, and a heart for the people whom you are called to serve. This first component is non-negotiable, and it is the easiest one for others to notice when it is missing in you. Leaders with naturally strong instincts as spiritual shepherds are often described as pastoral, warm, genuine, kind, easy to trust, everyone's friend. If this is your primary ministry component, you may derive great energy from comforting those who are hurting, praying with the needy, or offering scriptural support and counseling to those who are facing grief, loss, suffering, or illness. You may find your greatest enjoyment when facilitating a small group Bible study, or sharing a "faith journey" discussion with others over coffee. You have a knack for sensing where people are in their relationship with God, and you like to help foster their growth. For you, the most important part of any worship service, ministry project, committee meeting, or work task is the spiritual connection that people experience, and you are diligent to make sure it's the priority.

If your primary ministry leadership component is Spiritual Shepherd, and you are deficient in the other two, you might notice one or more tendencies like these in yourself:
- An inner sense of resistance when work or task accomplishment must come before offering someone a listening ear
- A preference to "go with the Spirit's leading" rather than working a plan
- Enjoyment in spending time with people more than spending time at the desk with administrative details
- Difficulty addressing people who need supervisory correction, preferring a pastoral counseling approach rather than bottom-line accountability

Meet Michael and his "Systems/Task Organizer" leadership story on the *Ultimately Responsible* DVD, chapter 1. It takes more than just your primary leadership component to lead with intention.

2. Systems/Task Organizer

A great ministry leader must have adequate skills to manage the internal systems and tasks necessary to support the practicalities of God's work. Developing or adopting systems to track and manage details, work assignments, time lines, and communication is usually what makes or breaks a leader's successful ministry growth. The speed of the leader is the speed of the team; and you know that if the leader cannot achieve a technique to make sure the nuts-and-bolts organization and deployment of what needs to happen is managed, those volunteering to serve alongside in any capacity will also struggle to succeed.

If your primary ministry leadership component is Systems/Task Organizer, and you are deficient in the other two, you might notice one or more tendencies like these in yourself:

- A preference to be productive rather than just sit and talk
- Dislike of "rabbit trails" or circuitous meetings
- A need to get decisions made, and frustration toward those who won't
- Occasional struggle to delegate work to others (worried it "won't get done right")
- Puzzled when people don't just "do" something and seem unmotivated
- Energized by completing tasks or organizing what needs to happen

3. Vision Crier

Even today, in a wireless world, the centuries-old role of town crier still exists in a few local communities to let citizens know what's going on at the moment and what's about to happen. If you can imagine the impact of a town crier racing through the streets in order to inform and motivate people, you can appreciate the impact and importance of the third essential component. Intentional leaders have learned how to talk about what potential is ahead for their church or ministry area, and they can also point toward a general route to the destination. It is through the Vision Crier component that people catch contagious excitement and energy to surge forward, to rally around a dream and pursue it. Without this leadership component, a church or ministry can stay stagnant for extended periods of time, content with the status quo. Those who have this primary component are sometimes "thought leaders," who like to challenge others by announcing new ideas and possibilities.

If your primary ministry leadership component is Vision Crier, and you are deficient in the other two, you might notice one or more tendencies like these in yourself:
- Successful at getting people fired up for a new idea or direction
- An awareness that you may threaten "godfathers and godmothers" in the church who are afraid to let change happen
- Frequent sense of discontent with the present reality
- Preference for discussion of new ideas and explaining new possibilities over hands-on ministry tasks
- More effective giving big picture descriptions of what needs to happen, rather than providing specifics for actual deployment

Did you take the Primary Components Assessment found on the DVD? Write your results here:
Spiritual Shepherd total _____
Systems/Task Organizer total

_____
Vision Crier total

_____

Your Results—and Next Steps

The Primary Components Assessment is only intended to help on your path to becoming self-aware of the primary direction toward which you naturally lean in your ministry leadership approach. Don't let it box you in, and certainly avoid any impression that these three natural proclivities are mutually exclusive. In reality, whatever you bring from all three

identities blends together and enhances the others as you learn to lever-
age them. Your first two basic steps are:

- *Allow yourself permission to "own" your own unique toolbox* of
  skills, strengths, and gifts for ministry leadership, rather than
  attempting to emulate a stereotype of someone else whom
  you've held as your gold standard, either consciously or unconsciously.
- *Identify what your primary ministry component (tool) is* that you
  instinctively try to utilize first when meeting new ministry challenges, dealing with people, bringing new potential to a stagnant situation or supporting persons in their spiritual journey.
  Whenever you take on a new phase of leadership growth, you
  will unconsciously grab your top tool, your most familiar com-
  ponent(s) first in order to try to solve, conquer, or address
  whatever is before you. Whether at the core you are a Spiritual
  Shepherd, a Systems/Task Organizer, or a Vision Crier, any of
  these will put a filter on how you initially see what needs to happen and what your instincts tell you to do. But by remaining
  aware that all three components may come into play, you'll
  avoid the failure that many church leaders make: pushing and
  trying harder with your primary component, while not understanding why it's not working, and never realizing that leverag-
  ing one or both of the other components is what it will take to
  succeed.

Check out Fran's
story, "Listen to
the Music," on
the *Ultimately
Responsible* DVD,
chapter 1—and see
how God can take
whoever you are
and maximize it
for leadership.

After teaching about shepherds, organizers, and criers, a poised and dig-
nified pastor approached me during a break and asked to speak with me
privately. "I have been in the ordained ministry for more than thirty
years. I have a seminary degree and did a doctor of ministry program
ten years ago. I'm a fine Bible scholar and have always made sure that
the pastoral responsibilities of any congregation I've served have been
well taken care of. My annual church reports are always reasonably in
order and turned in on time. What has frustrated me is seeing the people sitting in the pews every Sunday, intently listening to me preach—
but so few of them actually get involved in anything! Hardly any want
to volunteer, no one gets excited about what I tell them we could do. I
feel like I tell them all the time, but they just sit there. Are you suggesting that, after all these years, there are still skills I can learn to become
more of a Vision Crier? I don't think I'm naturally a salesman, you see."

If you are wondering something similar, the answer is yes! Yes, you can
learn what you need to know in order to bring an effective complement
of these three components into whatever setting God has called you to
lead. Yes, you can maximize your role of ultimate responsibility by changing gears, learning new approaches, and even finding strategic partner-

ships. All will be in proportion to your willingness to unlearn and relearn (no matter how uncomfortable), to maximize your innate abilities and enhance them with the right new skills.

What happens if you decide not to make an effort to grow in each of these primary ministry leadership components? You can chair your committee, or finish seminary and become pastor of your first church, or serve as the Sunday School superintendent, or continue on as senior minister, or even become a church staff employee—and perhaps do a passable job on the sheer strength of your primary component. But if you desire to embrace fully your capacity for ultimate responsibility as spiritual leader, commit to becoming a serious student of what it takes.

Ministry Success Equation

Ministry success can be summarized by a simple equation. It can help you diagnose why you are not experiencing God's definition of success in your own ministry leadership, by showing you what is missing and where you need to do some work. You will understand each of the factors in the equation more clearly as we define them one by one in the following chapters.

[Awareness of/leverage of your primary ministry components/strengths]
+
[Your daily living and growing relationship with God]
+
[Your contagious, ministry-movement strategy and communication]
+
[Your full embrace of the "Body of Christ" approach to Kingdom work]
+
[Your ability to develop strategic partnerships and teams]
+
[Your skills as a leader of change]

= Ministry "Success"

The following chapters contain topic-by-topic strategic information and instructions to help you learn and implement what you need for each element of the equation. Sidebar notes are placed throughout the text to provide extra tips, directions, and insights, depending upon your core primary ministry component. In the book and on the DVD, you will also encounter stories of ministry leaders who have taken the necessary steps to change, and the powerful results that God has brought. You'll also find worksheets to guide you and your team in learning and discussion.

No matter what type of leadership role you've received, God's intent is for your enduring accomplishment of Jesus' work through unleashing the lives of others. Be prepared for your own miraculous story to unfold.

ON THE DVD FOR CHAPTER 1:

-Primary Ministry Components Assessment Tool

-"The Intentional Leader" Worksheet for your team

-"The Intentional Leader" Bible Study

-Video Story: Michael—"Leadership"

-Video Story: Fran—"Listen to the Music"

"The ship that will not obey the
helm will have to obey the rocks."
-English Proverb

2

YOUR NORTH-STAR STRATEGY

Many leaders in the congregation shift their focus so completely to the tangible ministry challenge ahead that they overlook what must always come first.

James was angry, completely frustrated. "I can't believe those guys! I don't know why they even signed up to be leaders in the men's group!" His fist banged the table for emphasis. "I just think they are uninformed and totally off track. They don't seem interested in my ideas. They're not even acting like grown-ups, and I certainly don't know why they volunteered. I don't see any way to work with them, so what I want to do is just get rid of them! There's no solution except that. Otherwise, I'll never be able to get my plans to go forward. I don't know why they are opposing me! I could pull off our events better all by myself, without them!"

I thought for a minute before answering the impatient face expectantly looking at me for permission to "fire" his leadership team. He seemed caught off guard by the question I asked in reply. "What Scripture did you read or study in your devotional time with God today?" "I didn't do that this morning," he responded. "I had to get the kids ready for school. I have to get up early to get all that done. Why? Why do you ask?"

"I understand. What about last night? Did you have your Bible study and prayer time with God last night, then?"

"No, I was watching the football game. Monday night, you know. Then my wife wanted to talk to me about a few things. I was tired after that, and needed to go to bed."

"How about the day before? What did you read in your Bible study and prayer time?"

"Well, I didn't because it was Sunday. I came to the worship service. I don't really sit down every day and do Bible reading, actually. I do look

If your natural inclination is to focus upon tasks to be done, and if you feel impatience with those who seem to slow the progress, your primary leadership strength may be labeled as **Systems/Task Organizer**. As you learn to see the "big picture" that the ministry tasks you and your team perform are all tools of a spiritual growth process, your perspective will gradually change.

If your primary ministry strength is labeled as **Spiritual Shepherd**, your team partners who are like James (strong **Systems/Task Organizers**) may frustrate you. Use your **Spiritual Shepherd** style to gradually bring your entire ministry team along in their core commitment to personal spiritual development, as described in this chapter. Harness the energy of your team's **Systems/Task Organizers** to pull the project forward.

for a good Bible verse to share whenever we are having a men's ministry leadership team meeting so I can open with a verse and a prayer. But I figure that as the chair of the men's ministry, I already know enough about the Bible. I've grown up in the church, and have pretty much already heard all of the Scripture stories many times. Trust me, it's not like I haven't thought a lot about this men's ministry situation. As I drive to work, I've been talking to God about how angry I am at these guys who keep stirring things up and wanting to change my plans. Like I'm supposed to support them, instead of them supporting me as their leader! Being the leader, I feel like the lone ranger. Yes, I've been complaining to God a lot about it. That's been my prayer time!"

"And what has God answered?" I asked. James was completely silent, seemingly uncertain about what I meant. "Well…I assume God agrees with me. God didn't drop any little piece of paper from heaven, with a note telling me any different!"

Think about today. In what leadership circumstances do you find yourself right now? You may be like James—an unpaid leader who has attended church for years, chairing different committees and helping keep the church work going. You may be a student pursuing an academic degree and preparing for ministry, deep into Old or New Testament exegetical courses, perhaps immersed in theology or ethics classes. Perhaps you are a busy pastor or church staff employee, with a congregation that assumes you regularly practice personal spiritual disciplines.

No matter what your circumstances, one truth is crucial for all who are called to provide servant leadership for God's people: it is impossible to fully know and follow the heart of God as you lead without a "north-star" strategy—both for yourself, and for them. What it takes for you as leader to fulfill your God-calling is the same foundational groundwork it requires of those you lead. Establishing this strategy from the start will provide a framework within which you can bring your best, and serve as a vehicle by which God can summon the best from your constituency at the same time.

Use the "North-Star Strategy" worksheet found on the *Ultimately Responsible* DVD, chapter 2, to articulate and define your own strategy—for yourself, as well as for those you lead.

Jumping into a new leadership role and immediately putting your best energy into dealing with urgencies is a common approach for new, enthusiastic leaders. Like James, your initial focus may be consumed with attempting to remove perceived obstacles in order to get things moving, rather than strategizing. However, intentional leaders first know and practice their own personal strategy for spiritual maturity, and then implement a broad application of the same for their team, ministry, or church. When a crisis or problem comes along, the solutions put into action happen in harmony with the strategy already in place.

So, back to you. What would you say is the intentional strategy that you practice for your own spiritual growth as a leader? If you are the ultimately responsible leader, how about the one toward which you direct your congregation, team, or group---whether it's large or small? Could those you lead articulate it? If you were asked to write down or draw your basic north-star strategy, would it look like a patchwork quilt that contains random bits and pieces? Or is it a cohesive, logical picture for both you and for your constituency, which is easily understood?

A north-star strategy forms the foundation for all the leadership you'll need to provide in order to ignite your ministry. Get this right, and you'll be on your way. My north-star strategy, as it applies to my own growth as well to as the constituency I serve, can be summarized in three words: Bring—Grow—Serve. As I explain each part of this strategy, I'll describe my personal as well as the broader congregational applications. Use this example to help you identify your own strategy, according to your unique internal compass and landscape.

Bring

…is how my morning starts every day. As a leader, my natural human instinct is to rush ahead to check e-mail, tackle the current "to do" list, or dash out the door to get to the office. The daily practice of the Bring discipline, however, means that before everything else, I first seek to bring all I know of myself to God, to experience the celebration of Jesus in every corner of life. I want to live and to lead while aligned with the intentions of God as closely as possible. Without regular alignment checks and corrections, I drift gradually (or sometimes veer quickly) off course. For me, "true north" means strategically bringing myself to encounter the pattern for daily living that Jesus provided, and continuing to make decisions that move me closer to synchronizing with God's ideal design. I seek to bring myself into constant community with God both through prayer and through faithful demonstration of godly choices, every day.

I bring myself **physically**. If, as the Scriptures teach, my body is the temple of God, then how carefully and thoughtfully am I caring for it? In what I eat? The amount of rest I give it? Exercise? Self-care? The way I take care of myself physically reflects the level of obedience I've developed spiritually. In order for God to use me, I desire to be as physically fit and healthy as possible.

I bring myself **mentally**. I bring my thoughts to be taken "captive to Christ" (2 Corinthians 10:5), so I pray for my mind to be filled with the mind of Christ. Bringing myself into God's presence will result in trans-

Need help making a plan for total life health? Your best bet is to utilize *Momentum for Life: Sustaining Personal Health, Integrity, and Strategic Focus as a Leader* by Mike Slaughter, © 2005, Abingdon Press.

An excellent book to help you deal with unforgiveness is *Forgive for Good* by Dr. Fred Luskin, © 2003, HarperCollins Publishers. You'll learn how to rewrite your "victim" stories, let go of grudges, and reclaim your life.

Financial health and freedom are key parts of building a sure spiritual leader's foundation. *Money Matters: Financial Freedom for All God's Children* by Mike Slaughter, © 2005, Abingdon Press, comes complete with practical personal and congregational steps to health in this area.

formation by the renewing of my mind, so I can see what God's will is (Romans 12:2). I long for my thought life to reflect what Paul described: "whatever is true, whatever is noble, whatever is right, whatever is pure, whatever is lovely, whatever is admirable—if anything is excellent or praiseworthy—think about such things…and the God of peace will be with you" (Philippians 4:8-9). I ask God for wisdom and to show me the priorities of Jesus, no matter how painful or challenging.

I bring myself **emotionally**. I ask God to create in me a pure heart (Psalm 51:10), and for the eyes of my heart to be enlightened, so I can know the hope and embrace the power available to all believers (Ephesians 1:18-19). I request that God fill me with the love that is defined in 1 Corinthians 13—that it would flow through me to every person who crosses my path throughout the day.

I bring myself **relationally**. I honestly bring to my prayer with God whatever judgment or unforgiveness issues I may be harboring against anyone or any situation, and release my victim mentality in exchange for a victor mindset, one fitting for a follower of Jesus. I seek God's forgiveness for when and how I have been wrong. I ask to receive the ability to become an unimpeded vessel of the Spirit's kindness toward others. I bring my relationships—family, friends, team members, congregation—and ask God to teach me how to form good relationship habits in every area, to bring others to a whole-life-celebration of Jesus just as I seek myself.

I bring myself **materially**. I want how I handle my finances, my home, and my possessions to reflect the light of true, godly stewardship. All I have belongs to God, and my responsibility is as caretaker, the manager of what I've been given. Whole-life celebration of Jesus means I seek debt-free living, practice tithing, share generously with others, and remember that the best things in life are not things.

For a congregation-wide application, consider painting the words of this north-star strategy (or the one you develop) in large letters on a wall in the main lobby of your church, so that everyone can keep it in mind. For newcomers, an extra explanation for each element can be added:

- *Bring* seeking people into a life-celebration of Jesus
- *Grow* as disciples in cell community
- *Serve* out of our call and giftedness

The broad strategic aspect of Bring for our congregation refers to the active, intentional, spiritual preparation that we strive to make together in order to open the doors and bring those who are searching into God's community of believers. We constantly ask:

- *Are we successfully setting the stage for God's love to be extended to newcomers the moment they set foot inside the door?*
- *Is the church facility with which our congregation has been blessed clean, cared-for, and hospitable?*
- *How user-friendly is our language? Can everyone understand God's message of invitation to bring themselves into eternal community with God through Jesus?*
- *Can attendees easily understand and join in whatever is happening here, feeling included in the community of faith?*
- *Are we modeling for one another lifestyles of obedience in every area of living?*
- *Are we preparing and training our members to spiritually cultivate a Bring attitude, radiating the inviting love of Jesus to everyone they meet throughout their daily lives in the world?*

Bring-Grow-Serve is not only a potential overall spiritual growth template for the entire congregation, but also the questions listed in the text can be asked on behalf of individual ministry areas within the church, so all are aligned around the same strategy.

Bring for church attendees is accomplished corporately through deeply inviting and meaningful worship celebrations. It is there that we together bring all of ourselves to all we know God to be—through music, praise, inspiration, prayer, holy communion. Bring also happens through other entry points into the community of faith. Other Bring examples include training churchgoers in Jesus-style radical hospitality when sharing their faith.

Bring can be summed up by this central question: *How do we continually train and prepare ourselves at both the personal and the communal levels to bring ourselves and others to the celebrating, inviting, life-transforming love of Jesus?*

Designing Worship by Kim Miller, © 2004, Group Publishing, is a resource that can show you how to transform weekly worship into celebrations that irresistibly draw in newcomers and demonstrate the power of Bring. Find this resource at www.ginghamsburg resources.org.

Grow

… is the second part of my personal north-star strategy as a leader. If you're like me, you may be tempted to count time spent studying the nuances of a Scripture passage in the Greek language in preparation for a sermon, or reading a passage from the Bible as you prepare to teach Sunday School, as personal devotional time. While this may bring valuable biblical knowledge, personal one-on-one devotional time invested in God's word combines scriptural insight with corresponding heart and life transformation.

I've learned that I must always embrace daily time spent in the Bible in order to hear God's direction—not only through studying but also through praying and listening. By studying the Scripture for the purpose of personal, practical life application each day, God has the opportunity to reveal to me why things might not be working and what needs to change. Through daily time spent together, I learn more of God's intention and purpose. In seasons past when I have omitted the crucial one-on-one investment of such daily time in God's word, I fear for how far I went awry, how out of kilter my leadership direction may have gone. I've learned now that in order to lead well, I must actively grow in my regular personal investment in the living word of God.

Help your staff or team additionally appreciate the compelling need to be in God's word daily by viewing a short video segment by Mike Slaughter on "The Word," found on the *Ultimately Responsible* DVD, chapter 2.

In years of working with both unpaid ministry workers and paid church staff, I have never seen authentic, explosive, powerful Kingdom work take place unless the leader was committed to the daily practice of this one true thing—a sure foundation as just described. In fact, I have a rule for all paid ministry staff I supervise: *do not come to work each day until you have spent personal devotional time with God in Bible study and listening prayer*. I have the same expectation for unpaid ministry leaders, for the same reason: *we cannot lead others further spiritually than we ourselves have gone*. Daily personal time with God through Bible study is not just for those who earn their living by employment in the ministry. It's a necessity for all followers of Christ who desire God to use their lives fully. When an individual accepts an unpaid ministry leadership role—whether as a committee chair, a coordinator, a teacher, or other position—part of the job description I emphasize is always the stipulation of prioritizing daily time in God's word.

Pure talent (or a seminary degree) may bring a certain level of accomplishment, as can on-the-job ministry experience and training. But don't be fooled—though your ministry train may leave the station, it will never pick up speed (and it could even become derailed) unless you and God share intentional time together in the Scripture every single day. That time will shape you into the leader worthy of ultimate responsibility for your ministry, provide you with deep wisdom and direction, and keep you focused upon God's design. Otherwise, you'll build a ministry that's all about yourself, your own desires, and your own authority. You'll slowly meander in perspective until you, like James in the opening story of this chapter, see the very persons you're called to serve alongside as your greatest obstacles rather than the recipients of your enabling leadership.

In addition to time invested in personal Bible study alone with God, Grow, for me, means spiritual investment in *community accountability*. I'm referring to a small, close group of Christian friends who share a passion for personal growth with God, meeting together regularly to uphold one another, to share honestly and confidentially about struggles and triumphs, and to encourage each other. Some call this a small group, a cell group, or an accountability group. Whatever the label, its importance in fostering my quest for spiritual maturity is unquestionable. In addition to time alone with God daily, I must have an honest, laboratory-like context like this with others to nurture my development.

Several years ago, I moved to a new state and began serving a congregation in which I was acquainted with no one except the senior pastor and a few of the church leaders. Although relational connections with other staff members and unpaid leaders quickly developed, I realized that I needed a personal accountability group as soon as possible. It would have been easy to form one right away with the ministry leaders I supervised, but instead I wanted a group with whom I held only one identity, that of collegial Christian follower. During the first few months in my new setting, I prayed for guidance as one-by-one I met individuals who might be candidates for a personal cell group. When the number reached four, I invited each of them to connect together with me into an accountability group that would function around the guidelines of these mutual commitments:

- Attend the group meeting every other week.
- Come prepared both to listen and to learn.
- Practice personal spiritual growth through regular worship attendance, daily devotional time with God, and dedication to a servant (volunteer) activity that serves others in need.
- Agree to group confidentiality, encouragement, and honesty.
- View the group as Christians who have chosen to do life together, support and uphold each other.

Vision Criers often prefer an accountability group within which to talk about ministry ideas and goals, rather than personal growth issues. Yet without personal and spiritual accountability—a set of friends who will ask you the hard questions, push past your great ideas, and confront you about your spiritual maturity—God will not be able to develop you into the total package of the intentional leader.

After five years the group is still active, expanded to twelve members. Three of the original five group members are now married. A few new kindred spirits have connected into the group. Two have moved away. Personal accountability groups are not usually open groups that are seeking to grow, because the group experiences dynamic changes with the addition of a newcomer. Yet in our case, we have reached a consensus each time God has led a new individual into our circle. Trustworthiness and safe space must redevelop each time this happens. So consistency of group members helps strengthen and deepen the intimacy and honesty a personal accountability group can achieve.

I do not lead this cell group; I am a member of it. I am not the pastor of the other cell group members; I am a fellow believer. I experience spiritual and personal growth as a Christian follower within the context of a cell group of other Christians like me. I share about who I am on the inside, who I am honestly choosing to be, and what decisions of faithfulness I may be struggling to make. Cell group time may be about defining my steps as I learn to be a better spouse or parent, or what I discovered (or wrestled with) in my devotional time with God this week. Personal accountability in cell community provides an intimate arena in which to share, to listen to others share, to confront each other when necessary, and to tell each other the truth in love. Jesus declared, "Where two or three come together in my name, there am I with them" (Matthew 18:20). Not only did Jesus himself pull away for regular time alone with God, but he also invested in personal accountability together in community with his closest friends, the disciples. Practicing this type of accountability provides me with the same relational foundation Jesus enjoyed during his earthly life as a leader: a group of comrades who rejoice with me, travel life with me, ask me hard questions, seek answers together with me, and champion my calling as I likewise offer this to them.

What happens when you as a leader ignore the importance of developing a small group with whom to share personal spiritual accountability? Unfortunately, the human need to share the stories of a genuine, intimate, and sacred pilgrimage may blip out in inappropriate settings.

A highly gifted pastor I know (who never took the time to develop a personal accountability cell group) suffered disaster when he went through a messy divorce. His perspective became skewed as his emotional pain increased. Without a personal cell group to offer him confidential safe space to work through his situation and help him stay on course, he turned to using the pulpit as a venue to process his journey of pain and disappointment. Anger with his estranged wife, the resulting loneliness of separation, and even his propensity to go on resultant drinking binges all ended up blurted into several Sunday sermons. Don't misunderstand me: real-life, personal sermon illustrations are certainly valuable. But this pastor-in-crisis crossed the line into an inappropriate setting for personal disclosure and inadvertently exploited the attentiveness of his kindhearted parishioners who thought they had come for worship and spiritual inspiration. Unfortunately, this pastor also began utilizing office counseling sessions he had with church members to talk through his own problems rather than theirs. He even used part of the monthly administrative board meeting to do what he called "a little soul cleansing" as he admitted to the church leaders other graphic details of the downfalls within his marriage, rather than reviewing the monthly finance report with them.

This pastor was eventually placed on indefinite leave from his congregation. It took two full years of counseling and healing before he returned to church ministry, this time with a personal accountability group in place for himself as well as a practice of daily time alone with God. His example is a warning for everyone, whether you serve as a committee chair or a pastor or as a class teacher. In addition to your personal relationship with God, connect with a confidential personal cell group with whom you can share honestly and openly. You'll find yourself in a healthier state of mind and spirit for your ministry role, and it will reduce the temptation to use your committee, class, or congregation inappropriately as your personal impromptu support group.

Think through your circumstances. If you don't already have a group, with whom you could connect and form one? Perhaps it's with pastors in your town or district. Maybe it's with a group of personal friends. A personal accountability group with your ministry supervisor, or those you supervise or lead in ministry, brings a duplicity of roles and agendas into the dynamics. Whatever it is for you, make certain you develop a confidential group with whom you can share your personal life and spiritual journey. With this rootedness, you will be enabled to grow and bring your spiritual best to the ministry leadership role you hold.

Like my own personal north-star strategy, the broader aspect of Grow for our congregation emphasizes the need for both one-on-one time with God, as well as growth in cell community.

It's important to challenge yourself and your constituency to spend time with God's word every day. And most are interested in doing so. But one important question often surfaces with most persons in a congregation: *What should I read and study in the Bible during my daily time with God? Should I just read through the Psalms? Open the Bible and read whatever page it opens to? Buy a Bible study guide to follow? I'm not sure what to do....*

A great way to answer this question is to get the whole congregation involved in reading the same passages of Scripture. A team of leaders can choose scriptures for the entire church family to use in a daily personal devotional time with God. In my congregation, we have produced a Transformation Journal in several different formats (one year we published a month's worth of daily Bible study pages at a time; another year we published pages every quarter). The current format features each week's daily scripture readings (along with a couple of sentences of introduction plus two journal questions for each day) together with journaling space on a folded insert in the worship bulletin that attendees receive each weekend. This Transformation Journal is what our pastors, staff, and congregation use daily in their personal time with God. It is available in downloadable form on our church Web site for those who might have missed weekend worship and can even be completed daily from any computer via our free online *Transformation Journal* edition. The creation and availability of the all-church *Transformation Journal* achieved two major victories:

Create your church's own online daily devotional by downloading the free software template utilized by Ginghamsburg's *Transformation Journal.* Check it out along with other free church Web site resources at www.webempowered church.com.

An example of the *Transformation Journal* weekly bulletin insert can be found on the *Ultimately Responsible* DVD, chapter 2. Check out this week's *Transformation Journal* (or get a free subscription to the online version) at www.ginghamsburg.org/tj.

See how we introduced the online *Transformation Journal* to the church family with a short video, found on the *Ultimately Responsible* DVD, chapter 2. Use it to help implement the *Transformation Journal* in your setting!

Teen *Transformation Journal*, *FUEL*, and the **children's *TJ***, *Imagine*, can also be found at www.ginghamsburg .org/tj.

See an example of a **cell connection form** on the *Ultimately Responsible* DVD, chapter 2. Customize it to fit the needs of your own setting.

It took away the excuse that staff, leaders, and members often used: they simply didn't have what they needed to guide their daily scripture time with God, and therefore were unmotivated to prioritize it regularly. Now we all share the same verses and reflection questions, and we experience unity about the core topics of our spiritual growth. Leaders are encouraged to use insights from the daily *Transformation Journal* study to open their team meetings. Teachers are invited to start class time with a devotional insight that they discovered through their own *Transformation Journal* use. Staff members discuss the *Transformation Journal* to launch their staff meetings. The preachers make reference to what they've learned through the Transformation Journal in sermon messages.

The daily scriptures and journal questions developed for the adults' *Transformation Journal* are also adapted for both children and students. Teens use a daily version called *FUEL*, and families with children utilize a companion version named *Imagine*. In this way all ages may invest in personal growth time with God every day.

Every measure of deepening growth of spiritual maturity across the lives of members and attendees—servant/volunteer involvement, financial generosity, numerical growth, and passion for worship attendance to name a few—has developed and expanded. The *Transformation Journal* has indeed transformed our congregation. God is able to use our lives together collectively for greater purposes through this faithfulness.

To bring believers together to *grow through Christian community and accountability* (the other part of Grow), our cell (small) group system is continually refined and improved to provide effective connection into cells for adults, teens, and children. Several times each year "cell connection forms" are distributed to everyone during all weekend worship celebrations. Newcomers receive cell connection forms in their "Visitor Welcome" gift bags. Cell connection forms are distributed at the end of most classes or courses. And they are continually available at the information display in the church lobby. When individuals fill out and submit a cell connection form, each is matched into an already-existing cell group, or drawn together with other persons to form a new one. Monthly trainings are held to ensure ongoing cell group leader effectiveness. The cell groups do Bible study together, pray together, serve together, and socialize together. When concerns or needs arise, group members provide mutual support among themselves. And cell group members hold each other accountable to a faithful Christian walk and witness. Like me, many report their most significant spiritual growth comes through the Christian community of a cell group.

Our church received the following e-mail from a member of a newly-formed cell group. The mixture of ages, personalities, professional backgrounds, and stages of life was eclectic. Yet God works powerfully when Christians gather and practice true accountability in community.

Hello—Just thought I'd give you an update on our cell group we formed last fall.

We started with 11, and one couple dropped off. Along the way, we happened to meet at one woman's house whose dad also attends our church. He was really impressed by the group and has decided to join us.

This past weekend, Enrique (the young man from Peru) brought his aunt Julianna along. She attends a church in a nearby town with no cell group ministry. We suspect that she may end up joining our group as well.

Even though our group is fairly new, we're really starting to bond. A large number of our members attended a movie together one Sunday afternoon. I'm currently coordinating a date for all of us to serve together down at the soup kitchen (we're scheduled for May 7). And, we're collectively looking at other local mission opportunities we can participate in together.

But the most incredible thing about the cell group is how we're all growing spiritually and becoming a "family." I've provided 3-hole punched "prayer requests" sheets for our binders. At first, everyone would mention their prayer requests, and some would write them down, others wouldn't.

I finally strongly suggested that everyone should write down each prayer request, and then use those as part of their prayers EVERY day. We also go through the sheet before we close the meeting with prayer and include the requests at that time.

I eventually wrote out a "suggested outline" for the meetings. We rotate who leads each meeting, and some folks find it easier to have some meeting items in front of them (such as the opening prayer, discussing recent God moments, things that stood out in the weekend sermon, cell group questions from the weekly worship bulletin insert, prayer requests, closing prayer, etc.) In fact, the person leading the group this weekend referred to the outline throughout our meeting.

It's amazing how many of our prayers are being met. I think the group is really starting to understand that being part of a cell group is more than just coming every first and third Sunday...it really can make a BIG difference.

In just the few short months since we formed, I've been amazed at how much we've learned about each other...and how much some of us have shared. We've laughed and cried for each other. And with no judgment.

I can't begin to tell you how much the cell group has meant to my life and the lives of the others in the group. I just received an e-mail from one group member who was facing an MRI scan after a scary preliminary diagnosis. Thankfully, the images that showed up on the first scans are nowhere to be found, and the whole cell group has prayed for her health and recovery.

Community is essential for serious Christian growth. Mike Slaughter offers bottom-line motivation for Christian community in a short video segment found on the *Ultimately Responsible* DVD, chapter 2.

If I can ever be of any motivation for other cell groups, let me know. I would gladly come and encourage the...even very diverse groups such as ours. In fact, I can't imagine our group without the diversity. One of our youngest members e-mailed me this week to say that he was glad he had other older members in the group—we were able to help with some questions he had about the direction of his life.

Keep up the great work encouraging the formation of the cell groups. They can truly be life-changing opportunities.

Dave

The questions to ask in order to keep on track with the Grow aspect of the north-star strategy are:

- *How do we encourage and assist persons individually in their daily Bible study devotional time with God?*
- *How is growing spiritual maturity intentionally supported through relational cell community within the body of Christ?*

Serve

...is the third part of my personal north-star strategy as a leader, and the corresponding third part of the strategy for the congregation I support. Serve refers to the spiritual growth that comes through joining Jesus on mission to love and to serve the needs of God's children. By serving, we join together to bring the supernatural love of Jesus to those in desperate need of help and hope. God has equipped each of us to serve according to our unique mix of gifts, talents, strengths, and preparation. We demonstrate our love of God tangibly by joining Jesus on mission to serve.

My call to serve in a leadership capacity means embodying the servant leader role that Jesus exemplified while on earth. The leadership roles of pastor, church staff member, team leader, or committee chair are not intended to entitle anyone to privilege, prestige, or superiority over others. In Kingdom work, a leader is the servant of all. Leaders relinquish their worldly rights to assume spiritual responsibility for their constituencies. It's an upside-down paradigm from the world's point of view.

Living personally into a lifestyle of serving requires me to stay alert to every opportunity to serve others, even down into the smallest details, with both strangers and friends. My practices of servanthood through leadership come through commitment to pray for those I lead, to see my role as providing relationship, support, training, inspiration, and resources to enable their ability to serve. In fact, understanding that my love for God is embodied through serving has resulted in a deep paradigm shift within: serving is not something I choose to do; it is who I am as I seek to embody the active love of God.

At the corporate level, when implementing the north-star strategy for an entire congregation, most leaders are weakest and least prepared in the Serve aspect.

Traditional seminary training emphasizes the development of personal devotion and provides biblical and theological education, preparing most pastors to put all their energy into creating the Bring and Grow aspects of spiritual growth. Resources abound to assist church leaders with Bring and with Grow. But followers faithfully model the passion and focus of their leaders. So if creating worship experiences and offering Bible studies are what energizes the leader, then those will become the accepted growth strategy for everyone.

As a result, engagement in Serve lags far behind in most churches and ministries that focus primarily on Bring and Grow. Church leaders expect their members to automatically want to serve as an expression of their love for God. They may even admonish members to do so but overlook intentional development of this component as spiritual growth. As a result, participants love to attend worship and other church events and enjoy learning from the Bible and deepening their faith, but they fail to grasp that the culmination of their faith is to be lived out through active demonstration of service to their neighbor. Jesus was clear that the path of service in his name is what characterizes his true friends.

The only fully effective path to *igniting the ministry you lead*—of any type, size, setting, or age group—is igniting your constituency's individual and collective passion to serve.

The pastor of a small church created a free health clinic in the dilapidated, crime-ridden, downtown area of her city. The clinic was launched from the servant dream of two doctors in her congregation, whose hearts break over the lack of health care for at-risk children in the most poverty-stricken blocks of the local urban crisis, and who donate their time and supplies. The project met with so much success that doctors around the county began to volunteer their time to serve at the clinic. Then dentists were added. Nurses began to serve at the clinic to train young mothers about nutrition and care for their babies. Eventually, a clothing and furniture ministry was added in a storefront next to the clinic, filled with clothes and furniture contributed by the generous congregation. A local bakery started donating bread, and a nightly downtown soup kitchen was born. Dozens of servants of all ages from the small church staffed the evening meal, from cooking to serving to cleanup.

When I made a trip to that city on business, I made sure to attend the Sunday morning worship service at this church. The service was different from what I expected at a church with such explosive impact. The pastor had entered the ministry as a second career with no formal theological training, and her preaching would not get a high grade from an instructor. The music could best be described as a "joyful noise unto the Lord"; the choir loft was packed with a loud, enthusiastic, untrained cavalry of voices. Children scampered noisily through the aisles even during the prayer time. How, I wondered, can such an unprofessional and disorganized worship service exist at a church able to fuel such a vibrant, life-changing ministry downtown? After worship I had a chance to talk with the pastor.

> You know, I'm no Bible scholar or teacher. And coming into the pastorate like I did, I've had little previous background in organizing Sunday School or even knowing how a choir rehearsal is supposed to be run. I'm aware we probably don't make a good impression on newcomers who are looking for a snazzy worship service and a neatly arranged class schedule—and I'm working on that. I struggle to get my annual church reports put together and turned in on time every year.

> But I do have a passion to unleash individuals to serve, to help them identify their God-dreams and then provide the platform and support to go help change the world by living them out. I thrive on helping my congregation connect their faith to their actions, seeing the vision of what is possible in God's name. And what I've found out is that it's not my talent at preaching or my ability to organize educational classes that makes the most impact for God's work or helps our church become contagious. It's unleashing everyone to serve that's the most important part—that makes an eternal difference. And that I can do!

You are blessed if you are an accomplished Bible scholar or teacher, or if you have completed formal education or advanced training in church leadership. But even if you haven't, the good news is that you can become the intentional leader that makes an unforgettable impact on behalf of Jesus' mission. As you learn and practice Serve in your own life and likewise infect and deploy your church or team, you will ignite the ministry of which you're in charge. Serve is the fuel that propels the entire north-star strategy.

Getting Ready To Go

First, you identified your primary ministry leadership component. Now, you have seen the importance of clarifying and working with a north-star leadership strategy as your foundation.

The next two chapters explain what you may never have learned or fully understood about the fuel of Serve, which has the potential to ignite the ministry when you're in charge. Learn to stage a contagious ministry movement that will unleash unpaid ministry and help you become the intentional leader God intends.

ON THE DVD FOR CHAPTER 2:

-"North-Star Strategy" Worksheet for your staff, team, or committee

-Video: *Transformation Journal*

-Mike Slaughter video segment on "The Word"

-Mike Slaughter video segment on "Community"

-*Transformation Journal:* God's Word on...Itself (PDF)

-Cell Group Connection Form

"Our call is to create church grow-ers,
not just church goers..."
-Bishop Bruce Ough

3

ANATOMY OF
CONTAGIOUS MINISTRY MOVEMENT

They were polite, friendly, and reserved. The committee of five from a church in a neighboring state had come for the weekend to visit our church's singles ministry. They attended the Sunday singles class, led by a single adult volunteer. They joined a large group of adult singles for a planned lunch excursion out to a local restaurant after the last worship celebration, led and organized by a team of three single adult servant leaders.

That night, they stayed to observe the weekly Singles Night held in our largest facility called the Avenue. Its classrooms were occupied with a variety of singles study groups. Two different types of dance lessons filled the building with laughter and conversation from dozens of participants. Two courts of volleyball rotated through four informal pickup coed teams. Card tables were arranged in a special area where euchre and bridge teams of adult singles competed. A small side dining room swelled to standing room only as single adult karaoke vocalists and their cheering sections of loyal friends arrived, all facilitated by a professional karaoke deejay (a single adult) who donated her time and equipment. Two teams of welcome host servants greeted newcomers at the front doors, providing informational tours throughout all activities and helping every person connect into the variety of offerings.

Partway through the evening, the visiting committee asked if they could debrief their time with me—what they had seen and learned in their daylong fact-finding quest to help inform their own church's potential to start a single adult ministry. "We are really impressed with what you have going on here!" the committee chair began. "Everything seems pretty organized. And wow, I didn't know so many singles could gather in one place at one time. It has been fun to see!"

"I'm glad you could experience the energy of this ministry," I answered. "Please remember that everything about this morning's activities and tonight's Singles Night is all led by our single adult servants. Everything is done by teams of many servants and leaders."

"Well, that's just the problem," the committee chair answered sadly. "If we had the quality of single adults you have here, we could do this also! But we have tried for almost two years to get a singles ministry going, and we just don't have any leaders. No leaders at all. We keep putting an ad in our weekly bulletin insert asking for leaders, and we've had some attendees at a few things we've tried but no leaders after all this time. Do you have any ideas as to where we could get leaders?"

Their story and question sounded familiar. I thought back to less than three years earlier when the thriving singles ministry they had just observed was comprised of only twelve people who had been meeting together as a small support group. That limited collection of singles had also been perplexed by the dilemma of how to find more leaders, and they expressed a desire for their group to grow. Everything began to change when they learned about the anatomy of a contagious ministry movement. A strategy emerged that they could see and apply. Over time, their diligence to work the contagious ministry movement strategy gained momentum. Now their challenge is to create enough leadership roles to engage everyone ready to lead, not the reverse. And mature leaders from the singles ministry have migrated into various church-wide leadership roles as well.

Your honest answer to the following question will clarify what kind of a leader God is calling you to be: Are you called to be a small group facilitator, or are you called to be the leader of a contagious, growing ministry movement?

If your call is to be a **small group facilitator,** you are a leader who is fairly comfortable with the persons who are already involved in your church or ministry. You have your team or committee in place, and perhaps you've served together for years. You have your activities scheduled together for each season. You have become good friends with everyone, and you have grown and bonded closely. You are there for each other and support each other. Visitors are welcome, so long as they understand that their role is to join in with what you already have in place. The idea of rotating leadership doesn't seem necessary because you all already have your responsibilities and know what to do, and you enjoy working with each other. You may think that some newcomers have a tendency to disrupt the apple cart with their suggestions and new ideas, even though it's good to add to the church's numbers if possible. You feel some internal resistance to the suggestion of changing your ministry approach, even if it would mean connection and involvement for a potentially larger group.

If your call is to be a **contagious ministry movement leader**, you feel excitement when you read Acts 2:42-47. You see that when healthy principles of connection and community are practiced, God adds to your ministry numbers. Living organisms grow and—as part of the living body of Christ—so should your church or ministry. You and your team or committee feel willing and open to learn new strategies and to look anew at your ministry or church, and you seek to develop an ongoing plan to connect and involve more and more individuals into your purpose or mission. You are even willing to change your longstanding approach, add to the leadership team, and allow others the same rewarding opportunity that you've had when accepting various servant responsibilities. You need only direction on how to proceed.

If you are called to facilitate a contagious ministry movement (rather than a small group) but have struggled with the frustration of having no new leaders, few trustworthy volunteers, and little forward movement of your church or ministry despite what feels like your best efforts, the information below has the potential to transform your approach and multiply your results into contagious ministry movement. If you are starting a new ministry or are new to the church you serve, here's your opportunity to start in the right way.

Four Levels of a Contagious Ministry Movement

In order to construct a contagious ministry movement, please begin by assessing your existing church or ministry situation. The following four general descriptions are provided to help you identify four constituencies that must be present within every growing ministry movement. You can customize these general descriptions according to the unique church or ministry constituency you lead.

Level 1: Prospectors

"Prospectors" are those who have not yet ever attended your church or ministry, or who have been once or perhaps occasionally. These individuals are considering the possibility of connecting regularly to what you have going. A Prospector's typical internal questions about your

Prospectors

A worksheet to help you translate these four constituencies to your situation is located on the *Ultimately Responsible* DVD, chapter 3. Make copies of the worksheet for your team or committee, and together discuss and work through the questions. When you've completed this, you will have a shared view of the reality of your ministry situation, as well as what you need to work on next.

church or ministry are crucial to understand as you strategize how to attract them:

1. Will I meet other people like myself?

A desire for community is placed deep within every human by God, the One who desires community with us. So an important draw to your ministry for the Prospector is the possibility of meeting others in a similar life circumstance, people with whom the Prospector can make friends. If friendly servants reach out to newcomers and help them meet others with whom a common interest is likely, the chance for a "yes" is much more probable. A Prospector is encouraged to think, "I could be friends with these people—I'd like to be like them and spend time with them," and if applicable, "This would be good for my whole family, my children, and my spouse. We need to be with other families who share our type of lifestyle and challenges."

2. Will anyone else be new?

If the Prospector shows up at your ministry or church and everyone seems to already know each other, preoccupied with their own conversations, then the answer to this question is an obvious, "No." Other cues also alert a newcomer that the closed circle has already been drawn, leaving him or her on the outside. For example, imagine that a leader gives an announcement saying, "If you're interested in participating, please see John." The exclusive nature of such communication is not lost on a newcomer, who has no idea who John is, or where John is—yet clearly everyone else does. Or if the Prospector experiences a request for too much information when attending for the first time (this happens when well-meaning servants demand name, address, phone number, e-mail, and other information immediately upon a newcomer's arrival), it communicates desperation for new people and feels like a violation of personal privacy. Yet conversely, if a Prospector is ignored completely, the inadvertent message is that newcomers are not desired.

3. Will I learn something new, have fun, receive support, and/or connect with a deeper life?

The busy pace of our culture allows most people only a limited amount of time for extra involvement beyond work, family, and personal affairs. Prospectors are actively assessing the potential worthwhile nature of "outside activities" and looking for enhancements, which may be in the form of spiritual growth, emotional healing, new relationships, or opportunities to help others. When a Prospector comes to your church or ministry, are answers to this question readily evident? Or does the Prospector experience a group or congregation whose mission, relational potential, and purpose seem mysterious and poorly explained?

4. Is it high quality?

A Prospector often gauges the answer to this question with another one: "Could I bring my friends, family, or coworkers here, and not be embarrassed? Could I tell others that I am coming here, or would a connection with this church or ministry be uncomfortable to admit?" While no church or ministry needs to think of its work as a performance, it is absolutely essential to plan and carry out everything with excellence, to the best of its ability. In fact, the 10/5 theory is a useful concept to remember: A newcomer decides whether or not to return on the strength of what happened in the first ten minutes and the last five minutes of their time at your event. To be clear—that's their first ten minutes with you, not the first ten minutes after the event officially starts!

I was enlisted as the speaker at an evening outreach conference, which was held by a church unfamiliar to me. The planners of the conference scheduled my presentation at 7 PM and asked that I come early. The day of the event, I arrived at 6:15 PM and found that I was the first one in the meeting room. A few leaders showed up at 6:30, and I helped them set up chairs. After the setting was organized, the leaders, clearly good friends, retreated to the corner of the room and shared conversation to catch up on the week's activities and news while attendees begin to filter in and take a seat. None of the leaders staffed the greeter/nametag table at the door, so I (though a guest myself) positioned myself at the entrance to welcome each arrival. A few minutes before 7 PM, the room was two-thirds full of Prospectors sitting silently, as the corner full of leaders became more and more involved in the merriment of mutual banter. At 7:05 PM, another leader came rushing through the door and upon entering spoke loudly across the large room of newcomers to the other leaders huddled in the far corner. "Have we started yet?" he called out. "No," one of his friends loudly answered back, *"No one's here yet…."*

I found out afterwards that the event's start was delayed by the yet later arrival of the emcee and the song leader—thus explaining the statement, "No one's here yet." But as the response had boomed across the room, I cringed at the inference it made about the value—or lack of value—of the roomful of Prospectors who were seated patiently, having arrived on time and waiting for the event to begin. And I've wondered whether a single one of them returned after that night.

5. Is it easy or difficult to connect immediately into what's going on?

The "stained glass barrier" is a problem that deflects some Prospectors. This term refers to anything that you do or say that seems unintelligible to a church newcomer. It might be the pietistic language or an unexplained liturgy that you use, or speaking extensively about being "saved," or the "blood of the Lamb," or other loaded phrases that may not connect with the uninitiated. It might be an assumption that everyone knows how to look up a verse in the Bible, when in fact newcomers might not. You may neglect to give context to what you are explaining as the preacher or teacher, which is fine for those who heard your messages over the last four weeks but seems exclusive and alienating to the Prospector who is a first-timer.

A first-time visitor who was a true Prospector had attended worship the Sunday before. She approached me to ask if I could do her a favor. What was that beautiful poem everyone seemed to know by heart and say together, right after the offering? Was there any way she could get a copy of it? I realized that she was asking for a copy of the Lord's Prayer! We had unintentionally erected a "stained glass barrier" for her and for other Prospectors that Sunday by not printing the words in our worship bulletin or projecting them on a screen in full view for all.

Level 1 Prospector Strategies

If you understand the questions in the mind of a Prospector, your next step is to think about your church or ministry and consider what inviting entry points, or entrance ramps, you have (or need to create) that make it easy for a Prospector to enter your ministry or church and experience positive answers to these questions. Any contagious ministry movement must have clear ports of entry through which newcomers can connect. Your entrance ramps depend on the type of church or ministry you lead. They must be customized to your setting, your constituency, and your purpose.

In order to be effective, the ideas you deploy to attract Level 1 Prospectors must feature indigenous forms of the following characteristics. Otherwise, they will not serve their purpose of creating Level 1 ministry movement intake growth. Remember to think of an entrance ramp as an entry point into your church family as a whole—not just into a holding tank for newcomers, perpetually secluding them from the church body.

- Events are **easy and convenient to attend**. They are held at an easily located place, with plenty of parking. Avoid holding the entrance ramp event at an obscure location that requires detailed driving directions or at a private home that might raise questions about personal safety for a newcomer who was not acquainted with the host.
- If possible, **childcare or children's activities are provided** if the Prospectors you hope to draw have children.
- The entrance ramp must have **very few requirements** that must be met in order to attend. Otherwise, prerequisites may become

excuses not to come. Examples include: requiring pre-registration several weeks ahead of time, mandating a certain dress code, or requiring everyone to bring a potluck dish to share.

- An ideal entrance ramp into your church or ministry **does not threaten newcomers with the message that they'll leave with responsibilities.** One common church practice is to announce a planning meeting in an effort to draw new volunteers to a ministry. Few Prospectors find an appeal in that approach. The threat of becoming obligated to help plan a ministry about which the newcomer knows nothing (and conversely, you as leader who knows nothing about the newcomer and his/her leadership potential) is not an invitation most healthy Prospectors would find magnetic.

- At an effective entrance ramp event, **positive, energetic leaders** proactively meet and connect with every newcomer in a casual and friendly way. If unhealthy servants act as hosts, Prospectors may be chased away by their well-intentioned but inappropriate social skills. And if a newcomer comes and goes at your church or ministry without a single conversation or connection because your servant greeters are shy, the likelihood of further involvement is slim.

- While not necessary for everyone who attends a worship service, for most church activities and events the **provision of nametags** is essential. Nametags are the great equalizer—everyone is equally capable of knowing everyone else's name. How empowering for a newcomer! Otherwise, when only the Prospector is given a nametag, all those already on the "inside" seem like a private, anonymous club. Equally isolating is when the church members all have special plastic printed name badges, whereas newcomers stand out with only a hand-lettered nametag. Better to save the expense of purchasing engraved plastic badges for insiders and level the playing field for Prospectors by providing universal inexpensive paper tags for everyone.

- **Publicity information** about a good entrance ramp event is clearly communicated: specifically who it is for, when and where it will take place, and (most importantly) what benefits will be gained by attending. When listing the benefits in your publicity or announcements, think back to the five questions of the Prospector. The benefits you list should answer some of those questions.

- A great entrance ramp event will also provide **a reason to return** again to the ministry or church. A Prospector needs information and instructions in order to take advantage of the connection made at the initial entry event. *When will the next event be? How can I find out more information about what's going on at this* *church, and what else is offered?* If a Prospector has attended an event other than your weekly worship service, information about what time the weekend worship services are offered is essential to provide. Make certain the Prospector gains the big picture of what your church is about, and what place the entrance ramp event plays as part of the whole.

Consider the small singles group at the beginning of this chapter—the one that evolved into a full-fledged contagious ministry. A number of Level 1 strategies were necessary to help create an inflow of newcomers. One step to increase its "entrance ramp ability" was to move the group's traditional monthly singles dance out of a small, carpeted classroom in the church building and take it to an off-site location in a heavily populated area of town. A switch was made from Christian music to popular dance music, and the Bible study and long prayer time that had historically taken a chunk of the evening's dance time (and provided a stained-glass barrier to newcomers) was eliminated and moved to a Sunday class setting. Instead, at the dance, announcements were planned and given halfway through the evening by a carefully chosen, contagious servant leader who also provided information on other entry points into the singles ministry and into the church as a whole. An attractive information table with printed materials was placed strategically at the entrance of the dance location, staffed by friendly servants who greeted attendees, chatted with them, and answered questions from thirty minutes before the dance's start until thirty minutes after the dance officially ended. As the singles dances grew quickly from thirty-five to over three hundred, so did the inflow of connection of single adults into the ministry and into the church as a whole.

Although the entrance ramps that you create to facilitate the flow of Prospectors into your church or ministry will be specific to your setting, here are some additional common examples to stimulate your thinking. Use these not as recommendations for your setting but only as ideas to inspire your own.

Level 1 Entrance Ramp Examples

...for a children's ministry:
- An excellent children's vacation Bible school, for which the entire neighborhood or town is canvassed with invitations to attend
- Friday night or after-school outreach party with games, snacks, interactive fun, and a Bible message—to which kids can bring their friends

...for a teen ministry:
- Special youth group outings that are newcomer-friendly
- A skateboard or pickup basketball outreach on Saturdays
- A class series for teens whose parents have divorced

...for a women's ministry:
- Young moms' group
- Book groups, craft/scrapbooking nights, other special interest topics

...for a music ministry:
- "Bring a friend" impromptu choir weekend (no rehearsals, just show up and sing!)
- Free group lessons for those interested in singing better, playing the keyboard or guitar better, and so forth
- Noncompetitive "Star Search" evening where anyone in the church or the community is invited to participate—and everyone is invited to come enjoy the performances

...for an entire church:
- Every worship service, every week! (the church's main entrance ramp event)
- A planned after-church ride for motorcyclists from the community/area
- A concert to which the community is invited—and invited to return again for worship and other connection points
- Special dinners, festivals, other interest/felt-need outreaches
- Food pantry (invite food pantry recipients to connect with other aspects of your church or ministry in addition to receiving free resources)
- After-school tutoring for children (whose families are invited to begin connecting into the church/ministry)
- "Dinner for Eight" groups (informal, organized to last for six or eight weeks by drawing together newcomers for a weekly meal and social time together)
- Support groups (Christian 12 Step, divorce recovery, and others)
- Pizza with the Pastor (a no-reservation, no-strings-attached, pizza supper with the pastor or other leaders who share the DNA of your church/ministry, answer questions, and give information about how to become more involved)

Pause here—and discuss with your team the "Level 1 Questions" found on your worksheet from the DVD, chapter 3. Take an honest assessment of where you are, what you have now, and what needs to be reinvented or added. Write down your ideas, but hold off making firm plans until you have read and discussed the next three levels of contagious ministry movement.

Level 2: Regular Attendees

"Regular Attendees" are those who have decided to make your ministry or church a regular part of their lives. They like the answers they found when they were Prospectors and have shifted into a mindset that views your church or ministry as a reliable resource for friendship, learning, and/or deeper life meaning. Regular attendees' primary motivation generally comes through a desire for relational, spiritual, or informational life enhancement. They now think of you as *their* ministry or *their* church.

Regular Attendees

Prospectors

A Regular Attendee is also motivated to seek answers to a new set of internal questions. The more satisfactorily those questions are answered, the more commitment develops. Think through how a Regular Attendee's questions might get answered in your church or ministry:

1. Do I find ongoing appeal in what originally brought me to this church?

If an interest in relationships with like-minded people brought a Prospector to your setting, opportunities for ongoing and deeper connections with others are essential. Have the servant leaders who are friendly to new Prospectors moved on in their friendliness to other newcomers, leaving Regular Attendees isolated? If a Prospector initially came to find education and healing, is there more after the first class series ends? Is the quality of entry points for Prospectors excellent, yet disorganization or mediocrity the norm in your activities for Regular Attendees?

2. I'm interested in the whole picture of what this church is about. Is it difficult or easy for me to find out?

Because alignment with your church or ministry is growing in the mind of a Regular Attendee, a natural curiosity about the organization begins. Who leads it? How are things set up? What else is going on here in addition to that in which I'm personally involved? A Regular Attendee is encouraged if this information is easily obtainable and can be clearly explained by leaders they meet. If the explanation is vague, confusing, or illogical, the Regular Attendee is forced either to reconsider further involvement or to decide to simply embrace only the aspect of the church or ministry to which they have connected. Either way, persons at Level 2 stall out in their growth and movement within the overall ministry or church when bigger-picture information is not readily and clearly available.

3. Who is Jesus?

Presuming that your church or ministry has a Christ-centered emphasis throughout, a Regular Attendee will soon be confronted with this all-important internal question. If the attendee is already a Christian, the question may take the form of "How does this church or ministry teach and live out the message of Jesus?" If someone is not a Christian, it is at the Regular Attendee stage that he or she may begin to seriously consider, or is first receptive to, the opportunity to receive Christ.

4. Does it matter that I am here?

A Regular Attendee's main agenda may be to receive (information, friendship, life meaning, support), but nonetheless it also has begun to matter that others appreciate their presence. Who notices when I arrive? Is my attendance frequent enough now that it's noticed when I am absent? Who welcomes me to sit with them when I need a place? Are my comments and questions valued?

Level 2 Regular Attendee Strategies

While coaching and training many paid and unpaid ministry leaders, I have observed that strategies for individuals in Level 2 are usually misunderstood and the crucial nature of this level is often underestimated. It's possible for the majority of a congregation to stay perpetually at Level 2, never intentionally stimulated or invited to grow further. Regular Attendees may remain only regular, settling into spiritual consumerism of the church's or ministry's offerings for months or years, only making a change when they drift away out of boredom or lack of further challenge.

In fact, it's when most of those connected to your ministry or church are only at Level 2 that you're most likely to think you have no leaders and that no one will step up and assume significant responsibility. You are probably right! And, rather than trying to prematurely talk reluctant Regular Attendees into more pivotal roles than they're ready for, seek to deploy strategies that help kick start their further spiritual and personal commitment on to the next level. Here are steps to help facilitate this growth:

- **Invite Regular Attendees to join a cell (small) group.** By participating in a regular personal accountability group, Regular Attendees form deep friendships with others, grow spiritually, and begin to learn more about what the mature Christian life looks like from the cell group leader. Belonging to a cell group builds commitment in a Regular Attendee and creates a sense of belonging to the church or ministry.

  As the leader, you (and other leaders) have the proximity with those at Level 2 to build relationships and spot those with leadership potential. Regular Attendees are around regularly, so take advantage of their presence and make time to get to know individuals. Look for those who seem to show active interest in spiritual maturity, see the importance in the overall mission of what your church or ministry is doing, and perhaps ask if they can help. Notice areas of strength and skill they demonstrate, and pay attention to their relational interaction with others. Are they well received? Immature in their behavior? Well spoken? Shy?

- **Ask Regular Attendees to help.** At this level, it's appropriate and important to invite Level 2 persons to serve, starting with one-time tasks that take little or no preparation. It's not uncommon for Level 2 attendees to help set up chairs, prepare the coffee, serve as door greeters (if the right personality is present), answer the phones, stuff bulletins, or bring two dozen cookies for refreshments. Some at Level 2 are interested in larger servant tasks. Invite Level 2 attendees to assume responsibility for activities or tasks that have low-impact ramifications should their follow through not take place.

- **Encourage Regular Attendees to bring their friends and family.** Routinely ask gatherings where Regular Attendees are present: "Whom do you know that really should be here? Invite them this week to come with you next time!" Level 2 attendees can be excitable and contagious, and they are at the most likely level of a ministry movement to respond by surveying their workplace, neighborhood, and relatives to see whom they can bring along. Their personal circle of influence is still mostly outside the church or ministry. They may be eager to introduce those in their personal circle to their new ministry or church friends, and to you. When they do, respond and do your best to engage them as a new set of Prospectors to welcome.

- **Show and tell to Regular Attendees** stories of individuals who represent the commitment to service found in the next levels, 3 and 4. Regular Attendees will stagnate unless spurred on by real-life inspiration, which can be provided by those who are deeply engaged in selfless servanthood and servant leadership.

Perhaps you don't have ready examples in your church and ministry? Then use the stories of great Christians from history, video stories produced by other churches, or invite inspirational Christians you know to share about their commitment to serve in person.

Meet Leland via his short video story, "Spiritual Territory," on the Ultimately Responsible DVD, chapter 3. What a great example of how to use your life to expand God's spiritual territory!

Steer clear of **two typical mistakes** that are made often with Level 2 attendees. Avoid moving a Regular Attendee into a major leadership role too quickly—usually out of desperation to fill the leader spot. When a person has not been given ample time and opportunity to learn the "DNA" of what your purpose is, to establish spiritual maturity, and to demonstrate strong loyalty to your church or ministry (as well as allow you time to know the person's character), you may unintentionally set up a scenario that will pull everyone into confusion. "But," you may protest, "my church is small, and we don't have many newcomers. I want to get them involved quickly once they're here, so they'll stay!" Inviting people to increasing levels of responsibility is strategic. Jumping levels too quickly, however, puts a ministry at risk. Move right along, but practice wisdom.

The other common mistake is to invite a Regular Attendee to embrace a meaningful servant role, without assessing whether it fits the individual's strengths and gifts. Does the role match the person? Again, you may feel an urgency to fill the holes of servant or leadership in your church or ministry. Make yourself slow down and remember that it's better to hold off on moving ahead until the right persons who are the right match are ready and available. See more about this in chapter 4.

Need some examples? The singles group with a heart to become a contagious ministry movement did more than just move the monthly entry-point dances off site and change the format to attract more Prospectors. The new single adult Prospectors needed steps into Level 2 to encourage their progress toward becoming Regular Attendees. So the leadership made sure everyone attending a dance began receiving information and a personal invitation to attend a new weekly Sunday Singles Night on the church campus. The original version of Singles Night began with offering choices to newcomers of volleyball, cards, or a class called "Boundaries in Dating." Eventually the palette of Sunday night offerings grew as Prospectors became Regular Attendees and maturity of leadership developed. All were provided with the church's worship service schedule information and were invited to begin attending worship together with their new friends made at Singles Night.

Other Level 2 engagement examples vary widely according to setting, purpose, and constituency. The following examples are intended to give a sense of what can happen.

Level 2 Engagement Examples for Regular Attendees

...for a children's ministry:
- Weekly children's Sunday classes
- Children's choir with regular rehearsals and spiritual emphasis
- Frequent local service projects

...for a teen ministry:
- Weekly youth group gatherings
- Teen band/vocal group with scheduled rehearsals and spiritual emphasis
- Incorporation of teens in serving/supporting weekend worship services (greeting, ushering)

...for a women's ministry:
- "How To" Christian lifestyle classes and Bible study groups
- Serving others through a local soup kitchen

...for a music ministry:
- Adult Choir—including regular rehearsals with Bible study/spiritual emphasis
- Serving in the community by singing at retirement homes and hospitals

...for an entire church:
- Opportunities to help with worship service support (setup, teardown, greeting, ushering), church lawn care, church facility cleaning and organizing
- Basic Bible study classes, specialized lifestyle seminars (marriage enrichment, parenting)
- Short-term service opportunities in the community (food pantry, furniture ministry)

Pause here—and discuss with your team the "Level 2 Questions" found on your worksheet. Take an honest assessment of where you are, what you have now, and what needs to be reinvented or added. Write down your ideas, but hold off making firm plans until you have read and discussed the next two levels of contagious ministry movement.

Level 3: The Engaged

Regular Attendees who have found friendship, education, spiritual growth, and deeper life purpose as a result of involvement with your church or ministry are ready to move to Level 3 of your contagious ministry movement and become part of "The Engaged." A decision has been made in the heart and mind of the Regular Attendee to belong to your

The Engaged
Regular Attendees
Prospectors

constituency. Persons moving into Level 3 often buy shirts bearing the name of your church or ministry to wear proudly. Now their cadre of friendships has shifted to those who also are involved along with them, rather than with individuals on the "outside."

The Engaged face yet another set of internal questions to address that help deepen (or discourage) their growth and dedication. Your awareness of what triggers Level 3 progress will help you strategize to provide them with positive answers.

1. Should I become an official member?

Organizational engagement with your church or ministry is crucial for those moving into Level 3 commitment. The Engaged want to know more about what it takes to join officially. What does it require of me? For what will it qualify me, prepare me? Are there strings attached—and if so, what are they? What will the benefits be?

2. Am I growing spiritually?

The Engaged have made a decision for Jesus Christ and realize that life transformation is the result of Bible study, prayer, and obedience. Particular questions at Level 3 about spiritual engagement may include: What about this church or ministry helps me with my personal spiritual growth? Am I receiving sound teaching? Am I learning Bible study skills? Who is praying for me, with me? The Engaged want to make sure that the ministry or church where they are becoming more deeply involved will also provide an ongoing spiritual feedbox for guidance and growth.

3. What about time, tithing, and lifestyle?

At Level 3, a person realizes that deeper commitment is likely to affect lifestyle practices and even the resources of time and money. Pressing, specific, internal questions emerge as The Engaged consider the price of moving further forward: What expectations about financial giving come with more involvement here? Is there any behavior in my daily lifestyle that will have to change or improve if I assume more ministry responsibility? Am I willing to reorganize priorities in my financial and time allocations to become more generous on behalf of God's work through this ministry or church?

4. Can I get into leadership, or is it impossible to break in?

At The Engaged stage, an individual has clear proximity to the leadership structure of your ministry or church. The Engaged have already become involved in serving opportunities, and they are close enough to the action to see who is in charge of organizing and deploying people and tasks. If it's obvious that the same people are always in charge of everything and no new ideas from "outsiders" are considered, The Engaged will sense internal frustration as their desire to become more and more strategically involved in God's work grows. Specific auxiliary questions to this one: Does my input count? If I assume more leadership, will someone train me? Is there a custom-fit niche to serve just for me, and how can I find it?

Level 3 Strategies for The Engaged

Your goal with The Engaged is to help set the stage for their ever-growing spiritual, relational, and service investment. Typically, little intention is put into helping the progress of those who are at Level 3. The reality in many churches or ministries is that Level 3 is viewed as the ultimate point of involvement, and it's assumed that The Engaged don't require active encouragement and support. The Engaged are frequently taken for granted. Yet without your diligence, those at Level 3 never move to Level 4. Consider these specific steps that you can take to secure the progress of The Engaged in your setting:

Need material? Utilize Ginghamsburg's signature membership course curriculum, *A Follower's Life* by Carolyn Slaughter and Sherry Douglas, available at www.ginghamsburg resources.org.

- **Provide an in-depth membership course.** Some churches invite everyone, including Level 1 Prospectors, to come forward and join the church on a given Sunday. Membership, however, at its best is a Level 3 commitment. Ideally, those who are only Regular Attendees will emerge from a membership course at Level 3, and Level 3 participants will be primed for serious leadership. Core elements in a membership course include foundational, interactive teaching about Christ as personal Savior and Lord of your life from now through eternity; living the daily Spirit-led lifestyle; learning how to invest in daily, personal devotional time with God; God's priorities for a believer's finances, including tithing; why engagement in a cell group is essential; spiritual gifts and how to utilize them in serving; and expectations of an official church member (regular worship attendance, cell group involvement, tithing, and regular serving). High-commitment churches often have fewer official members in ministry or church than the number who attend worship on weekends. Membership is a function of those who are at The Engaged level and should be taken seriously.

- **Create educational opportunities that teach how to manage money and get out of debt.** The Engaged have grown spiritually to the point that they understand that what is out of alignment in their lives needs to be corrected or healed. Finances, especially debt, are a huge issue for many seeking life wholeness. Get serious about providing help for those who are looking for a new set of financial practices and priorities to embrace.

- **Connect The Engaged with servant teams.** While Regular Attendees agree to occasional or low responsibility servant spots, at Level 3 it's important to strategically help individuals find custom-fit servant roles of influence in a team atmosphere. The Engaged seek ever greater windows to bring Kingdom impact and influence.
- **Provide constant training.** As The Engaged agree to more responsibility in serving, they'll need help to do it well. Provide skill training for specific roles, or connect The Engaged with other experienced servant mentors who can help show them the ropes. Level 3 commitment requires support and resources to facilitate an expanding confidence and sense of ministry ownership.
- **Invite The Engaged into small-scale leadership roles.** An ideal position for Level 3 is as a cell group (small group) leader or as a team leader for a task-based servant team. These trial settings help The Engaged experience a greater sense of responsibility and test their growth and training.
- **Create settings in which The Engaged's voice can be heard.** Periodically hold open brainstorming meetings to which Level 3 persons are welcome. Allow all ideas to be considered and every opinion honored as the direction of the church, ministry, or project is discussed. Every idea may not be implemented, and final decisions may be reserved for Level 4 leaders to firm up later. But make sure the creative thinking of The Engaged (and sometimes the Regular Attendees) is included.
- **Make certain The Engaged have regular opportunities to change areas of service.** Some churches or ministries leave a Level 3 servant in the same role for months or even years, guaranteeing ministry fatigue and burnout that may drag others down as well. Limit terms of service, and encourage change to keep fresh.
- **Offer a variety of forms of recognition and appreciation** for the contributions of The Engaged. This acknowledges and reinforces the value of their investment in the church or ministry.

As you challenge The Engaged with these strategies, keep in mind that their base of support must stay intact in order for their overall growth to continue. In the excitement of a small new leadership role or placement into a significant position on a servant team, The Engaged's focus may drift away from practices of organizational engagement (membership commitments), spiritual engagement (daily time with God), and even relational engagement (personal accountability with a cell group). The result is eventual decline of perspective and passion for mission. Stay alert to keep the fires alive with Level 3 in personal practices that fuel growth and maturity.

The singles ministry, after moving Prospectors into Level 2 Regular Attendees through lifestyle classes and social activities, then strengthened and multiplied Bible class offerings for single adults on both Saturday nights and Sunday mornings. Those who became involved attending classes were also invited to join cell groups and challenged to serve within the singles outreach in short-term commitment roles. As Regular Attendees moved into Level 3 commitment, information about church membership was provided to them. Scheduled leadership training began one Saturday morning each month, and The Engaged (few in number at first) sorted themselves to servant team leadership positions according to their areas of interest and passion. The monthly training showed them the strategy for overall contagious ministry growth, so they understood the urgency to connect with Prospectors and invite them further in. Vital movement had begun as more and more adult singles moved through increasing levels of engagement.

It's helpful for individuals at Levels 2 and 3 when your church or ministry establishes a clearly identified discipleship path for growth. See an example called **the Core5** on the *Ultimately Responsible* DVD, chapter 3.

Additional Level 3 engagement examples vary widely according to setting, purpose, and constituency. The following examples are intended to give you a sense of what can happen, not to provide exact steps for you to put into place.

Level 3 Connection Examples for The Engaged

...for a children's ministry:
- Team leader roles for children within Sunday class setting
- "Ministry shadowing" opportunities with the pastor or ministry leader
- Cell group involvement for children where the adult leader has proximity for intentional discipling

...for a teen ministry:
- Membership course
- Brainstorming teams for the future direction of teen activities
- Key roles in helping coordinate service projects
- Leadership training to prepare for more responsibility

...for a women's ministry:
- Leadership training on how to connect with and engage women of all ages
- Women's cell (small) group leadership roles
- Team leader for service projects

...for a music ministry:
- Apprentice in training with choir director, accompanist, or other role

Pause here—and discuss with your team the "Level 3 Questions" found on your worksheet. Take an honest assessment of where you are, what you have now, and what needs to be reinvented or added. Write down your ideas, but hold off making firm plans until you have read and discussed the fourth level of contagious ministry movement.

- Coordinator of small vocal or instrumental ensemble
- Organizer of rehearsal logistics and/or communication

...for an entire church:
- Apprentice training for serving as committee chair, service team leader, or other role of specialized responsibility
- Cell (small) group leadership
- Classroom teacher (after training)
- Membership course

Level 4: The Invested

The change from Level 3 to Level 4 often happens as a result of a major spiritual juncture, challenge, or growth experience. Sometimes it's after a mission trip or all-weekend spiritual life retreat. A powerfully successful (by God's criteria of success) ministry initiative can also propel one of The Engaged into The Invested readiness. Still to others it happens as a result of an intense season of spiritual obedience and engagement. Whatever the trigger, be ready to recognize a candidate for Level 4 when it happens. When The Engaged bridge into the final level, you'll be able to identify this transition by a number of signs, rather than internal questions for which they need answers.

1. I am hungry to cash in all my chips and live 100 percent for Christ.

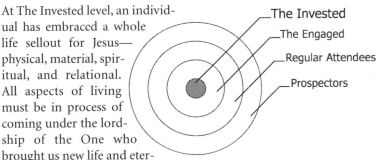

At The Invested level, an individual has embraced a whole life sellout for Jesus—physical, material, spiritual, and relational. All aspects of living must be in process of coming under the lordship of the One who brought us new life and eternal hope. No pride or need for attention, power, or control is evident. Invested servants are ready to accept whatever assignment will help further the Kingdom.

2. I view serving in this ministry/church as my real job.

Your day job is what you do to survive physically—it provides financial income to pay the rent and bills and to buy the groceries. Your real job is what you do that feeds your soul and spirit, regardless of whether monetary gain comes from it. Your reward is the spiritual joy it brings you to fulfill your passion. At The Invested level, serving the mission of Jesus has become a real job.

3. I embrace the vision of the church or ministry, rather than argue with or criticize it.

Level 4 individuals not only understand what the mission and direction is, but they also seek to explain it to others with excitement. All their questions have been answered, and they stand ready to represent the overall vision in tangible ways.

4. I am excited when others join the Leadership Core.

Those at Level 4 do not seek exclusivity but instead encourage and mentor others in their path of spiritual maturity to the all-out commitment level of invested participation. Level 4 leaders are contagious.

5. I have a heart for those at Level 1, the Prospectors, and desire to see them move further and further into our contagious ministry movement.

Newcomers are not invisible or unimportant to those at The Invested level. Just the opposite—Level 4 leaders invest great time and consideration into how Level 1 entrance ramps are created, how Prospectors are welcomed and gain initial connection, and what happens through the other levels. The motto of Level 4 is that of Jesus, when he said, "[I] did not come to be served, but to serve" (Matthew 20:25-28).

It takes time to develop leaders like this. It's tempting to recruit a group of The Engaged (Level 3) as your Invested. And if you have not yet developed Level 4 leaders, you must work with those your circumstances provide. However, keep in mind the signs of a Level 4 leader, and remember this is your goal in contagious ministry development. Here are some telltale signals that you do not yet have a core leadership team of Level 4 leaders:

- The team struggles with power and control issues.
- Persons want to join the leadership team to be close to you (or the others already on the team), not to serve.
- The leadership team has a reputation of a prestige group.
- The team is uninterested in relating to the Level 1 newcomers.
- The team is resistant to sharing their responsibilities with other new leaders or struggles to rotate out of a set of particular roles so others may gain the experience.
- Team members put energy into promoting their personal agendas.
- Certain leaders insist on always having the up-front microphone even when someone else might do a better job or is ready for the opportunity.

- When the team is together, team members pull each other down rather than build one another up.

Level 4 Strategies for The Invested

Any church or ministry with a healthy Level 4 has worked intentionally with its ministry movement growth strategy to raise up leaders like those described above. And it takes time. Do not expect The Engaged to understand and grow toward full investment without describing the process over and over, training them about it, and demonstrating it yourself. Work on the following action steps to encourage Level 3 transitions into Level 4 surrendered leadership:

- Constantly explain and demonstrate to the overall entire constituency, "We all share responsibility for this ministry/church together." Make certain the **demonstrated shared ownership** of what's happening is made real by the involvement of as many servants as possible at every opportunity. If the constituency sees only you (plus a few others) planning, organizing, and deploying everything, they'll receive the message that it's *your* job to do the ministry and their job to receive the benefits. Level 4 leaders grow out of the vision provided by your faithfully demonstrated, team-based servant leadership.
- Allow Level 4 leaders to **own a specific chunk of the action**. The greatest discouragement to Level 4 leaders comes when you refuse to relinquish responsibility, even when the Leadership Core has had the training and has demonstrated the maturity to handle it. Will it get done exactly as you would have handled it? Perhaps not. Is there more than one way to carry out a ministry responsibility? Certainly. Let it happen, and cheer it on.
- **Practice fluidity of vision.** Those who have matured into Level 4 have developed such ownership of the ministry or church that God may provide them additional insight on next stages for your plans. Welcome their wisdom, and stay flexible when necessary on how details are planned out. Leadership Core commitment is discouraged when input into the vision shaping is refused.
- Make sure **leadership rotation** happens on a regular basis. As great a contribution as Level 4 leaders can make, their usefulness diminishes if they are left in the same positions of responsibility for an overextended length of time. Make room for new Invested to rise up and assume responsibility, and create new roles for experienced Level 4 leaders. Require this rotation as insurance to keep the church or ministry fresh.
- **Repeatedly define Level 4 leadership** for those who participate at the most invested core. As committed as Level 4 leaders have become, human nature can pull perspective from "the servant of all" thinking to "I'm more important than all" thinking. Each

time The Invested gather, remind them of the nature of this calling to serve. As more and more ministry responsibilities are assumed, more and more rights are given up. This, after all, is the way of the Cross.

Learn more about terms of leadership responsibility in chapter 5, "Leading A Team."

As the singles ministry matured and one-by-one several of The Engaged became ready for Level 4 responsibilities, they each were invited to greater accountability and contribution, and each assumed specific duties according to spiritual gifts and strengths. As these new Level 4 single adults moved into key leadership with enthusiasm and ideas, several longtime established leaders resisted their addition and decided to leave. Instead of begging them to stay in leadership, the long timers were shown appreciation and recognition for their contributions, encouraged to stay active in the ministry as a whole, and guided to different new Level 3 servant roles with more specialized focus. This set the pattern for rotating leaders through one or more seasons of invested leadership without letting the ministry build a fortress that barred new leaders from contribution.

Additional Level 4 engagement examples vary widely according to setting, purpose and constituency. The following examples are intended only to give you a sense of what can happen, not to provide exact steps for you to put into place.

Level 4 Engagement Examples for The Invested

Meet a Level 4 servant, Char, who began as a Prospector. Hear what motivated her to become part of a contagious ministry movement through her short video story, "Unfinished Canvas," found on the *Ultimately Responsible* DVD, chapter 3.

...for a children's ministry:
- Older Level 4 children trained to mentor and teach younger children
- Leadership training classes for children who have demonstrated spiritual maturity and commitment
- Leadership opportunities for children to facilitate projects and coordinate ongoing ministry activities

...for a teen ministry:
- Older teens trained to mentor, teach classes, and lead cell groups for younger teens or children
- Level 4 teens included on church-wide servant teams as leaders
- Leadership Level 4 teens trained to assume upfront worship or preaching role when needed
- Teen training in ministry vision, actively contributing to specific future plans

...for a women's ministry:
- Chief planner for an entire women's spiritual life weekend retreat
- Coordinator of support team available to respond to women in crisis
- Large group Bible study teacher

...for a music ministry:
- Lead choir, worship, or band both during rehearsals and during worship
- Train new vocalists or musicians for worship participation
- Take responsibility to create the process of recruitment and welcome of newcomers to the music ministry

...for an entire church:
- Serve on key church boards and vision teams
- Spearhead mission trips and community service initiatives
- Hold leadership training classes for those in Levels 2 and 3
- Lead and coordinate an entire ministry area of the church's mission, including servant recruitment, training, and deployment

Pause here—and discuss with your team the "Level 4 Questions" found on your worksheet. Take an honest assessment of where you are, what you have now, and what needs to be reinvented or added. Write down your ideas. Now that you've discussed all four levels, spend some time brainstorming what needs to happen next to implement an overall plan for contagious ministry growth.

What's Next?

Once you've understood the overall strategy for contagious ministry movement, you're now ready to move on to the next subject that all intentional leaders take seriously: how to unleash unpaid ministry. You've seen the importance of connecting Levels 2, 3, and 4 into servant responsibility. But did you know it doesn't just happen? Learn the art of unpaid servanthood now.

ON THE DVD FOR CHAPTER 3:

-"Contagious Ministry Strategy" worksheet for your team

-"Core5" discipleship path listing (PDF)

-Video story: Leland—"Spiritual Territory"

-Video story: Char—"Unfinished Canvas"

"Of all the things I have done, the most vital is
coordinating the talents of those who work for us
and pointing them towards a certain goal."
-Walt Disney

CHAPTER

4

UNLEASHING SERVANTHOOD

I received an e-mail from a woman who had attended our church for at least a year. Barbara was in worship every Sunday with increasing regularity. She was in "Basic Training," a class for those who want to learn the fundamentals about how to use the Bible, develop a prayer life, and live out the practices of a Jesus follower every day. Barbara volunteered to sack groceries at our most recent food pantry drive, and I had seen her helping weed the church's front lawn on an early summer Saturday when those who enjoy yard work were invited to "beauty-blitz" the church grounds. She fit perfectly with the profile of a Level 2 Regular Attendee who had found spiritual growth and new friends within our church family. But despite my invitations to consider greater servant investment and responsibility (which would help move her on into the ranks of The Engaged), Barbara held back. Everything I suggested received a no. I assumed Barbara was stuck in a comfort zone common to many Regular Attendees: it felt safer and more enriching to stay chiefly on the receiving end by attending worship and class, serving only occasionally when it conveniently fit her schedule.

Learn the anatomy of contagious ministry movement by reviewing the four levels described in chapter 3: Prospectors, Regular Attendees, The Engaged, and The Invested.

But Barbara heard something in the previous weekend's sermon that jumpstarted her deep inside.

> Dear Pastor Sue, I have to say that the message Sunday has changed my life. I never (up till now) understood what serving had to do with spiritual growth and my relationship to God. I guess I always thought the ministers are on the payroll to do the ministry. I don't know why I never understood it before. Please call me, or have someone call me. I can see now I need to sign up for a regular servant role, and want to talk more about some ideas.
>
> Love in Christ, Barbara

View an excerpt from the message by Ginghamsburg's senior pastor, Mike Slaughter, that provided Barbara with a mind shift about **Servanthood** on the *Ultimately Responsible* DVD, chapter 4.

This chapter is in honor of Barbara, and in honor of all the Barbaras who are still waiting in your church or ministry to be awakened to the true call to serve.

It's typical that a ministry leader, who is responsible for enlisting servants, approaches the task out of a personal need. "I've got to find someone to do this!" And often the enlistment of servants is the least-liked, most-dreaded aspect of leadership for many pastors. Perhaps you have said to a colleague, "I'm not good at selling; I hate this!"

No matter what wiring you've got, building an effervescent servant team is within your reach—but first you must have a clear understanding of servanthood from a biblical perspective. So the first step is for you to appreciate what serving is all about, according to Jesus himself. Then we'll move to the second step, which is understanding how potential servants think—and how to help them experience a mind shift toward serving. Your third step will be to learn and understand your own role as leader in the servant engagement process.

Serving: Not Optional

Leaders start by deepening the personal perspective about the role of service in the spiritual growth of every Christian. It is impossible to infect anyone in your constituency with the passion to serve unless you understand the non-negotiable purpose that God has for serving. If your constituency seems only to listen and learn but not rise up and serve, it's a telltale sign that you must first get your own thinking grounded about this aspect of the Christian life. You may be the reason they are not getting the message about the imbedded mission to serve that's woven into a life lived for Jesus.

During his life on earth, Jesus ushered in a whole new paradigm for his followers about their purpose and mission. Jesus modeled the lifestyle of servanthood, emphasizing over and over to those around him that this was the work God had called him and sent him to do. *"Whoever wants to become great among you must be your servant, and whoever wants to be first must be your slave—just as the Son of Man did not come to be served, but to serve, and to give his life as a ransom for many"* (Matthew 20:26-28). The powerful truth is that when a person makes a decision for Christ, the old life is gone and the new life of Jesus fills the believer. So if the life of Jesus lives and is embodied in you, then you have joined Jesus on mission to serve the needs of the world. Not serving is not an option. You have been invaded by the life of Jesus in you, empowered by the Holy Spirit. No longer is serving a choice based on convenience. It is a lifestyle in which you now live every moment. The life of Jesus in you will lead you to join in where God is working, wherever God needs your hands, your feet, and your gifts. Nowhere does Scripture validate the mistaken belief that a Christian's purpose is simply to read and learn the Bible and hang out with other believers having potluck dinners and Sunday School classes. Those activities are intended only to prepare you for your real mission: to serve.

In clearly-defined terms, Jesus explained repeatedly what God's intention is for the work of believers: bringing healing and hope to those in need. This is the sole purpose of a life lived in harmony with God's intention.

> When the Son of Man comes in his glory, and all the angels with him, he will sit on his glorious throne. All the nations will be gathered before him, and he will separate the people one from another as a shepherd separates the sheep from the goats. He will put the sheep on his right and the goats on his left.
>
> Then the King will say to those on his right, "Come, you who are blessed by my Father; take your inheritance, the kingdom prepared for you since the creation of the world. For I was hungry and you gave me something to eat, I was thirsty and you gave me something to drink, I was a stranger and you invited me in, I needed clothes and you clothed me, I was sick and you looked after me, I was in prison and you came to visit me."
>
> Then the righteous will answer him, "Lord, when did we see you hungry and feed you, or thirsty and give you something to drink? When did we see you a stranger and invite you in, or needing clothes and clothe you? When did we see you sick or in prison and go to visit you?"
>
> The King will reply, "Truly I tell you, whatever you did for one of the least of these brothers and sisters of mine, you did for me."
>
> Then he will say to those on his left, "Depart from me, you who are cursed, into the eternal fire prepared for the devil and his angels. For I was hungry and you gave me nothing to eat, I was thirsty and you gave me nothing to drink, I was a stranger and you did not invite me in, I needed clothes and you did not clothe me, I was sick and in prison and you did not look after me."
>
> They also will answer, "Lord, when did we see you hungry or thirsty or a stranger or needing clothes or sick or in prison, and did not help you?"
>
> He will reply, "Truly I tell you, whatever you did not do for one of the least of these, you did not do for me."
>
> Then they will go away to eternal punishment, but the righteous to eternal life.
>
> Matthew 25:31-46

In the language of the Kingdom, those who serve are called "servants" by Jesus. "Volunteers," the terminology used in many churches, is the language of the club. Volunteers give of their time when it is convenient and whenever they personally choose. Servants, however, have a Master who is in charge, and servants obey for a lifetime. Serving is not something a servant chooses when it's easy or convenient. It's a way of life, an identity.

For Systems/Task Organizers, you must make certain you grasp the biblical understanding of servanthood. Otherwise, you'll be the first to default into seeing persons simply as instruments through which to accomplish work—your "to do" list. Keep developing your **Spiritual Shepherd** skills to support your servant teams.

Spiritual Shepherds—keep in mind that your primary ministry component may lead you to want to care for and help potential servants get their own needs met, postponing their servant involvement until they're better or healed. Yet it's clear that healing and purpose also comes through serving others, even when you are a "wounded healer."

If you as the ultimately responsible leader understand that serving is what we *do* as believers—rather than a choice we make—your entire approach will be different. You'll educate your constituency about the lifestyle of a servant that naturally comes along with choosing to have Christ as your center. It will also change your approach when inviting persons to servant roles. You will no longer think your job is to persuade them to give of their precious spare time to help out the church (or an even more misguided perspective, to help you out). You'll know you are actually igniting the life of Jesus in persons as they connect with a productive niche in which to serve. Your next task is to help lead them to the mind shifts necessary to embrace the servant life that identifies faithful Christians together in contagious ministry.

Mindsets versus Mind Shifts

Understanding the mindset, the perspective of a potential servant at any level of a contagious ministry, is crucial for your effectiveness as the one ultimately responsible for servant deployment. Even paid staff on ministry teams, pastors included, often do this poorly. The typical default of ministry leaders is to feel panicked about filling holes and to see themselves in the unpleasant role of convincing individuals to help out. Unfortunately, it's not unusual to hear a preacher trying to guilt the congregation into serving out of duty. Persons do not respond to a call to duty out of the same conviction that our grandparents did. In fact, demanding that believers must serve out of obligation is a sure way to alienate your constituency and inadvertently communicate to them that serving is a necessary evil.

Now that you understand the organic servant calling within all Christians, however, you're ready to look inside the minds of those you lead in a whole new way. You are ready to help unleash them for incredible servanthood.

Let's start by defining **four different mindsets** that potential servants may represent. You may hear a version of any of the four of these mindsets when you invite someone to serve. As the leader in charge, you can learn how to help elicit a healthy mind shift in each.

Mindset #1: Wait a second— isn't that your job as the ministry leader/pastor?

Like Barbara who sent me the e-mail, entry-level Prospectors (and even some Regular Attendees) may view the work of the ministry as your responsibility. They are focused on the potential of the ministry

traditional church model of ministry

or church to provide for their personal needs of friendship, education, fun, and life enhancement, not on the idea of making a contribution. In addition, these individuals may see the church or ministry from a traditional church point of view. Their assumption may be that the pastor, staff, and leaders of the ministry are the ones who do the actual work of the ministry. They assume that any committees the ministry or church has formed exist to offer support to the chosen few who are actually "in ministry." And the role of the attendees is to simply support the entire paradigm as well as benefit from the ministry work of the chosen few.

The contagious ministry movement version of this prototype, however, is based upon the priesthood principle found in 1 Peter 2:9-10:

people

teams/committees

ministers/staff

biblical model of ministry

But you are a chosen people, a royal priesthood, a holy nation, a people belonging to God, that you may declare the praises of him who called you out of darkness into his wonderful light. Once you were not a people, but now you are the people of God; once you had not received mercy, but now you have received mercy.

Through the liberating message of Jesus, all believers are transformed into the role of priests, united and commissioned in ministry together on behalf of a hurting, broken world. No believer is just a spectator! And in 1 Corinthians 12, the body of Christ (consisting of all believers) is depicted as an empowered collection of contributors for a common cause, each playing a unique and equally-valuable role in the overall mission. Any church or ministry that practices a traditional church model of ministry, reserving servanthood only for the select few and rendering the rest of the gathering as only observers and recipients, stands in direct contradiction to the biblical intention of what God expects your church or ministry to model. I also like to call this the body of Christ principle:

Just as a body, though one, has many parts, but all its parts form one body, so it is with Christ. For we were all baptized by one Spirit so as to form one body—whether Jews or Gentiles, slave or free—and we were all given the one Spirit to drink. Even so the body is not made up of one part but of many.

If the foot should say, "Because I am not a hand, I do not belong to the body," it would not for that reason cease to be part of the body. And if the ear should say, "Because I am not an eye, I do not belong to the body," it would not for that reason cease to be part of the body. If the whole body were an eye, where would the sense of hearing be? If the whole body were

Vision Criers are capable of explaining the body of Christ principle and casting vision to your constituency to help bring a mind shift to the contagious ministry movement prototype. Whether or not casting this vision comes naturally to you, practice sharing it on a regular basis with those you lead, even with newcomers.

an ear, where would the sense of smell be? But in fact God has placed the parts in the body, every one of them, just as he wanted them to be. If they were all one part, where would the body be? As it is, there are many parts, but one body.

The eye cannot say to the hand, "I don't need you!" And the head cannot say to the feet, "I don't need you!" On the contrary, those parts of the body that seem to be weaker are indispensable, and the parts that we think are less honorable we treat with special honor. And the parts that are unpresentable are treated with special modesty, while our presentable parts need no special treatment. But God put the body together, giving greater honor to the parts that lacked it, so that there should be no division in the body, but that its parts should have equal concern for each other. If one part suffers, every part suffers with it; if one part is honored, every part rejoices with it.

Now you are the body of Christ, and each one of you is a part of it.

1 Corinthians 12:12-27

You can recognize when potential servants are settled into Mindset #1. It may be expressed in some version of the following responses when they are asked to serve:

- "I am so busy; it's all I can do just to show up. There's no more time in my schedule to do anything more. I'm lucky to be here at all."
- "Oh, no, I could never do that. I have no training or education for it like you do."
- "This is my only time to see and catch up with my friends. I don't have any other time to be with them than when I'm here."
- "I'm not mature enough in my faith to help with anything. I have to spend all my time soaking in the teaching and truth I'm learning."
- "I put in offering every week, and I don't expect to have to help the pastor/staff do the jobs we pay them to do."

Creating a Mind Shift for Mindset #1:

I stood at the front, looking out across the room at their faces—complacent, content. It was a ministry group that had been led for a number of years by a hardworking pastor whose primary ministry component was Spiritual Shepherd. He had cared for this group, taught them, nurtured them, and responded to their needs. And they had loved receiving his dedicated attention. But now he was gone, and I had inherited responsibility for this ministry's constituency. I heard every one of the Mindset #1 responses listed in the previous section as I started working to awaken within them the yet hibernating call to serve, to replace what had become their customary expectation to be served by staff and leaders.

I planned a strategy to help trigger a mind shift among the talented yet stagnant group of believers who expected me to "do" the ministry to and for them. The first action I implemented was a new opening statement I made each time the group met for any reason. I made sure a version of it was also printed in their monthly newsletter.

"Welcome to our church," I would begin. "Our church exists to help prepare and equip you to become the hands and feet of Jesus in the world. Every class we offer, every worship service we plan, every committee that meets—everything we do has the same purpose: to prepare us to be unleashed to serve the needs of our world through the powerful love of God. You see, when the new life of Jesus lives inside you—when you have accepted Jesus as your Lord and Savior—you join Jesus on mission to serve those around you. As Jesus said, '[I] did not come to be served, but to serve, and to give [my life] as a ransom for many' (Matthew 20:28)."

At first, a few of the long-time attendees asked me about this "new" purpose I shared at the opening of each gathering. "Well, you see—we get together to learn and have fun. What you are saying may turn some people off. Most people have no interest in becoming missionaries or something."

I would smile, and then answer, "Yes, I feel pretty busy, too. But you know, none of us has an option if Jesus is alive in us. That is what Jesus was about while on earth, and the good news is that he's still about it today through us. Don't worry—we will learn more about this as we go."

Soon I added something else to the opening statement at every gathering. I also told a servant story, or interviewed a servant who was dedicated to servant work in Jesus' name. At other times I showed a brief video story of a servant's work. The video stories were poor quality, because I took my home camcorder and filmed them myself—but surprisingly, the ministry loved them. I did my best to choose someone who most persons in the room knew, if at all possible. By telling stories of servants and their dedication, a new picture of our goal as Christians was illustrated each week for the attendees, a new measure of how we were defining success. Those who served began to be seen as our heroes and became minor celebrities among us. It was motivating to everyone.

At the same time, we began to distribute a "Top Ten Ways to Serve" list to the group every time it met. These included opportunities to serve within that ministry as well as church-wide. The "Top Ten" list changed every week, and included a "Yes, I'm interested!" portion at the bottom so that it could be completed and returned for follow-up. I often acknowledged and thanked new servants by name each week during announcement time, further highlighting the importance of serving.

Systems/Tasks Organizers may tend to most value servant roles that require the greatest responsibility. Instead, be intentional to acknowledge every role, no matter how small. Remember, they all count!

Vision Criers often excel at telling great servant stories and casting the vision that we all are called to serve. Pay attention that immediate connection and support are provided for those who indicate an interest in serving.

More specifically, I made sure that every servant role was equally acknowledged, in keeping with the 1 Corinthians 12 body of Christ model. I refused to allow teachers and up front, visible servants to be viewed as more valuable than others. The more humble the servant role might appear to the secular mind, the more I publicly compared that task to Jesus washing the disciples' feet, the ultimate in servanthood. Gradually the ministry constituency began to say yes when opportunities to serve were named. The energy of the ministry grew, and so did its numbers.

John was a Regular Attendee of the ministry group, but, due to under-developed social skills and outdated clothing, he seemed unapproach-able, communicated little with others, and often sat alone on the back row. I knew little about John, a young man of perhaps thirty years old, a physical laborer by trade. I could see he would not be a great candi-date to become a door greeter, an emcee, or a teacher. I pondered what servant role would be just right for him.

You'll find a list of "Always/Nevers"— What to Say to a Servant—on the *Ultimately Responsible* DVD in chapter 4. Review these with your leadership team or staff as they improve their skills with enlisting servants.

After a few months of working the servant engagement strategy I've just described, I knew John had heard over and over, along with the others about our ministry's purpose to equip Jesus followers to become hands and feet of service to others. One week as John was leaving, I simply asked him if he saw any particular way he would like to serve. He looked away shyly, was quiet for several moments, and then smiled. "Well, I can see a better way we should be setting up the chairs in this meeting room." His words stumbled over each other in his awkwardness. He grabbed a sheet of paper off the table and sketched a quick design. "If I came early and set up the chairs this way, we could get a lot more people in the room and everyone could see each other better, and see the speaker better. If you want, I could come early next week and try it…?"

The next week, John was already in the meeting room when I arrived. Every chair was perfectly spaced in a new configuration that the min-istry participants found they loved. Even the welcome table had been placed at a different angle, the trash can for disposing of paper nametags now handily located. John had found his place to serve. He was methodical, never absent, consistently arriving early to make cer-tain the room logistics were ideal. I highlighted John as one of our star servants in the weekly announcements, and he began to be viewed as one of the ministry's favorites. Gone were the days of sitting alone on the back row of the room. John had found a place among what had become a community of fellow servants. He had become one of The Engaged, a transition achieved through serving.

One day I received an unexpected phone call from John. His voice was hoarse, frightened. "Pastor Sue, I just got the doctor's report. They diagnosed me with Hodgkin's disease today. My cousin is taking me to the medical center in the city for treatment. I'll be there for eight weeks. Please tell the ministry group to pray for me. I'm sorry, I won't be there for the chairs. I hope you can find someone else...."

It was only then that I learned John had no family other than the cousin, a farmer, who drove him sixty miles that day to leave him at the medical center specializing in cancer treatment. John eventually underwent a bone marrow transplant and could not have visitors. But the ministry group passed out pre-addressed "get well" postcards for John and set up a rotation for mailing them so that he would receive a few cards every single day. They formed a prayer team, recruiting servants who would pray for John each day of the week. At first, John called me occasionally from the medical center. But after eight weeks we heard nothing more from or about John and had no contact information to reach his cousin. Our concern was great.

John had been gone for twelve weeks when I remember arriving early to the weekly meeting room for the ministry group's gathering. The lights weren't on, but through the spring evening dimness I could see a thin figure moving slowly, dragging chairs across the room. A large bandage still covered part of his neck. I flipped on the lights and recognized John! "Hi! I talked the doctor into dismissing me from the medical center today instead of this weekend, so that I could make it for tonight's meeting. My cousin had to leave his work to pick me up and bring me here in time. But I know our group needs to have the chairs just right so they can learn and grow as they study God's word. I didn't want to miss my opportunity to serve. Serving is what I was born to do, and this group needs me...."

By the time the ministry participants arrived, John had completed his signature chair and room arrangement. Though he was so tired and weak he could barely sit up through the evening's event, the smile never left his face. He glowed with the life of Jesus from within, the spiritual energy that comes from true servanthood.

Shift your ministry or church out of Mindset #1 by:
- Regularly painting the picture of the contagious ministry movement model, the body of Christ principle
- Bombarding all attendees with descriptions of servant opportunities, introducing new possibilities and ideas
- Telling servant stories, spotlighting servant heroes in your midst whose witness will inspire and motivate others

- Teaching and emphasizing that God's intended result of spiritual growth in Christ is expanding dedication to the expression of Jesus' servant lifestyle through us.

Mindset #2: I want a calling, not just a job.

Though some Prospectors and Regular Attendees prefer servant tasks that require little thought and no preparation or particular skills to perform, most individuals who make your church or ministry a regular part of their lives have a desire for something more. Passionate Level 3 and 4 servants ideally grow toward a wholehearted willingness to do whatever it takes to accomplish God's work, even the most menial of tasks. But most who are on an active spiritual journey of faith long for a servant contribution that is more than just a job. They want something that not just anyone can do, something that fits their unique strengths, gifts, and experience. They are looking to connect with a purpose to which they can contribute that is bigger than themselves. They seek a calling.

A calling doesn't necessarily refer to a Mother-Teresa-sized, lifelong ministry role in Calcutta. What it describes is a specific servant task God has for you right now. A believer may pursue a number of different callings during a lifetime. Recognizing a calling comes when you notice what it is for which you have spiritual passion, over what it is that your heart breaks. A calling brings with it a sense of desire for contribution to a bigger cause for Christ. Those who serve out of a calling may actually perform routine work, but their spirits are fed through the satisfaction and contentment they receive by contributing an integral ingredient to something they see as large, miraculous, and extraordinary for God. Most notably, serving out of a calling allows you to see your servant work through different eyes, a different perspective than those around you. You connect with the bigger God-picture of which your call to serve is a vital part.

Servant Mindset #2 reveals itself in various forms. When asking Mindset #2 individuals to serve, the responses may sound like:
- "I don't think that's how I want to spend my time."
- "I need some type of service to really sink my teeth into. I don't think what you're asking me to do is it."
- "Well, I'd rather do something that really matters if I'm going to serve."
- "Yes, I heard you announce that we need servants to do that (or saw the sign-up sheet). I figured other people could do it."

When you hear a statement that represents a version of Mindset #2, you can know that the person who said it has failed to connect a particular servant task to the bigger picture of God's work and mission.

Creating a Mind Shift for Mindset #2:

Posting or passing around a sign-up sheet asking people to serve in a given role, while a common practice at many churches (including my own), isn't ultimately the most effective way to involve people deeply. As I pointed out earlier, a sense of duty might have motivated our grandparents' generation to serve, but not those succeeding it. If you receive blank stares as you plead with individuals who seem uninterested in helping own the action of your church or ministry, it may be because they are not looking for a servant job that just anyone can do. They may each long for a role that touches a deep sense of mission and passion.

During the first two years I served in a paid ministry leadership role, I had the responsibility to support a new, fast-growing young adult outreach ministry that attracted newcomers every week. Their regular gatherings were social, noisy, and energetic. I loved the enthusiasm of the community they were building together. I had figured out servant Mindset #1 and realized I needed to engage them to serve and support their own events. But I didn't understand Mindset #2, and as a leader I was stressed, frustrated, and disillusioned.

One specific challenge I faced was enlisting persons to come early to make the coffee and lay out the cookies for the fellowship time offered at the end of their gatherings. Clearly the group enjoyed the evening's refreshment and social conclusion that they regularly shared—so, I reasoned, shouldn't some of them see the need to help it happen? I tried walking around at their events to recruit workers in person with little success. My next attempt was via the phone, calling through alphabetized sections of the constituency. Again I received minimal response despite what felt akin to begging on my part. I knew it was not right for me to continue to come early and do the refreshment setup myself, because this represented the traditional church model rather than the body of Christ principle of shared servanthood—yet I found myself doing just that. I was confounded by the refusal of the constituency to come early and handle the coffee and cookies. I became downright angry the week I called thirty-two different Regular Attendees on the phone, and not one of them believed they had time or availability to come early and commandeer the refreshment table.

So I made a decision. At their next gathering, the kitchen area adjacent to their meeting room was visibly dark and empty. During the opening announcements, I explained that the young adult events would no longer offer a coffee and cookies refreshment time at the end of the evening. "Since no one feels the call to take responsibility for doing this, it must mean it's not an essential part of the group's time together," I said in conclusion. Silence filled the room for a few moments, and then the evening

Check out chapter 6, **Building a Team**, to learn more about servants who prefer a "Worker" role. Workers respond well to sign-up sheets for serving—though many other potential servants do not.

My **Systems/Task Organizer** leadership component was in overdrive throughout most of this story. I don't remember taking time to pause during those phone calls to be a **Spiritual Shepherd** to those I was attempting to enlist, considering each conversation a potential opportunity to minister. And my **Vision Crier** skills were on vacation! Work to intentionally engage all three leadership components when recruiting others to serve.

went on. Afterwards, the room emptied quickly as everyone went home instead of staying to socialize and bond over snacks. I felt defeated.

But the next day, I received a call from a woman identifying herself as Jane. "You don't know me, but I've been coming to the young adult ministry events for the last month or so," she explained. "I was there last night when you announced something about not having coffee and cookies because no one thought they were important enough to help out with." I cringed as I heard her version of what I had said to the group, and again felt the frustration inside of what I believed was my own leadership failure to enlist servants to do the job.

Then Jane made a statement that brought me a profound mind shift. "You know—the truth is you don't really need people just to do the job of laying out the cookies and making the coffee for our group. What you need is a *kitchen ministry*... You see, it's not actually about the coffee and cookies. It's about creating an atmosphere at the event...like the warm, inviting atmosphere of Grandma's kitchen. When persons walk into one of our gatherings, you want them to feel welcome, invited, and included—like family. The cookies and coffee are a part of that, but so are some other things."

Of course, I was thinking as she spoke, *of course!* Jane had just connected the simple task of coordinating refreshments with the big-picture mission of creating community, God's intention for believers who gather together. Suddenly even I wanted to help with the cookies. Jane had helped me see a new valued perspective of a simple servant role when it connected as part of a bigger calling.

"I'd like to make you an offer. A few friends and I, well, we would love to help create the sense of warmth of Grandma's kitchen. Could we be the new kitchen servant team for the young adult ministry? I'll call them, and we'll show up early and take care of everything. Don't worry. I see what can happen with this."

My mind was working fast. I had never met Jane, and I didn't know her friends. And I was turning the church kitchen over to strangers? What might they do? What if it wasn't appropriate? What if I trusted Jane's offer, and then they didn't really show up? I quickly decided we would not be any worse off if they were no shows. After all, I had announced we would not be having refreshments. "Jane, you're on. See you later this week!"

I came even earlier than usual the evening of the young adult outreach gathering, anxious about what I might find. The church kitchen lights were already on, and the air was alive with laughter and cheerful voices.

I could smell the inviting aroma of brewing coffee. I was drawn to the window counter separating our meeting room and the kitchen. "Hi, I'm Jane!" a cheerful woman with red hair greeted me. "These are my friends. We're having a great time!"

I could see that—as could the other attendees of the young adult ministry who began to arrive for the evening's activities. The activity, the energy coming from the kitchen area drew them irresistibly over to the counter window, too. Soon it was time to start, but nearly two-thirds of the attendance was crowded in and around the kitchen, engaged in the friendly banter of the new kitchen team! It reminded me of a large party to which everyone was invited. I had to use the microphone to ask everyone to sit down so we could start. And at the end, the social time lasted far later than usual due to more engaging frivolity extended by the kitchen crew. Persons I'd never seen serve before were now helping out at the kitchen sink wearing aprons along with Jane's crew, chatting and joking as they assisted with clean up.

"We had such fun, we'll take care of this every time," Jane assured me as they finally departed. And they did—for three straight years, at every single gathering of that ministry, Jane and her friends gradually identified kindred spirits who understood the power of the calling to kitchen ministry. Their recruits eventually inherited the responsibility and later raised up their own successors as well.

The mind shift Jane helped me and others make has permanently shaped my approach to recruiting. When inviting persons to serve, I no longer ask individuals simply to do a task. I first explain the overall mission, the big picture we are working together to fulfill. Then I explain what part the servant role has in accomplishing this mission. Like Jane, I paint the big picture of the contribution the task makes to heartfelt purposes such as the needs of others, the atmosphere of the room, the spiritual growth of the attendees and other soul-satisfying results. I've found this helps servants at all levels also make the mind shift necessary to live out the passion of a servant's heart, to embrace a servant role with the sense of fulfilling a calling.

Shift your ministry or church out of Mindset #2 by:

- Operating out of the awareness that many servants aren't just looking for a job—that their desire is to do something on behalf of Jesus' work that makes an important contribution to something bigger than themselves
- Explaining the unique contribution of every servant role to the bigger mission
- Trusting God to connect the deep calling of servants to specific tasks, and allowing them to fulfill it

• Encouraging servants to connect with others who share their calling, and to multiply themselves in their Kingdom work

Mindset #3: I want to serve, but the servant tasks our church/ministry offers don't really interest me.

Most ministries and churches struggle to break through the 20/80 barrier. Perhaps you're familiar with the term?

The 20/80 barrier in ministry appears when 20 percent of the persons in your church or ministry do all the work of serving, and the other 80 percent seem to do nothing other than attend. The 20 percent stay busy doing the core five or ten tasks that typically keep the church or ministry going—standing at the door as greeters, singing in the choir, teaching the children, or holding positions on committees. They perform the essential servant tasks that are necessary for maintenance of the church or ministry.

The 20 percent are tired because they believe they are carrying too much of the load. And they become frustrated when trying to get the 80 percent to help them with what they are doing. In fact, the missional focus of the 20 percent may be gradually pulled off their own serving, distracted instead with complaining about the 80 percent who appear to remain perpetually in Level 1 or 2: persons interested in what's going on but content to simply receive rather than serve.

Truth is, I believe that the 80 percent in a church or ministry situation such as this do indeed want to serve, to contribute to the mission and work of Jesus. *They're simply not interested in the servant tasks in which the 20 percent are engaged!* And it may appear to the 80 percent that the only servant role choices offered them are those same five or ten ministry tasks. They are usually the only servant roles identified and presented (and pushed or honored) by the ministry leadership. Since those don't appeal or trigger a sense of calling, the 80 percent are stuck. They are stuck inside your ministry or church, a place that has become like a fortress requiring all who enter to serve only by helping with the customary maintenance work of the fortress itself.

You might be thinking that service involving the core tasks of ministry or church support and maintenance are essential, and some of us are indeed called to those roles. You, as a reader of this book, may be a 20 percent specialist! But in the spirit of 1 Corinthians 12, an ideal metaphor of the body of Christ, the church cannot thrive or survive if only 20 percent of the body is working or contributing to its dreams and passions. Instead, the church must be a **launching pad**, offering springboards from which believers can dream and fulfill all kinds of unique passions for serving Christ. This is what it means to unleash servanthood in your setting. It is the true manifestation of the body of Christ principle, in which individuals are living out their unique giftedness and utilizing their special strengths and skills in the grand unity of Kingdom work.

You may hear a variety of versions of Mindset #3 as you invite potential servants to embrace a ministry task, particularly if you are offering a core 20 percent ministry role to someone who has been hanging out in the 80 percent crowd:

- "I need some type of service that will jazz me, and so far nothing I've seen here really has."
- "Nope, that's not for me. I think there is something God wants me to do, but I haven't seen it yet."
- "I feel like a round peg in a square hole. I wish I could teach kids or be outgoing enough to be a greeter, but I just don't seem to fit."
- "I appreciate everyone who does all the work around here—the committees and everything—but I'm just not a committee-type person."

Creating a Mind Shift for Mindset #3:

One of the basic mandates of contagious ministry movement strategy is to accomplish all Kingdom work with a surplus of servants, rather than an economy of servants. Ministry momentum occurs when as many persons as possible become owners of the action. And in order for that to happen in any sized setting, a wide variety of servant opportunities need to be offered.

One significant route that can help your church overcome the inertia of the 20/80 barrier is the creation of an annual "servant catalog." In my current church setting, all teams and committees across the church family work to identify as many different servant roles in their areas as possible, writing an appealing description and identifying a contact person for each. These are compiled every July and published every August in a servant catalog, inviting everyone to sign up for a yearlong commitment to a servant role. Servant sign-up forms to complete are provided with the catalog. When the sign-up forms are returned, they are distributed to the designated leaders or ministry teams for immediate follow-up, training, and deployment. The servant catalog is available all year long and is distributed regularly to new attendees and new members for servant engagement.

The servant catalog has appealed to all, particularly to the 80 percent who did not realize how many options for serving were possible. They were not interested in the traditional servant roles of the church (though

If your primary leadership component is **Systems/Task Organizer**, you may think it's satisfactory to get the work done efficiently with only enough servants to cover what needs to happen. Instead, train yourself always to think of giving as many as possible the experience of involvement. When your most faithful servants move on to other roles, you'll have a new generation of servants ready to step up.

these are listed in the servant catalog and have many who respond to them), but stepped up to the plate when they saw the wide variety of possible unique and creative servant roles.

Robert's eclectic background had led him to explore many avenues of spirituality through his adult years. He found himself in mid-life, haunted by a growing desire to fill the God-void deep inside. Robert began attending church and caught the vision for what a life fully lived in Christ is like. After committing as a follower of Jesus, Robert began learning about the call to serve. But he was frustrated at what he believed was his own lack of passion for working with children or students—obvious servant roles in our setting. Robert was shy and introverted, so joining a large team of other servants on any project also didn't appeal. As a faithful Regular Attendee, Robert's guilt grew as he became painfully aware of his lack of servant contribution.

Check out Ginghamsburg's online servant catalog at **www.ginghamsburg .org/serve**. Want to create your own online servant catalog? Download the free software template called "Servant Connector" from **www .webempowered church.com** and customize with your own church's servant roles!

That is, until Robert searched through the servant catalog. "Stage Artist," the role was titled. "Help arrange and decorate the stage for worship, according to the weekly worship theme. Requires a servant heart, creative and artistic flair, and a willingness to work in conjunction with the worship design team." Robert's mind flitted to his garage and basement, delightfully disorganized collection areas for a plethora of unique and unusual objects and items. He thought of his craft table, the birth location of countless arrangements, displays and artistic efforts over the years. He remembered his enjoyment of browsing garage sales, choosing flowers for distinctive bouquets. Suddenly, everything clicked. He marveled that his outwardly diverse interests and hobbies might miraculously come together in a servant role that could utilize them all.

Some of his church's most inspiring and amazing visuals for worship since that epiphany have come through the servant energy of Robert. Robert gets his direction from the worship team and then works alone to create what become creative and eye-catching displays that help the church family experience multisensory worship. Robert also occasionally helps create the artistic settings for informational booths in the church lobby and other projects as he is led. All this—launched from a servant catalog.

This simple tool, a servant catalog, is applicable in all types of church sizes and settings for igniting the servant activity of otherwise complacent Regular Attendees. Here's what I've learned—words to the wise—if you decide to create one for your ministry or church:

List only servant roles that are truly open for anyone to serve. Do not advertise for an adult class teacher, for example, if you are really looking for a special someone who is dynamic and already experienced in front of groups. You may have a person sign up who does not meet these qualifications—and then you are in the uncomfortable position of saying no. Recruit personally for servant roles that require a specific level of expertise.

List servant roles for which, with training, most interested potential servants could accomplish. Ask yourself these questions: *Is there anything I need to put in the description of this role that would help persons know if they would enjoy it or have the natural gifts for it? Am I prepared to offer training if necessary for this role—and if so, who would be the trainer? Can I support this servant role, if someone signs up for it?*

Brainstorm as many facets of each ministry area as possible in which a servant could contribute. Within every task area (even within the 20 percent servant work of the church), a multitude of unique roles could exist. For example, a servant may not desire to teach children in a Sunday morning classroom but would be excited to serve as "Children's ministry workroom organizer" and come in regularly to straighten shelves, re-stock teacher supplies, sort curriculum, and organize crayons and scissors. Similarly, not everyone feels led to help with the weekly worship service through joining the choir, ushering, or reading the Bible lectionary from the pulpit, but a person might be enthused to be a sermon researcher on the Internet, culling through Web sites to find interesting and useful data and information relating to the next week's sermon topic to send to the preacher as he or she prepares.

Make sure you also list the basic 20 percent roles in the servant catalog. With a clear description, some may sense a call after all to help with the core work of the church. Well-written descriptions emphasizing the contribution to the overall mission of your congregation may help redefine stereotypical assumptions about what it means to serve in these roles.

Remember that you must always keep actively and personally recruiting servants. A servant catalog is at best a supplement to help ignite and expand the options for engaging the 80 percent, not a substitute for making personal connections and invitations. A crippling mistake would be to assume that all servant recruitment will be accomplished through paper or electronic means. Your key leaders and servants must be identified and invited in person. Using a servant catalog adds a "both-and" approach to igniting servanthood.

Shift your ministry or church out of Mindset #3 by:

- Assessing whether you have unintentionally created a 20/80 barrier at your church or ministry

Systems/Task Organizers, orchestrating the creation of a servant catalog may be right up your alley. Pay attention to the descriptions of each servant role you place in it, making sure the connection to the bigger mission is mentioned as well as the specific work tasks it involves. A servant catalog is not appealing unless it creates the sense of adventure and excitement.

Even typical church ministry areas offer a wide diversity of opportunities to contribute—as limitless as your imagination. View the video story about **UltraLive** on the *Ultimately Responsible* DVD, chapter 4. All are student ministry servants, but each fulfills a unique role.

- Brainstorming the possibilities for service in your setting
- Creating a mechanism through which attendees may be informed about the variety of opportunities open to them
- Carefully crafting your requests for servants to fill the 20 percent roles, in order to avoid creating the impression that these are the only tasks available through which to serve

Mindset #4: I want to find a custom-made serving niche that uses my unique gifts and strengths, but I'm not sure what they are.

Those who have served faithfully as Regular Attendees—even those who have become The Engaged—often present with the fourth Mindset. They understand the mandate of servanthood that comes with following Christ. They have likely already served, some even in significant leadership roles. Occasionally this mindset is found in a Prospector or in a Regular Attendee who experiences a desire for self-discovery. That desire comes from a growing awareness and wonderment at how carefully a loving God crafted each one of us—especially oneself.

To maximize the servant impact of those with Mindset #4, first appreciate the reality that we have all been raised in a remedial society. By this I mean an environment in which, from kindergarten forward, your focus has been directed toward childhood and adolescent report cards, then the annual performance reviews of working adulthood. On those report cards and performance reviews, you have been faithfully reminded of what you need to improve. What you do well may be taken for granted, in order for time and energy to be fully invested instead in improving your limitations. Gradually this remedial emphasis becomes such a way of thinking about yourself that now, fully grown, you are much better at identifying what you are not good at, rather than what gifts and strengths you've been given. If asked to make one list at what you are truly talented, and another listing what you need to improve about yourself, most persons could quickly create the second list. The first list might pose a challenge. For you and many others, the environment in which we live has simply not provided focus on our abilities, what we do well. To some, it even seems conceited or inappropriate to name your own giftedness.

So, keep in mind that the persons in your ministry or church may live with a continual mental critique of what they're not good at threaded through their daily self-talk, a self-critical running commentary about what they need to improve. This inner voice has been so consistent for so long that it is difficult for some to acknowledge and embrace their own God-given gift mix for service. So when confronted with new servant opportunities of any kind, your community of attendees may default to a remedial mindset, convinced they don't have the talent or gifts for what it takes.

Mindset #4 expresses itself in a number of ways. You'll recognize when potential servants are struggling within this mindset when you hear comments along these lines:

- "I think God has some bigger purpose for me, but I don't know what it is."
- "There's something else God wants me to do, and I believe I've been prepared for it. I wish I could find it."
- "God gives us all strengths and gifts—I know—but I have no idea what mine might be!"
- "It's not that I'm unwilling to serve in my current position. I just believe God has something more for me to do."

Creating a Mind Shift For Mindset #4:

As we mature in our faith, I believe followers of Jesus become deeply aware of a God-authored heart-tug, urging us to serve fully out of our unique strengths and giftedness. This heart-tug is identified several times throughout Scripture. One passage is Psalm 37: 4-6a:

> Take delight in the LORD and he will give you the desires of your heart.
> Commit your way to the LORD; trust in him and he will do this:
> He will make your righteous reward shine like the dawn…."

"Shining like the dawn" is certainly descriptive of a role more customized and indigenized to who a person is than a role in which one simply agrees to help lay out pens and paper on the tables before class. It speaks of the energy that is released in and through a person when the talents and gifts inside have opportunity for full fruition on behalf of God's work and God's children. As Jesus pointed out, *"You are the light of the world. A city on a hill cannot be hidden…Let your light shine before others, that they may see your good deeds and glorify your Father in heaven"* (Matthew 5:14-16).

Your church or ministry must create an intentional route by which persons may seek to self-identify and embrace their God-given talents and gifts, and find a corresponding launching pad for utilizing them. Within the ideal route, individuals are retrained first to identify and focus on what they are good at (their gifts and strengths) and then to listen to God's guidance on how to utilize those gifts and strengths. These are the two essentials in helping to provide leadership to servants who long to connect with a custom-fit servant role. Identifying gifts and talents alone isn't enough. Learning to spend time with God every day and connect with God's guidance for how to serve and "shine like the dawn" also isn't enough. Both must be provided together to help believers learn a

Spiritual Shepherds are particularly effective at helping believers consider what it means to have a "shine like the dawn" tug inside. Your patience as you encourage persons to take off a remedial mentality and replace it with focus upon personal gifts and strengths will help many. Use **Systems/Task Organizer** skills to create a structured environment (class or small group) within which this process can take place.

lifestyle of utilizing and maximizing their giftedness according to God's unique direction.

You can set the stage for deploying Mindset #4 servants in more than one way. Find the right means to assure that an ongoing process exists within your own church or ministry.

Ministry By Strengths is an approach I've created and developed over the last eight years to help accomplish both these objectives for staff and for unpaid servants: identification of gifts and natural talents, and the corresponding utilization of them for custom-fit service. Learn more at www.ginghamsburg resources.org.

Create a course or class series to help participants self-discover their gifts and strengths, along with how to listen to God for their utilization. Fortunately, today's church curriculum market offers a variety of choices you can use for this purpose, complete with a leader's guide and student workbooks. Some incorporate a spiritual gifts inventory, and others help the class attendees self-identify their strengths or talents. As you assess what course material to utilize, make certain that it encompasses both aspects—not only recognizing gifts and strengths but also providing structure through which students learn to connect with God's guidance for employing them. Otherwise, the course will provide head knowledge to the participants ("Hmmm, isn't it interesting that God has gifted me in these ways") without motivation to actually use them for service.

Add a spiritual gifts inventory (plus training on how to deploy those gifts) to your church membership class. Some churches ask everyone who plans to become an official church member to take a spiritual gifts inventory, and learn more about God's intended use of them through serving. It becomes an enabling part of the responsibilities accepted with membership.

Work one-on-one or in a small group setting to unpack and uncover ownership of personal gifts and talents, as well as God's directive for use of them. A safe space setting in which Mindset #4 servants may express and process this is pivotal for many. Receiving validation (and honesty) from others about giftedness, as well as affirmation of God's leadership of potential direction for serving, is life changing.

As the ultimately responsible leader, you have a thoughtful role to play in the process of assisting servants on their journey to discover a custom fit role. Resist the desire to tell servants what God has created them to do. Like a wrapped Christmas gift, what's inside each servant's unique toolbox of gifts, strengths, spiritual growth, and lessons learned through life experience can be known only through the servant's willingness to do a self-inventory—not by your guesses from the outside. Though feedback about what gifts and talents you have observed in them is appropriate, your job is definitely not to focus only on fitting persons into what you believe are gaping needs in your servant corps. Mindset #4 servants require you to make a leader mind shift, viewing them as individuals setting sail on a journey and not as something to be shaped into accomplishing your own goals for the church or ministry. Focus on arranging and providing a launching pad of support for their unique God-directions.

Gwen was warm, friendly, and supportive. Her intentional efforts to introduce herself and welcome me were wonderful. I immediately asked Gwen how long she had been attending the church where I was new to the staff, and how she was involved in serving.

"Right now I'm not serving—I just haven't found God's right place for me to do that," she replied. "I've been going here for several years and have already served in all sorts of ways. I think I've found myself in a time now of asking what God really wants me to do."

Over the next several weekends, I saw Gwen and enjoyed warm conversation with her. Each time our paths crossed, I had a few suggestions for ways in which she could serve. "Huggers and Rockers" ministry in the nursery area, where her grandmotherly charm could comfort babies while their parents were in worship? Front door greeter, where her friendliness could assure other newcomers as it did me? But each possibility I mentioned had a drawback. "I've done that," Gwen would say. "And I could serve in those places. Right now I think God has something more for me, but I'm just not sure what it is."

A few months later, I launched a course I designed to help individuals shed their "remedial society" acclimatization and reorient into claiming their gifts and talents, along with guidance on how to see the path for practically investing them in Kingdom work. Gwen was one of the first to enroll in "Ministry By Strengths." I remember feeling a twinge of anxiety the first night of class: what if Gwen still didn't see what God wanted her to do, even after completing the course? How would that reflect on me, the new leader?

Immediately I experienced one of those reassuring moments when God's wisdom came gently to mind. *"Sue, it's not your job to help Gwen find what I want her to do next. It's Mine! All you need to do is to set the stage for her to hear Me speaking...."*

By the end of the Ministry By Strengths course, Gwen had connected with God's next means of service and had gotten started. The energy and joy that came through using her amazing strengths on behalf of others was contagious. We shared Gwen's inspiring story with our entire congregation, and because of her example many others chose to seek a deeply fulfilling, specialized servant role. Whenever I see Gwen, I think of my initial attempts to

Here's where you may need to be careful if your primary leadership component is **Vision Crier.** Your articulate vision-casting may so inspire listeners that they try to pursue servant roles out of the power of your persuasion rather than a careful self-inventory as described here, along with a listening ear for God's leading. Lean on **Spiritual Shepherd** skills to pastor believers through their individual discovery/ discernment process.

View Gwen's servant story and learn of her calling on the *Ultimately Responsible* DVD, chapter 4, and share it with your Mindset #4 servants for inspiration. God's divine design for serving is not about gaining us attention and spotlight—it's about deep spiritual fulfillment and affirmation of God's direction.

Use your **Systems/Task Organizer** leadership skills to develop a system by which those who discover a new ministry direction may be followed up, connected with others of similar interests, trained and/or set into motion. Without this structure, even the most stalwart servants may become frustrated. See the **"New Ministry Idea" development sheet** on the *Ultimately Responsible* DVD, chapter 4.

recommend servant tasks instead of recognizing that she was in Mindset #4. What amazing influence can happen when individuals like Gwen recognize their own tools and embrace God's guidance!

Shift your ministry or church out of Mindset #4 by:

- Affirming the quest of servants at all levels who feel led to seek specific ministry through their gifts and talents
- Working toward establishing intentional settings through which servants may take stock of their life experiences, spiritual journey, and evidence of giftedness—as well as receive feedback and support from servant colleagues willing to listen
- Inspiring others by sharing stories like Gwen's, which offer permission to others to forego their remedial self-perspective and have courage to "shine like the dawn"

What Servants Want To Know

A little-acknowledged fact about any church or ministry manifesting successful servanthood is that behind the scenes are leaders (paid or unpaid) who understand how to set up servants of any mindset, at any level, for success. If your primary leadership component is Spiritual Shepherd, you may be outstanding at helping potential servants understand the biblical call for all believers to serve. If your strongest component is Systems/Task Organizer, servants may love you because of your ability to get all the supportive details covered. And if you are naturally a Vision Crier, your inspiration may motivate attendees to line up for a chance to contribute to the work of the mission.

But the bottom line is that no matter what your strongest leadership component, you must also make sure that the non-negotiables to support servant ministry are consistently supplied. Otherwise, even the most passionate servants will falter, then lose interest (or go elsewhere) if what they need to succeed isn't available.

Here are the top questions servants want you to answer—by your words or your actions. Train yourself to excel in these areas.

Will I Be Allowed to Actually Do This Servant Work?

Ironically, some servants leave discouraged because others will not share responsibility or opportunity. The culprits may be part of a long-time servant team that has always performed a certain set of servant tasks. Or you may be the guilty party! Many ultimately responsible leaders have such a tight grip on making sure the right things happen that they struggle to relinquish servant opportunities to newcomer servants. For example, though you may ask some servants to come early and arrange the supplies needed for an event, you worry that they won't come. And instead of letting them work on the task they have agreed to do, you arrive first and have it almost completed when the servants arrive. Another unfortunate version of this scenario is when you as leader repeatedly call or e-mail the servant to verify that the task will be or has been completed. On the other end of the spectrum, it's also possible to destroy servant interest by endowing them with a far greater task than what you originally described, requiring more time, energy, or experience than the servant anticipated.

Systems/Task Organizers—watch out for falling into these traps!

Your leadership mantras (repeat and practice as many times as necessary to retrain your own thinking and approach):
- My God-given leadership responsibility is to share the work of the ministry with as many others as possible (body of Christ principle), not do it all myself.
- Outlining the actual scope and expectations for a servant role is essential as I communicate with a potential servant, including the length of term or time frame of the servant task.
- I must remember to inform already-active servants of what I've asked newcomers to do—so that others will not stand in the way of their contributions.
- It's always best to accomplish any ministry initiative with a surplus of servants, rather than an economy of servants.

Who Will Train Me?

Nothing frustrates a servant more than agreeing to a new servant role and then being abandoned to muddle through alone. If you have connected a servant to a new opportunity, you must also provide training and support as needed to provide the person with confidence and assurance. Even when enlisting individuals for basic tasks, take time to think through what questions they will need answered: Where do I park? What door will be unlocked for me? Will I have space? Where will I find the supplies I may need? Who are the other servants with whom I am teaming? Is there anything I should expect? Who should I call if I don't have what I need? What time will I finish? You get the picture.

Your leadership mantras (repeat and practice as many times as necessary to retrain your own thinking and approach):
- My job as leader does not end when a person has said yes to a servant role. I must then make certain that training, supplies, and information will be provided and that space logistics have been arranged.
- Part of training a servant is providing the emotional and spiritual support and encouragement for the task. I will remember how important it is for me to be a Spiritual Shepherd to servants,

taking time to connect with their lives as well instructing them about the tasks I need them to do.

- If a servant fails, I must take first responsibility and do a check to see if I made sure beforehand that training, supplies, information, and logistics were covered adequately.

What Does Success Look Like for This Role?

Your unconscious tendency may be to define a servant's success by whether or not his or her task was done just the way *you* would have done it. And if that's the definition you use, your ability to see growth and increase in the numbers on your servant teams will be limited. Why? No one may live up to your unique style and exact expectations.

"If only I could find three of myself to hire onto my staff, I'd be happy," a pastor whose primary leadership component was Systems/Task Organizer told me. "I just can't trust others to do things the way I would do them and need them done. So at my church, I do a lot myself. I don't think my administrative board appreciates how tired and overworked I am. And they certainly don't pay me enough for all I do!"

That pastor's insistence that every task be done his own way was the reason his church had stagnated and was gradually experiencing membership loss. Great leaders learn that it's a sure-fire method of stifling your servants to hold your own bar of success at too obscure an angle for them to reach. Excellence and quality do matter. But learn to gauge servant success by an independent set of criteria free of your unique style standards.

Your leadership mantras (repeat and practice as many times as necessary to retrain your own thinking and approach):
- My assessment of success for servants in the church or ministry I lead will be based upon the intended goal of the servant task.
- The first question I will ask is, "Was the intended goal accomplished?"
- The second question I will ask is, "Was God honored and was excellence displayed in this servant task?"
- The third question I will ask is, "Did this servant task fit the gifts and talents of the servant performing it?"
- The fourth question I will ask is, "Was the work of this servant harmonious with the overall mission of our church or ministry?"
- The fifth question I will ask is, "Were others honored, served, and/or included in the completion of this task?"

If the answers are yes to all five questions, the servant has been successful—even if the work was done differently from how I would have performed the same task.

Will Anyone Notice What I've Done?

When servants pour their heart and energy into serving in the name of Jesus, it feels affirming to have a leader acknowledge their efforts and the results. Yet it's a common omission of leaders to ignore offering recognition for diligent servants. Somehow it seems to some leaders that a "thank you" shouldn't be necessary for those whose mandate through life in Christ is to serve.

However, good leaders know that recognition of servant efforts is actually like throwing gasoline on a fire. It confirms for servants that they are on the right track, that what they are doing matters, and that Jesus' work is being accomplished. Whether you write thank you notes, acknowledge servants before the whole group or congregation, have occasional gratitude gatherings at which you offer your thanks for servant efforts, or come up with some other means, make servant recognition a non-negotiable part of your leader practices.

Your leadership mantras (repeat and practice as many times as necessary to retrain your own thinking and approach):
- My responsibility is not only to engage servants in Kingdom work. Equally important is my commitment to encourage them with positive feedback.
- Recognition for all servants, whether brand new or longtime, will become part of my focus.
- I will become creative, enlisting help when necessary, to learn new and personal ways of acknowledging and thanking those who serve in my church or ministry—including by writing, telling stories of great servants, holding special thank-you occasions, and other means.

What If I'm Failing?

Ultimately responsible leaders also notice when a servant is not in a role that's a fit—even when the servant may not be self-aware of a shortfall. When the thrill of a servant role is significant, it becomes difficult for the servant to own any consciousness that the right gifts, strengths, skills, or spiritual maturity are not present. Or it may be that the servant's availability for or compatibility with the actual task is not congruent. Whatever the circumstances, when the criteria for success have not been fulfilled, it's time for you to help the servant find a role more in compliance with gifts and strengths.

Systems/Task Organizers and Vision Criers—pay attention to this and lean on your Spiritual Shepherd skills to truly show heartfelt appreciation to those who serve.

Those who have Spiritual Shepherd as their primary leadership component may struggle here. Ask God to show you a courageous, loving perspective of what it means to help someone connect with their most successful servant role, rather than allowing them to stay and struggle in one that's not a good fit.

"What?" you may think, "'fire' a servant? I can't do that! A servant is, after all, giving free time. I don't want to seem unappreciative or hurt anyone's feelings...."

A better tactic is to remember that in the body of Christ, it's all a process of exploring where each person can serve in an all-star capacity. A hand is not a foot or an eye or an ear. So, too, with servants. As a leader, you're responsible to do everything possible to assist servants as they find just the right spot from which they can hit a home run. In fact, it's a sin to allow a servant to continue in a role that isn't the right fit for maximum Kingdom success.

If the servant is a long-time, faithful servant who is no longer effective in the role, one approach might be to say, "Tom, you must be tired. You have held this servant position for a long time now. You have made important contributions. It seems to me that we need to allow you to shift to a new servant role, give you a break, and let someone else have the opportunity you have had to do this. Do you need a break before you start serving in a new way, or shall we start exploring that for you right away?"

If the servant resists, you may continue, "I know it has been fulfilling, and I give thanks for that! But I think that it fits with the body of Christ principle for our ministry to give others the same kind of serving opportunity you have had. It may be that you return again later for another term. Or who knows what God has been preparing you for next? I'm excited to see!"

If the servant is fairly new in the role and it's not working out, you might approach it this way: "Jennifer, I love your enthusiasm and know God is pleased that you have said yes to serving. But I'm not convinced we have found your perfect fit for the right role. You have gifts and strengths that are clearly not being utilized right now. I'd like to suggest we rotate you to try [name of the new servant task]. Let's just have you try it. I'll make sure you get the training that you need. One of the great things about our church is that we don't have any permanent servant roles—we just try different roles until we discover the one that fits the best. Let's do that with you. You have too much talent to be in a servant spot that doesn't play to your strengths."

More information on this topic is in chapter 7, "Leading Successful Change." For now, promise yourself that you'll proactively keep the church or ministry healthy by helping people out of ill-fitting servant roles, and into happier ones.

Your leadership mantras (repeat and practice as many times as necessary to retrain your own thinking and approach):

- Servants who are not succeeding in their servant role need an opportunity to move to one more appropriate for their skills and strengths.
- It's my responsibility to make sure prompt action is taken to address any situation where a servant change has become necessary.
- As servant roles are arranged, no winning or losing is involved. Rather, it's all about fitting the right persons to the right roles.

Next Steps

Now it's time to learn how to lead and to build servant teams, unpaid or paid. If you have grasped the principles of servanthood, understand the mindsets, are alert to incorporate what it takes to bring mind shifts capable of unleashing servant energy, and are knowledgeable about how to answer the questions every servant wants to know, then you are ready to move ahead. You're in the process of igniting your ministry!

Inspire your servants with the short video story of Stephanie, a believer who found her own way to serve the mission of Jesus, on the *Ultimately Responsible* DVD, chapter 4.

ON THE DVD FOR CHAPTER 4:

-Video segment by Mike Slaughter on "Servanthood"

-"Always/Nevers: What To Say To A Servant" sheet

-Video story: "Ultralive Servants" (diversity of roles)

-Video story: Gwen—"Serving Through Strengths"

-"New Ministry Idea" development worksheet

-Video story: Stephanie—"Divine Direction"

"A competent leader can get efficient service from
poor troops, while on the contrary an incapable
leader can demoralize the best of troops."
-John J. Pershing

CHAPTER

5

LEADING A TEAM

He was impressive: a senior pastor, blessed with a personality as big as Texas. Any church attendee within twenty feet was always enveloped in the radiance of his genuine warmth and enthusiasm. He had an uncanny gift for remembering names, grandchildren, and prayer requests. When he hugged you (which was every time he saw you), he looked you right in the eyes with such a pastoral heart and aura of care that you felt drawn to tell him even your deepest confessions. This pastor's persona also projected from the pulpit in an equally personal and magnetic fashion. The churches he served had always grown quickly and become large.

And yet—even though his dynamic gifts of charisma and energetic presence were undeniable, his staff and church leadership resembled a revolving door. They privately shared with me both their admiration for the pastor's vision and his ability to provide spiritual guidance as well as their frustration with him as a day-to-day manager. As a result, the accomplishment of every church's mission he led was slow and chaotic. Ongoing engagement of servants was at a minimum.

The senior pastor told me he couldn't understand why he was unable to establish stability with staff and leader longevity. "After all," he pointed out, "I'm doing the hard work of casting vision and spiritually nurturing the congregation. It shouldn't be that difficult for them to do the rest!" When asked about his leadership style and team building techniques, he brushed off any idea that some skill development might be needed. "I lead as well as any pastor, I'm sure. I'm not very detail-oriented, but I have never worried about it much. I expect the staff and leaders around me to accommodate my idiosyncrasies and my individuality. That's their job. I can't change any of that, and I don't have time to worry about it."

If you can relate to any part of this story so far, this chapter is for you. Many ultimately responsible leaders are like this one: they have never taken the time to honestly assess the state of their own leadership style and skills and create an intentional plan for improvement—let alone learn the basics of how to wisely build the teams around them (unpaid or paid). The senior pastor was a natural with primary ministry components of Spiritual Shepherd and Vision Crier, and had unconsciously come to rely on them exclusively. His skills as a Systems/Task Organizer were sorely lacking, creating havoc as every congregation he led grew larger. The solution? He did not need to become an all-star in orchestration and execution of details. What he did need to learn was a baseline comprehension and appreciation of Systems/Task Organizer skills, along with how to choose and build the right team around himself to augment that particular leadership component so desperately needed by the church.

Chapter 6 offers additional specifics to guide those who build and supervise paid staff teams.

Whether you have had a little or a lot of ministry leadership experience—you can learn what intentional leaders purposely practice in order to serve the persons for whom God has given them responsibility. All applies to both paid and unpaid settings for leaders and teams.

How Do You Lead?

The speed of the leader is the speed of the team. In ministry this means that your thoughtful, practiced, intentional leadership style; the skills you learn and practice; and your ability to build a team around yourself all directly influence the deployment and effectiveness of the servants (and staff), the ministry, and the church you lead.

Review chapter 1 to refresh yourself on the three primary ministry leadership components. Find the "Primary Ministry Leadership Component" assessment tool on the *Ultimately Responsible* DVD, chapter 1, and use it to clarify which is your most dominant component.

Only self-focused leaders who are not actively engaged in life-transforming growth in Christ take the dysfunctional attitude that it is the team's job to live with their leadership shortcomings. The statement, "Well, that's just the way I am!" has no valid place in the life of any Christian, unless it refers to spiritual gifts or natural talents with which God has endowed you. By its very nature, the life of a true, committed follower of Jesus is in process of transformation and growth into the likeness of Christ. You may not ever reach the publicly acknowledged level of a Billy Graham-type of Vision Crier, a Robert Schuller-type of Spiritual Shepherd, or a Bill Hybels-type of Systems/Task Organizer. But active, ongoing spiritual growth means you grow into harmony with the rest of the body of Christ, so that all are released to do what they do best. If you are resistant to recognizing and acknowledging changes and improvements that God may desire you to make in your leadership approach, don't expect God to be able to use you fully. God eventually goes around or sidelines leaders who resist growing and developing into their full leadership and team-building potential.

Leadership Styles

No matter what your primary leadership component, you as a leader also bring along a backpack of life experiences and assumptions that shape your style of leading others. We'll begin with defining **eight common leadership styles** I've seen play out in the church setting. These don't always present themselves in church or ministry leaders as pure styles—two or more may combine with each other. The intent is to give each of these styles a name and then arm you with knowledge about how you can transform whatever your style (or combination of styles) into greater effectiveness. Whether manifested in a paid or unpaid leadership capacity, any of these will affect the accomplishment of God's work. Think carefully as you read further about which style honestly represents you. The details of the following stories and the names of the persons involved have been adjusted for anonymity, but all represent actual situations I've observed and experienced in both paid and unpaid settings.

Leadership by Parenting

Sharla had been a stay-at-home mother during her years of raising four children. The give-and-take of keeping the peace between her brood had led her to offer indulgent, unconditional love to them, no matter what. Even when one became rebellious and violated the house rules, Sharla took the tolerant approach of listening and peacemaking, loving the naughty child back into the family dynamics rather than saying the hard things and enforcing necessary consequences. Sharla's dislike of conflict and her desire for her children's affection had produced inventive children ("spoiled," by outsiders' standards) who lacked life focus or goals but cherished the unconditional environment of the family home.

When Sharla became a team leader at her church, it was a new experience. Without leadership training, Sharla unconsciously defaulted to her parenting skills and created an unconditional environment for those on her team. Rather than providing overall missional direction, Sharla focused on understanding each team member, making exceptions to the team rules to accommodate uncooperative attitudes, and allowing team meetings to be driven by whatever complaints, criticisms, or disagreements they brought to the table—just as she did at home around the family dinner table. She slipped easily into the familiar role of peacemaker, spending long hours on the phone to explain to one team member where another team member "was coming from." Yet when the senior pastor expressed concern about negativity coming from her team members, she was fiercely defensive. Like a mother bear protecting her cubs, Sharla deflected the pastor's unease by assuring him they were a better, more special, and talented set of team members than any other team and that she would "take care of them." A year later, Sharla's team remained

As you review these eight leadership styles, evaluate not only which one you embody but also which represents any leader who has led a team on which you've served. What do you remember about how it affected the team's productivity and morale? What do you wish would have been handled differently?

relatively unproductive and self-focused. Sharla continued to be enmeshed in their individual personal issues rather than provide proactive encouragement and a challenge to grow and mature.

Leadership by Mind Reading

Everyone said Bob had graduated at the top of his seminary class. Though the years had streaked gray through his hair and well-trimmed beard, the pastor's intent gaze through small, round, silver glasses as he listened to his team members reinforced the assumption of truth to the rumor. No doubt about it, he was highly intelligent and a classic introvert. It added to his aura of authority as he stood in the pulpit each week to teach from the Scriptures.

But what he was really thinking as he stroked his beard at the team meetings was anyone's speculation. He shared little in the way of specific instruction or guidance as team members fumbled to plan details in fleshing out the pastor's overall plan. When one team member called him on the phone to ask for clarification, the secretary replied that he was busy all week and was unavailable. Another servant made an appointment with the pastor in person, shared frustration at the lack of specific direction, and received only silence and a penetrating gaze in response. Finally the pastor said, "You've been at our team meetings. If you were really sharp, you'd know what to do on your own without having to ask me. That's how I tell great servants from average ones. Great servants just know what needs to happen. They're self-starters. They don't need someone to explain it to them."

Leadership by Loyalty

Without a doubt, Charles radiated love and affection to his team. His approval was affirming and addictive, and team members found themselves willing to do anything to stay in its warm sunshine. Charles' opinions about what should happen in the ministry were strong. He encircled his team members with a sense of unity and trust. After all, Charles often repeated, "When servants join together for a common cause, anything is possible!"

All things are possible—unless, as a few team members discovered, you happened to disagree with Charles' plan. Then it became personal, a tense matter of loyalty. The meeting room temperature would shift from its customary warm acceptance to cold judgment. "You're either with me, or you're not," Charles would declare, staring at the person who had offered a contrasting opinion. His face would fill with suspicion, focused upon the dissenter. "After all I've done for you—trained you, supported you—do you mean you're not part of this mission after all?" The offending party would usually begin to reply, only to be interrupted by Charles' escalating challenge. "I have gone to the mat for you and personally chose you to be on my team. I have prayed with you, supporting you through your family crisis. I have been there for you! And now, when I need you to really help make it happen, I wonder if maybe we haven't had the relationship I thought was there after all. I believed in you and thought we were on the same team. This is how God's mission begins to fail: when someone decides not to be faithful to the leader, the one to whom God gave the vision."

At this point, the pressure was usually too great to resist. Whoever had triggered Charles' articulate call to reaffirmation of loyalty always defaulted back to Charles' plan. Charles would beam, hugging the team member and wiping tears from his eyes. "I knew you would stay with me, buddy. I just needed to make sure you were on my side! Yes, you're one of my people!"

Leadership by Command

Miriam didn't have a military background, though her team often wondered if that might have been a more suitable career track for her. From the moment she accepted the team leader role, her communication took the form of issuing orders and instructions. At every meeting, Miriam brought not only an agenda but also instructions of exactly what each team member was to do that week. When challenged, Miriam's standard response was always, "I'm in charge here, remember?" or "That's just the way it's going to be, period."

Miriam's top-down approach left her team members feeling like mindless, opinion-less slaves who were expected to carry out her every wish. It was apparent that Miriam viewed herself as superior to her team, more knowledgeable and capable. At one memorable team meeting, a member suggested a more efficient method of accomplishing a task than Miriam's customary orders had dictated. Miriam paused, then smiled condescendingly. "Wow, there are rare occasions when you all surprise me by coming up with an idea or two yourselves. And that was actually a good one. I'm impressed!"

Even though Miriam was a talented strategist and ministry architect, her CEO demeanor and refusal to allow her team any decision-making input or authority produced their passive, resentful attitudes and a lack of respect for their leader. Miriam, however, didn't mind. After all, she was the leader, above it all—and from her perspective, they were simply workers whose purpose was to scurry to accomplish her instructions.

Leadership by Inclusiveness

"Sure, we'd love to have you!" was the constant exclamation of Nancy, a jovial pastor who sought to involve as many as possible in the work of the ministry. Nancy even had an eye for enlisting those who were quiet wall-standers and others whose social skills needed development. She was agreeable whenever someone asked to assume any servant role that was open. "Sure, why not. You'll be good at it!" she encouraged, as anyone available and willing took on teaching roles, chairing committees, visiting the homebound, and even performing funerals as laypersons. Nancy saw every set of hands and every pair of feet as valuable assets to get the work of the ministry accomplished— the more, the merrier.

But her church didn't thrive. Because Nancy's core goal was to include everyone, she did not slow down to include the crucial step of making sure individuals had the right skills, experience, and spiritual maturity for the servant role they wanted. The reason? She didn't like to disappoint anyone with a no. And once servants seized a role, they usually kept it for months, even years. As a result, the quality of ministry lagged. A few church leaders approached Nancy about the need to screen servants who served in key roles, but Nancy refused point-blank. After all, she protested, didn't Jesus say we are to go after every sheep possible to bring into the fold, not just the ninety-nine but also the one last, lost one? How would individuals feel if they were told their term of service had ended, that somehow they weren't good enough for the job! The church leaders who approached Nancy tried to explain, but she wouldn't listen. The servants had all become her close friends. It was unthinkable that their feelings might get hurt over something as simple as serving at the church. After all, making sure no one's feelings were hurt was a more important priority to Nancy than whether the work of the ministry was top quality.

Leadership by Punishment

Dan seemed to have a good way with church members. He knew how to give spiritual leadership and seemed to do fine with organizing what needed to happen. When Dan invited churchgoers to join his servant teams, they usually accepted. Dan was generous with allowing servants to assume significant roles of responsibility. But one thing that puzzled the church administrative board was how servants sometimes abruptly disappeared off Dan's teams.

Insiders who teamed with Dan knew that Dan's punishment moved swiftly when a servant failed to complete a task the way Dan wanted it to happen, or if the servant chose to disagree—or simply didn't follow through. No redemption was possible. Dan punished servants who didn't go with the flow for any reason by removing them on the spot, citing to others vague grounds like, "He just wasn't spiritually mature enough yet for the role," or, "She really had a commitment problem, and that doesn't work in our ministry." What was worse, Dan's leadership influence extended to other ministry teams. He often mentioned to other team leaders that he had removed an individual for reasons he "couldn't repeat," simply saying, "Trust me on this," and advising them not to add the person to their servant teams. Servants whom Dan removed usually left the church entirely, due to the punitive nature of Dan's leadership style and the resulting shutout from any other servant opportunity. Yet those who performed to Dan's standards never realized the lurking retaliatory side of his leadership style.

Leadership by Incompetence

Thomas was thrilled to accept the leadership role for his team. He was a logical choice—an attorney by profession, with a sharp outer appearance. Thomas liked people, enjoyed the team meetings, and was excited about the mission. It wasn't difficult to recruit servants to join his team. Thomas' articulate demeanor and professionalism brought everyone initial confidence in his selection as team leader. He relished identifying himself as the team leader and always introduced himself to church newcomers with his leadership title.

However, it became painfully clear to the team members that Thomas was not up to the leadership task. His lack of experience in leading teams and organizing ministry became obvious, as did his spiritual immaturity. When a question or conflict was brought up at a team meeting, Thomas became anxious and seemed uncertain what to do. He would begin to ramble about the general importance of their work, sharing instead about his prayer time that day or a Scripture verse that had puzzled him. When asked about how to get resources for ministry work, what direction to take in accomplishing team goals, or even how to reserve a meeting room in the church building, Thomas responded by either admitting he wasn't sure or agreeing to take care of it—and then later didn't follow through. If conflict arose on the team, Thomas' low leadership courage led him to ignore it as though it didn't exist.

As a result, Thomas' team members began to go around Thomas. He became only a figurehead, irrelevant to the team's progress. Team members began to call the church secretary instead, asking the same questions of her and proceeding with plans about which Thomas had no knowledge. The church secretary was uncomfortable but liked Thomas, and she didn't think it was her place to address him about her concern.

Chapter 2 describes the north-star strategy for an intentional leader. This forms the foundation upon which this chapter's information is built. Further leadership development is limited without ongoing commitment to personal spiritual growth, community accountability, and passion to serve.

[This leadership style may also take the form of a slightly different version, "leadership by irresponsibility." These are leaders who have the schooling, training, or experience—yet through procrastination, disinterest, or other issues refuse to follow through, and thus bring about the same incompetent result.]

Leadership by Intention

Karen's leadership mantra is to "build a team environment that the best servants [or staff] will love." An early mentor in Karen's leadership learning warned her that those she led would faithfully model her attitude, words, work ethic, and focus. So Karen pays careful attention to keeping her personal walk with Christ alive and fresh, her prayer life vital, her attitude positive, and her wholistic health practices active. She assumes that by her own personal investment in a sure foundation, those who serve with her will have the right kind of example.

Karen does not envision her team as an old-fashioned hierarchy, with herself in the presiding spot. Instead she imagines herself, the leader, as the hub of a flat wheel when it comes to forming teams. She explains to those she leads that her purpose is to:
- Provide the team with spiritual nurture and challenge
- Translate the mission into practical, accomplishable steps
- Make sure everyone on the team has what they need to do their ministry work
- Provide support, teamwork, training, problem-solving, and encouragement as needed
- Lead and manage so the best servants will love the team environment

Karen doesn't see herself as superior to any person on the team. She sees herself as the servant of all, in true Christ-like behavior (Matthew 20:26-28). She works tirelessly in her role as hub, helping align the team's efforts for maximum productivity. When a team member complains, she listens carefully and helps troubleshoot the issue. Karen is careful not to use the leadership role as ammunition to think that she is more competent and more knowledgeable than her team members. Rather, she views each of them as a rich resource, all contributors to the mission, each possessed with unique strengths, gifts, and life experiences that no one else in the body of Christ brings to the table in exactly the same way. To Karen, not to take advantage of their personal and spiritual resources in the team context would be a terrible leadership failure.

Karen reminds her team regularly that there are no individual winners in Kingdom work—"we all win together or lose together." She emphasizes that everyone's contributions affect the other team members either positively or negatively. All must engage fully in the mission for God to maximize the overall team effort. No member of the body of Christ is more special or praiseworthy than the others.

Karen's motto is that when it comes to deployment of team members or servants, everyone is equally important to God, but *not everyone is equally strategic to everything*. Rather than indiscriminately assigning tasks according to who voices interest, Karen works carefully to match individuals with tasks at which they can bring their best skills and talents. She often creates mentor relationships in which a person with the right talents but little experience can team with someone more experienced who can provide training and support.

Print out a Leadership Styles worksheet to complete about your own team or ministry, as you proceed through this section of the book. It's on the *Ultimately Responsible* DVD, chapter 5.

What Great Leaders Practice: Credibility

Karen illustrates the hands-on competence of unforgettable leadership, the embodiment of what you're now aiming to learn as the one who is ultimately responsible in your setting. Let's look more in detail at Karen's approach and examine the prototype that great leaders use to shape an intentional leadership style, both in the paid and the unpaid, or servant, setting.

Think now of a time in the past when you willingly followed a leader. How did you feel when you were around the leader? What impressed you? What did you admire about the individual? What motivated you to trust the leader enough to follow?

It's the perceived *credibility* of a leader that triggers openness within the constituency to proposed new ideas and direction. Credibility on the leader's part results in trust shown by those who are led. Evaluate your current leadership approach as you consider the following concrete action steps, credibility markers, that convert leader credibility into practices you can learn.

Marker #1: You can explain the vision.
Peter M. Senge is credited with saying, "In the absence of a great dream, pettiness prevails." Healthy teams are built around shared vision, and it's the leader's responsibility to be able to articulate it and keep it at the center of all ministry efforts. Without a vision in simple, clear terms that everyone understands, a team turns inward and builds a golden calf unto itself, based on its own wishes and desires.

Check out the results that Moses faced when his "team" exchanged God's vision for their own gain (Exodus 32) and ended up with an idol (of another god) to which they had shifted their worship. The contemporary version of the golden calf might be found in your own church—in committees that exist to spend their meeting time debating the flavor of cookies to have at the next event, the color of paper onto which the worship bulletin should be copied, and whether Sunday morning coffee drinkers should be allowed to bring their cups into the sanctuary. In the absence of vision, teams forget why they were created in the first place, and small-mindedness takes over. If you lead a committee or team that struggles with such issues, look inside and focus on the vision to correct your own focus.

If you're honestly not sure why the entity you lead (ministry, team, or committee) exists, ask the person who recruited you to lead it, or ask your pastor. If you are the pastor or staff person and you can't see what the purpose or vision for an existing committee or team is, then it's time to disband it. Effective ministry work is only accomplished around vision. Without vision, we are wasting the time of Jesus' servants by keeping ineffective systems of committees going—and that's a sin.

If you're a natural **Vision Crier**, articulating the vision may come easily for you. But if not, you must intentionally plan ahead how to tie the specific work of the team into a bigger picture connection. As you prepare any team agenda, think through how each item relates to the mission the team exists to accomplish. Otherwise, the preparation you've made ahead of time may go unappreciated.

Unfortunately, an inability to explain the vision can happen at all levels of responsibility. I sat fidgeting for two straight hours as one meeting unwound at an excruciatingly slow pace. The leader, a director responsible for a dozen paid executive staff and hundreds of clergy serving in local churches, had invested months of painstaking preparation to create a carefully-crafted proposal for adding a new staff person to her executive team. She had convened a think tank of clergy from across her constituency with whom she wanted to share the proposal and receive feedback. Now, if ever, was an occasion for this leader to provide an authoritative, positive, and persuasive case for what she fervently believed was the right vision for improving the quality of local church ministry in her state.

Yet the director, an individual gifted in strategic thinking and high energy, now sat silently as an assistant shared her written proposal with the group. She sat silently as the meeting's attendees began to ask questions and, without receiving real answers, proceeded to dismantle the proposal out of ignorance of its place in any overall vision. The discussion began to drift far afield from the subject of the proposed new position and turned to negativity and frustration with the current denominational system. Still not a word came from the leader to rally the group around the big-picture vision and the proposal's purpose to help accomplish it.

At only a single point, the leader responded to a challenge that the proposal received, yet she quickly concluded her remarks with, "But I'm not trying to sway or convince anyone either way. It's the decision of this group." That statement effectively gave away the last of her leadership credibility and influence to the various opinions, some of them uninformed, present in the room that day. Finally, her assistant spoke up near the end of the meeting's two-hour time allotment in a panicked last-ditch effort to gain support. "We here in the director's office think this is the only way to go for the future," she desperately blurted. "It will be impossible to truly raise the effectiveness of our local churches without someone who works full-time in helping orchestrate this. We'll never make progress if this doesn't get approved!"

The room fell silent. One opinionated pastor, who had only moments earlier eloquently discredited the proposal, expressed surprise. "Well, why didn't you say so before? Actually, I think the proposal is okay." And to the director he said, "Do you really feel strongly about this proposal going forward?" And she replied, "Well, yes…I do. But I don't want to overly influence the group today. You are the people with wisdom."

If your strongest leadership component is **Spiritual Shepherd**, think about how to couch the vision in language that ties it to the team members' spiritual call. If you're naturally a **Systems/Task Organizer**, put it on your checklist to reiterate the purpose and direction of the team at every gathering, so you'll remember to do that before getting started on the nuts and bolts of team business.

As I looked around the room, I saw no one, other than the director herself, who would have possibly had the inside perspective of the internal dynamics of the executive staff. I saw no one who had been in the work team meetings that had taken place to create the masterful document before us that day. I saw no one who had done the same careful national research on how to help increase local church effectiveness and what kind of staff position it would take to help organize it. All present at the meeting were solo pastors of small and medium-sized churches, along with two retired pastors. I was mystified about how this eclectic group who had been invited to the think tank meeting could have anywhere near the professional wisdom and acuity of the director, our leader, in their ability to judge the viability of the proposal. Yet we left the meeting without hearing even one statement of her knowledge, insight, or the overall vision of where the aim was to go. Afterward in the hallway outside the meeting room, the director stepped up to me privately. "Whew!" she said. "That meeting was a miracle! I'm so glad the proposal ended up getting positive feedback. I don't know what we would have done if it hadn't—I've worked on this for months! It's the only way we are ever going to get anywhere."

Great leaders get the vision named and help team members connect how their specific work is all part of accomplishing God's bigger picture. Write it out for yourself if you need to, and read it at the beginning of every team gathering. When your team is at a decision point, refer to the vision and ask, "Is this proposal in accordance with accomplishing what God has brought us together to do?" Think of yourself, the leader, as the compass that consistently indicates the overall direction.

Marker #2: Your leadership attitude is contagious.

Find a printable copy of the "Rights vs. Responsibilities" graphic on the *Ultimately Responsible* DVD, chapter 5, to print off for those you lead.

Whatever demeanor you demonstrate as you react to surprising obstacles, resistant individuals, or roadblocks will be the demeanor that your team members, paid and unpaid, will adopt. A co-worker arrived at the door of my office waving the printout of an angry e-mail from one of our most talented adult education teachers. The teacher was disgruntled because she had forgotten to let us know about some teaching supplies she needed, and felt unprepared in her classroom the evening before as a result. Yet her e-mail (unjustly) blamed my co-worker for the oversight.

As team leader, I had a choice. I could have said to my co-worker, "Wow, what's wrong with this woman? She is really out to lunch. Zing her back with an email that lets her know in no uncertain terms that it's her fault, not yours!" With a reply like that, I would have immediately given my co-worker permission to become angry and retaliatory towards the teacher. It would have given her an excuse to feel superior to one of our servants.

But instead, I quickly thought through how to keep my colleague's servant leadership attitude intact, keeping her connected to her call to serve our servants, not to look down on any of them. So what I said was, "Hmmmm…I wonder how the miscommunication happened between the two of you? I'll bet she did feel frustrated not to have everything she needed, since she places such a high value on teaching her class well—and we certainly appreciate that. Why don't you email her and apologize for whatever communication breakdown happened. It's really not necessary to spend time trying to pinpoint whose fault it was. Then maybe you can suggest a new route by which she can alert you by a certain day of the week about her upcoming classroom needs. Come up with a schedule that you can both agree to and put on your calendar to remember. Or ask her if she has a better idea on how the two of you can communicate about her needs every week so that she will feel totally prepared and supported—that might help also."

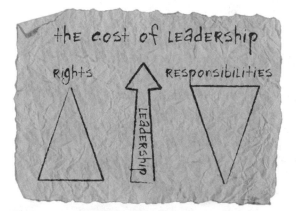

Make a habit of giving the benefit of the doubt—believing the best of individuals, seeing their strengths and gifts, and looking for solutions—rather than nitpicking for what you can disparage. The purpose of criticizing others is only an unhealthy attempt to make yourself feel smarter, more important, and superior. Choose to keep your servant attitude: you are in your leader role to serve others, not to have others serve you. The way down is the way up, according to Jesus. And as your leadership responsibilities increase, you give up more and more of your rights and privileges. This is the path of Christ-like leadership, lived out through you.

Practice a servant-leader attitude in every way you can. If you're physically capable of walking, park in the furthest parking place away from the church door, in order to give others the more convenient spots. Have you "earned" the right to park in the closest opportune place? Perhaps. Is it modeling the servant style of our true leader, Jesus? No. Make certain no one on your team has a task you would not be willing to do yourself if necessary. Hold yourself to a higher standard than you hold even your team members in integrity, morality, faithfulness, and positivity. Never gossip; keep confidences. Be a solution-finder and a problem-solver, not an obstacle of negativity for those with whom you serve. React calmly to whatever calamity or issue is presented to you by your team—paid or unpaid. It's a liability when a leader is so reactionary that a team fears (or avoids) telling him or her what is happening! Practice presenting words and an attitude that convince those whom you lead that a solution will be found, God will guide, resources will be provided, and a path through whatever is ahead will show itself. Your team desperately needs you to demonstrate contagious confidence in both God's provision and adequacy as well as the team's ability to forge ahead and conquer.

Marker #3: You're willing to look and talk like a leader.
Leadership credibility is established through a range of practices, and one sometimes overlooked is a willingness to embody the look of a leader whom others can respect.

Betty, a deeply committed Christian and married mother of two, was hired at her church as the Christian education director. The thrilling milestone of entering a paid ministry position was evident through her enthusiasm at quickly becoming knowledgeable in the areas of her new employment responsibilities. She bought several books on Christian education and read them immediately. During the first month of employment, Betty also attended a two-day conference that featured specialized training and displays of new curriculum for adult and children's classes. While there, Betty took the initiative to meet other staff colleagues who worked at churches around her state. Her hope was to network with them regularly as a means of keeping herself current in the field, eventually forming a ministry-accountability group together.

Entering the workplace after eleven years as a stay-at-home mom, Betty looked every bit the part of a frazzled parent of busy adolescent children. She showed up at work and committee meetings with hair uncombed, often wearing gray sweatpants, tennis shoes, and tee shirts pulled from her husband's "day off clothing" drawer. For Betty, feeling comfortable was important, plus it made things easier for her when she got home and quickly transitioned into an evening of fixing supper, helping her sons with school projects, caring for the dogs, and fitting in housework tasks. But for the congregation and the unpaid leaders who worked with Betty, her appearance was distracting. To some, it seemed disrespectful to the importance of the leadership to which she was called. Others misjudged Betty's competence because she just "didn't look the part," as one unimpressed church member frequently complained.

It was not only her disheveled appearance that transmitted a false perception of disorganized leadership. Betty chatted candidly before and after team meetings with church members about her husband's up and down income as an insurance salesman, the debt load from old college student loans under which they still staggered, and their frequent arguments about her ballooning weight and dislike of exercise. She received and made long personal calls during the workday, arguing with her children or dealing with personal affairs within easy earshot of hallway passers-by.

Betty rightly suspected she didn't have the respect of her leaders and co-workers. But she was mystified by what the reasons might be. Hadn't her work at the church raised the educational programs to a whole new level? Didn't she stay up-to-date with the latest new curricula, church educational trends, and teacher training techniques?

Fortunately, Betty's credibility as a leader could be improved by habits she could change. Unfortunately, she remained oblivious until eight months after she started her church position. Betty finally confided her frustrations to the ministry-accountability group she formed from the area-wide colleagues she met back at the two-day conference, who were now good friends. "I'm just as competent as anyone on our staff team and certainly have been much more successful than my predecessor in this position!" she told them. "But the administrative board always ignores me at the monthly meetings, like I'm invisible. And even though it would make sense to have me present on the platform occasionally in worship services, maybe reading the Scripture or even giving announcements, I'm never invited like the other staff. What do you think is going on? Do they just not like me at my church?"

One of Betty's colleagues cared enough about her to respond honestly. "Betty, being a credible leader means more than just being knowledgeable about your job and being spiritually mature. It's also about professionalism. Does anyone care that you always wear sweatpants and tennis shoes, even on Sundays? Certainly the church represents the unconditional love of God for all God's children, but remember: that doesn't mean the human beings who fill the church will always unconditionally accept everything—a careless appearance, for example. That goes for what we as leaders talk about, too—not everything is appropriate for every setting. Maybe looking the part and talking the part are your next steps of growth."

The following two-hour transparent discussion with her ministry-accountability group changed Betty's entire perspective about the type of credible perception she wanted to bring to her leadership role. Never before had it occurred to her that choices about appearance, healthy lifestyle practices, and appropriateness of conversational topics with the congregation were part of great leadership. Betty had to decide it was worth the time and effort to change her habits: to get up earlier in order to take more care with her appearance, to find time privately over lunch break to deal with family matters on the phone, and to allow church members to share about themselves before and after meetings rather than using them as a captive audience to hear all about her own personal affairs. Betty's credibility with the church staff and the congregation improved dramatically, thanks to her willingness to look and talk like a leader.

Marker #4: You tell stories and nourish possibility.

Use stories to enhance your leader credibility. They give show-and-tell, tangible evidence of what God is doing in and through your ministry and point out what everyone involved is entitled to celebrate together. Sharing stories about how the common intended purpose is being actively fulfilled gives everyone permission to personalize the ministry success, marvel at God's supernatural work in and among you, and encourage others to become storytellers who bear witness to their own miracles of grace.

Telling stories also accomplishes the creation of a "possibility atmosphere" in your team or ministry. Many leaders mistakenly focus exclusively on specific planning and deployment rather than on nurturing hope. A profound difference exists between *what is* and *what if.* Knowing when and how to fuel an atmosphere of possibility is an essential part of leadership credibility. Stories help nurture openness to exciting possibilities of what God can do. Jesus himself was a master storyteller. Stories helped his listeners visualize the possibilities God had for their lives and their faith—and they will do the same for yours.

Systems/Task **Organizers** may prefer to cover the nuts and bolts when it comes to explaining future plans and possibilities to their group. While those details are always important, consider how to assume the mantle of a **Vision Crier** and awaken the desire for new potential and hope within others.

As the new leader of a small ministry that I hoped to jumpstart, I was convinced that the only way to disrupt the status quo environment was to assist as many as possible in beginning a spiritual-growth spurt. I was familiar with an opportunity that could provide such growth: a weekend away on retreat. I had the promotional materials ready to share and group transportation reserved. But I feared the monumental task of trying to convince an inertia-bound group of adults who had never been on a retreat before that boarding a bus for a fifteen-hour (one way) bus ride to get to a place they had never been, and never heard of, was an appealing idea.

So that next Sunday morning when the ministry attendees met together for class, I held up a red maple leaf. It was a gorgeous souvenir of autumn, carefully carried home, pressed and dried between the pages of a thick book. For a few moments before I spoke, all eyes in the room feasted upon its fragile beauty.

> This leaf symbolizes something far greater to me than what it is—a beautiful leaf. It came from a place like none other. On a tree-covered hilltop deep in the Ozarks of Arkansas sits a conference center called Mount Sequoyah. And every year for the last thirteen years of my life, I have invested one long weekend each fall at a very special spiritual life retreat held at that sacred place.
>
> Every year for thirteen years I have sat on the porch of Mount Sequoyah's Parker Hall with friends I've met there in years gone by who also return to this sacred place, laughing and talking as we drink hot cider. Every year I join my voice with others as we sing our praises in worship. I listen as we learn from speakers who speak truth and wisdom for faith and ministry. And every year I have a personal ritual. I take time in the early morning to walk alone with God the perimeter road around the hilltop of Mount Sequoyah, scuffing my feet through the red and golden leaves that have fallen, doing a review of everything that's taken place in the year since last I was there. I feel the warmth of the sunlight filtering through the branches above. I gaze out across the foliage-covered countryside from the high point of the cross at the lookout point. And I think the long, long thoughts of God about where I've been, where God will lead me next, and who God is now calling me to be.
>
> For those who have already made the journey to Mount Sequoyah, seeing this leaf would have required no explanation. All those from everywhere around the country who have taken the Mount Sequoyah fall pilgrimage I've described share a bond of memories and powerful God-experiences that no real words can capture. All it takes is the symbol of this leaf to remember and to look forward to the next time you journey to Mount Sequoyah—to the setting like none other where you can hear God speak truth and direction into you.

This year, I'd like to invite all of you to go with me to "the Mountain," as some fondly call it. I'd like you to join me as we travel via bus for a weekend from which you will return changed forever. Will you make new friends? Absolutely. Will you learn and grow, laugh and have fun? Without question. And you, too, can take a walk alone with God at sunrise, where you're finally away from the hubbub of the usual routine and are where you can hear that Voice clearly. And then you, like me and countless others, will share a bond through bringing back a red maple leaf to help you remember for the rest of your life.

I've put informational brochures on the table by the door, for those of you the Spirit may be prompting to answer this call to journey to "the Mountain," to come away with me this fall to Mount Sequoyah. We have chartered a bus for the trip. And I think there's a seat on it just for you.

The room was completely silent when I finished. After class was over, I stood talking with a few persons as everyone began to leave. But soon the conversation was interrupted. "Pastor Sue, where did you say you put those brochures about the Mount Sequoyah retreat?" one man asked. I quickly looked at the table where I had stacked a few dozen—and they were all gone! "I'll bring more next week," I assured him. "Well, could you mail me one instead?" he asked. "I want to make sure that no one else gets my seat on that bus...."

Meet **Jane**, one of those who pursued possibility and took the bus ride to Mount Sequoyah, through her short video story on the *Ultimately Responsible* DVD, chapter 5.

When I think back now on the extremely long bus ride, I don't remember whether the seats were comfortable or whether I got much sleep as we drove. What I hold fast are the memories of a full bus, of many who left as strangers and returned as close friends. I remember watching each of them step out when we finally arrived and look around in wonder at the place in the Ozarks that held great possibility for profound encounter with God. I cherish the recollections of their laughter, their camaraderie and the long walks they chose to take alone around the perimeter road. Most of all, I recall my amazement at seeing them gather handfuls of red maple leaves to press in the pages of their Bibles on the long ride home. Upon our return, the bonded Mount Sequoyah sojourners formed a leadership coalition that indeed drove the ministry forward with explosive growth.

Visual Leadership: The Church Leader As ImageSmith by Rob Weber, © 2004, Abingdon Press, is a helpful book that teaches how to lead with stories.

Include stories as you lead, and commit yourself to the intentional creation of an atmosphere of God-possibility in your church or ministry to which individuals can respond. Do you always talk of what can't happen, or do you instead cast the intoxicating spell of what might? Just as Jesus used loaves and fishes and bread and wine, use symbols, logos, and anything else that connects your group with hope and the magnetism of potential up ahead. Believe and remind the persons you lead that, in Christ, this is the best and most important season of their lives so far, they have never been better prepared for what God has for them next, this is their time, and their story will be the next one told to inspire others with hope.

Marker #5: It's not about you.

The Purpose-Driven Life by Rick Warren reminds everyone of this fact, and it's not only true in your spiritual life. It's also true of great leaders, for whom another identity marker is keeping the team focused upon the mission rather than shifting all the focus to themselves. Unfortunately, some who receive a leadership role mistakenly see themselves as the spotlighted, center-stage dancer in the entire production. They see their team members as admiring fans with whom to share all about themselves—their thoughts, their relationships, and their personal issues—at every team meeting. Leaders who don't understand this identity marker insist on always having the microphone, the podium, the recognition, and the final word. Let's face the truth—it is a satisfying feeling when individuals want to serve on your team in order to spend time with you! But a great leader avoids falling prey to the ego-fueling temptation of allowing team members to attach themselves primarily to him or herself as the center of the ministry.

Credible leaders are masters at instead helping their flock bond around shared identity and mission. As a gathering of individuals grows into a group formed with an "us" identity, a uniting of powerful energy as God's community emerges. Leaders whose credibility is strong have learned the art of coalescing their followers around mutual purpose.

Great leaders do not take advantage of their team members with unrealistic or selfish expectations. "I almost lost my marriage," a youth pastor admitted apologetically as he explained why he had left the staff team of a well-known church that televised regionally in his state. "But Pastor [the senior pastor] did teach us that our responsibility was to be there for him, whatever he needed, whenever he needed it. I took that seriously. It was the summer he needed the staff team to come help plant the large flower garden on his estate that really hurt my family life. My wife had just given birth to our first child. She didn't understand why the choir director needed to be out planting the pastor's flowers! But we all knew that if Pastor wasn't happy, no one would be happy. And, of course, for the sake of the church we had to keep him happy, so we dropped everything and responded whenever he told us to." What a tragic story of a senior pastor who ignored this leadership credibility marker!

Instead of *personality-driven* ministry, *mission-driven* ministry keeps the team members focused upon the purpose for which they serve. It's not personality-dependent. In fact, I think of team leaders as middle managers in Kingdom work. Middle managers can come or go as God calls, but the Kingdom work they facilitate ideally continues on uninterrupted. If you retain a middle-manager's mindset, you'll avoid promoting team members' allegiance to you rather than to your collective God-dream.

Marker # 6: You share authority and responsibility.

Ben was a go-getter when it came to heading up the missions committee. He worked long and hard to set up meticulous files, one for each missionary that the church supported financially. He faithfully attended the quarterly denominational mission gatherings to represent his congregation, took notes, and e-mailed them to his fellow mission committee members. He talked to the cyber-ministry team in charge of the Web site for his church and gave them instructions on how to create a Web page on the Internet with photos and bios of the homegrown missionaries whom God had raised out of the church family.

All seemed to be going well, except with the other mission committee members. They had nothing to do other than to sit through the monthly mission meetings and hear Ben talk about what he'd done. Whenever any of the members asked to help or offered to do anything, Ben was quick to refuse. "No, that really needs to be done by the committee chair," he replied to one willing offer. "Have that already under control, no problem!" he triumphantly rebuffed another. The message was subtle but unmistakable: Ben's opinion was that his committee members weren't capable of doing the "real" work to support missions at the church. Despite his efficient competence, Ben's leader credibility was low. And when his term was up, Ben's committee was happy to get a new leader.

Martha was like a breath of fresh air. "I think we need to fully take advantage of the talent we have represented on this team," she told them at the first meeting. Their entire evening was spent giving each an opportunity to share about particular areas of passion regarding missions and what dreams each had for the future of missions within the church family. Martha made careful notes as each one talked, and climaxed the evening by distributing responsibilities. "What an exciting idea you have about supporting child protection in the Sudan!" she said to one. "Can you find out more about what we could realistically do to assist them as a congregation by next month's meeting?" "Yes, you are right," she agreed with another. "It would really encourage our missionaries in the field if we identified five church members who would commit to staying in touch with each one of them every few weeks. Do you want to sketch out a potential plan on how we could make that happen and bring it back next month for discussion and decision?"

If your primary leadership component is **Systems/Task Organizer**, Marker #7 may come naturally to you. If you're a **Spiritual Shepherd** or **Vision Crier** at heart, however, it's perfectly acceptable to team with someone who can make sure details are completed—as long as you continue to take ultimate responsibility to make sure the task is carried through.

At the end of Martha's year as missions chair, her credibility with the committee members was high as they begged her to renew for another term. Her willingness to see the leadership role as one of facilitation, service, and teamwork had brought them a powerful sense of shared responsibility and authority. Unlike Ben, Martha had a mindset of collective community and purpose that made it natural for her to include everyone in on the action.

Marker #7: Communicate, communicate, communicate.

Karen, the "Leadership by Intention" example from the previous "Leadership Styles" section, is fond of emphasizing that "communicate, communicate, and communicate" are the three most important tasks of a leader. Those on your team must be convinced that you have heard them and will respond. Great leaders prioritize communication by a variety of venues so that all involved can stay well informed. Knowing what's going on reassures team members that they are on the right track and that their input is valued, and it motivates them to move forward.

What form of communication is most important in your leadership role? If it's through e-mail or voice mail, try to respond within twenty-four hours. On e-mail, copy all players on the original message so they know the answer or that the issue was addressed. If project plans change or more information surfaces about a meeting made by the team, communicate it as soon as appropriate. Remember that bad news never improves with age.

Let your team see you taking notes during meetings and in hallway conversations with any team member; it will give them confidence that you're paying attention to details. Make sure you follow up on the notes! Provide a phone number where you or another contact can be reached should urgencies arise (make sure your team can count on someone to answer). If you're a staff leader and will be out of the office, tell someone when you're leaving and when you'll return; leave a note by your office door as well as a message on your outgoing voice mail stating this same information.

No matter which is your primary leadership component, cultivate your **Spiritual Shepherd** skill in order to provide safe space for your team members and the ministry you serve. Confidentiality is essential, except for a few select scenarios governed by law (check with an attorney for specifics).

As important as thorough communication is, great ministry leaders also develop discretion in terms of who needs to know what. Part of leadership is the awareness that you don't tell everyone everything. Full personal emotional disclosure to your team members who look to you for leadership—and to those you serve who look to you for competence—may not always be appropriate, for example. (Save that for those in your personal accountability or cell group.) Leaders don't have the luxury of wearing their hearts on their sleeves about every thought or feeling. In your discretion, include the discipline of keeping an important confidence if necessary. Team members lose respect for a leader who cannot demonstrate their ability to offer safe space.

Marker #8: You resolve conflict as it happens.

The tension hung like a wet towel over the atmosphere of the meeting room. Team members sat like statues frozen in time, all eyes riveted on me as one of their long-time team members named Kendra proceeded to deliver the most scathing berating I have ever received as a leader. "It doesn't matter to me whether you are a pastor or not. You have no people skills, have no idea what this ministry needs, and never follow through on anything. You never even return voice mails we leave you! You are trying to ruin everything we have ever built in the great traditions of this ministry, and you don't care. We know how to run our own ministry, and you don't. You're not even a nice person to know or talk to—and everyone here knows it!"

I quickly took stock of the situation. I had become the leader of this team of servants only two months before. Kendra had been provoked to anger that day by my presentation of the four levels of a contagious ministry movement, and the team members' subsequent discussion of what could happen if they shifted approaches in order to ignite such a movement in their ministry efforts. It threatened Kendra's sense of familiarity and control when I talked of new attendees, new servants, and renewed outreach. Rather than simply stating that the new information made her uncomfortable, she leveled her anger straight at me in front of everyone by mounting an aggressive personal attack with a flock of unfounded accusations.

I felt unappreciated and frustrated inside. Didn't she—didn't they— understand I was working to help their tiny, ingrown ministry group become an outwardly-focused God movement? For a brief moment I felt the temptation to get up and walk out, to leave and drive home and let them go on as they were before I ever became their leader. Then I considered merely ignoring her outburst, acting like it never happened, and going on with the discussion. But I had already learned that though ultimately responsible leaders don't seek conflict, they have to be willing to proactively seek peaceful resolution to team conflict as promptly as possible. I took the first step I'd learned about how to diffuse and resolve differences.

1. Clarify what the issue is.

Looking across the table directly at Kendra, I stayed calm. "Wow! Well, that felt like you were attacking me personally, but since the information I presented today wasn't about me personally—it was about the contagious ministry movement model—I am going to assume what you are really angry about has something to do with that. Am I right?"

I heard someone in the room let out a sigh of relief. By shifting the discussion back to the issue of conflict, I had re-engaged the entire team. "Darn right I don't like the model," the angry leader shot back. "Well, tell me what you don't like about it, and then we can all share our opinions," I invited her.

2. Establish healthy ground rules for talking through issues of conflict.

Then I turned and looked at everyone. "Here will be our ground rules for this discussion—and any others in the future, when we don't all agree. Let's respect them together." I wrote these in abbreviated fashion on the white board so all could see as I named each one:

- We are all sharing our opinions about the future of our ministry together. It is not about any of us personally. We are only talking about the ideas presented.
- Our opinions are not right or wrong; they are simply opinions. It's okay if we don't all share the same opinion.
- Our goal is to figure out what accomplishes the mission most effectively for those we are called to serve.
- It's not what each of us wants personally; it's what would best serve our constituency. We are not here just to please or serve ourselves.
- There's more than one way to do most anything, including approaches to doing ministry together. It's not wrong or sinful to try new things.
- No ministry approach is wrong unless it violates Scripture or discriminates against any of God's children.
- Remember that conflicts about power and authority neither honor God nor respect the priorities of Jesus.

"And," I said in conclusion, "there's nothing we are called to do as a team that is about personal power or authority issues. If there is, our team has a problem bigger than we realize. In Christ, our egos and desires for attention and power are now dead, buried, and out of the way. We are new persons in Christ. We are called to serve together, work together, and value each other. If that's not where you are, maybe serving on this team is not for you. Maybe serving at one of our events might be better, becoming a servant who helps out with what our ministry is doing. Being on a team like this where we are responsible for charting the future of the ministry requires greater spiritual maturity and willingness to work together. It's a more serious call."

Words of agreement came from around the room when I finished. Kendra, however, angrily picked up her coat and walked out the door. I didn't follow her. I told the group that I would call her later, and simply proceeded with the meeting and its discussion. By the end of the hour, the team had decided to reformat their ministry and work to develop the contagious ministry movement model. They were positive and enthusiastic.

3. Work to resolve team conflict and quickly find healthy solutions.
That evening I called Kendra at home but only got her voice mail. I tried again for the next two days, and finally she answered. "You and I have a personality conflict!" she started our conversation. "We can't work together!"

"That disappoints me, because I'd like for us to be able to serve together," I told her. "But I understand; not everyone teams comfortably with everyone. I've got an idea, though. I hear you enjoy the mission trips the ministry has taken each year. Would you like to coordinate a special team of servants to focus exclusively on developing them more fully? I will continue with the leadership team, and you can invest in the mission trip planning—you'll be a specialist. I think this would really maximize the gifts you bring to serving."

It's best to bring along another leader when meeting someone for conflict resolution. This provides accountability and helps assure integrity on your part. Meet with your partner ahead of the meeting to pray and to go over the communication you plan to employ with the angry party. And don't let things get personal! Stay focused on the issue.

Kendra liked this idea, and it acknowledged the fact that some personalities don't work well together. We implemented the plan. But unfortunately, as the ministry's goals shifted over the following months and contagious ministry strategy resulted in attendance growth, Kendra became outspoken in her negativity. She began to spend every evening on the phone, calling those she knew at church to complain about what was happening. I received near-daily reports from concerned ministry attendees who had been offended by Kendra's vocal and unconstructive critique she shared at every event.

4. Take responsibility to keep the ministry or church safe space.
When Kendra's criticism escalated and became directed personally at several faithful servants on the leadership team, I took action. I asked Kendra to meet together with me and another staff person. We met at the church, neutral ground for everyone. I opened the meeting with prayer.

"Kendra, you have been a member of this church for some time," I told her. "We would like to keep you as a positive part of our ministry for many more years. But you are unhappy and critical about all of our newest initiatives. What will it take to help you get yourself back on track?"

"Well, if everything went back to the way it was six months ago, all would be fine with me!" she replied. "I've always been one of the ministry's leaders, you know. So I have a right to my own opinion, you said."

"You absolutely have that right, but when you're using negativity in order to destroy others' focus upon what God has called them to do, you've misused it and you'll have to stop. If you continue, you will need to take a break from participating in any part of the ministry's activities until you have worked through your anger and can bring a positive attitude instead."

"You can't throw me out of this ministry! This is a church, and anyone can come!" Kendra was caught completely off guard. She was confused, thinking the nature of God's unconditional love somehow meant it was permissible for her to become destructive and aggressively distracting within the community of God's faithful.

"We're not throwing you out. You're taking a break for a while, let's say six months. We'll talk again in six months, and if you see this ministry as a place where you can thrive and contribute in a positive way, then we'll go forward with your attendance again." Kendra was shocked and left the room slowly. That afternoon I wrote Kendra a kind letter summarizing the message of our meeting so that we all had a record of the criteria necessary for Kendra's return to participation at that ministry. I weathered weeks of feedback from ministry attendees that Kendra's version of the conversation was that I "threw her out" of the ministry. I wasn't surprised, and, though her comments were aimed at me, I focused on remembering that her unhappiness actually stemmed from the new ministry changes and growth.

5. Aim for healthy restoration if at all possible.
I sent Kendra a friendly e-mail every month, asking her how she was doing and reminding her I was praying for her. Though she attended weekend worship services and still participated in her cell group, it was nearly a year before Kendra contacted me and said she was ready to return as a participant to the ministry whose leadership she had left. "Sure, Kendra—we would be glad to have you back. Do you think you are seeing things in a more positive light now?" I asked. "I'm ready to be open to that," she answered. "I think change is hard for me, and I took it out on you last year. I apologize."

I believe someone like Kendra may be in leadership or service at your church or ministry right now, and I encourage you to take these steps to address and resolve the conflict. If you don't, the valuable energy of your team will be siphoned off into concern and worry about the situation rather than on what they are called to do.

Marker #9: You get decisions made and details covered.
More complaints about team leaders revolve around this marker than any of the others. The concerns voiced by team members fall into one of two categories. **The first** is that the team leader either fails to see or fails to follow through on crucial particulars necessary for team members to do the work of the ministry.

"Those things just aren't important to me!" I heard a pastor retort to one of his staff team members who had challenged him about his lack of follow-through on details he'd agreed to complete. "Yes, but they are to me!" she answered. Represented in their brief, heated exchange is the summary of what great leaders know and prioritize: the criteria for successful detailed follow through is set by the needs of your team, not whether you personally think details are important or necessary. As leader, you give up your rights to choose to invest your time on only the things you care about, and you instead assume the broad mantle of servanthood as you stay faithful to focus on what the team needs from you for them to succeed. Your faithfulness in this area is one factor that builds credibility with your team and constituency. Related to this is timeliness in finalizing decisions. Even if you're not adept at making a decision on the spot, give your team a time frame within which you will finalize a decision—and then stick to it. Remember to communicate details and decisions to those who need to know.

The second category of common complaints related to this leadership marker springs from whether you are a status quo team leader or a possibility leader. Status quo leaders are glued to completion of details and decisions with which they are familiar, have done before, and feel confident.

John had devoted several years to serving through his church's men's ministry. From the start he had served at every event, quickly gaining responsibility due to his reliable Systems/Task Organizer skills. Over time John became an excellent historian on the men's ministry, keeping detailed records in multiple files on everything the men's ministry had ever staged. When John eventually became the team leader, he constantly utilized his file notes to guide every decision the team tried to make. "Yes, we did something like that two years ago," he would say. "Let's stick to that plan. We have it ready to go and know everything that needs to happen from my records." If someone suggested a new idea, John was quick to remind everyone that, after all, it would be easier to go with what had been done last year. "Yes, Father's Day is important. But I think the fathers liked just fine the picnic we held at the park last year. Why change something that worked well? After all, the picnic will be easy to do again this year since we've already done it before. I even have the lists of servants from last year, so we know exactly who did what. We can just call them and use them again." John's team members became resentful, then apathetic. Their leader, though enthusiastic about their mission to reach men, had a clamp blocking any new surges of creativity from the team.

John's feelings were hurt the next year, when his term of team leadership was up and a new leader was put in place. After all, didn't his extensive files and records entitle him to tenure? But Ted, the new leader, was a radical change to the men's ministry. Ted valued the history of men's ministry and the mission they had accomplished in the past. He worked to uphold the traditions that were still effective, but he challenged his team to pray about new possibilities they could explore to outreach further and more strategically.

If you're a **Spiritual Shepherd,** you may fear hurting a team member's strong feelings, like John's. Learn to follow Ted's example of non-confrontational leadership: acknowledge the team member's opinion and also affirm the opportunity for other perspectives to be voiced.

"What new thing might God be encouraging us to try?" Ted would ask at each team meeting. John, still attending the team's planning meetings, would chime in every time: "Well, last year we did a breakfast [or other effort]. I see no reason we need to change that." "We don't need to change anything for the sake of change only," Ted would reply calmly, "But we do need to be open to the freshness of the Spirit's direction. God is always in the business of making all things new. Let's explore whether this is one of those times." Ted's words gave the rest of the group permission to brainstorm and discuss, even though John's face would resemble a storm cloud. Ted knew that John was capable of stalemating the team with his tenacious hold on the familiar status quo, even when he was not the team leader anymore. So Ted made sure he was always ready to speak up and give the team permission to dream whenever John tried to close down the discussion by reports of "what we did last year."

Great leaders help decisions happen by tactfully yet directly keeping negativity and naysayers from blocking the forward flow of progress. Remember, your team expects you to do this. If you don't, team dysfunction and futility will result.

Marker #10: You care about and invest in your team members.
In the pursuit of accomplishing ministry mission, some leaders charge ahead with project tasks and de-prioritize efforts to connect personally with team members. The dream of igniting a ministry to encompass large numbers of persons and orchestrating spectacular outreaches pushes some leaders to view team members only as co-workers in the mission, rather than as individuals whose personal lives and spiritual journeys matter.

I had been invited to train a women's ministry leadership team at a neighboring church and was impressed by the group of nine women waiting for me when I arrived. The team leader was easy to identify. She was younger than the rest, with short, dark hair; businesslike attire; and high energy. Though I was early, the team was already seated around a large round table, with one chair open for me. The leader pointed me to my place right next to her and immediately launched the meeting. "Pastor Sue is here today to train us on how to recruit more servants.

Sue, go ahead and get started. We only have till noon, so we don't want to waste a moment of our time."

I felt unsettled. I had been in the room less than sixty seconds and had no idea who these women were or what their context for ministry was like. I had no idea even what their goals were, yet their leader had instructed me to get started with the training program. "Wait," I protested. "You all know who I am, but I don't know any of you. I think we'll enjoy our morning together more if I can get to know you a little first."

The team leader frowned. "Well, we already know each other! Don't worry, you're fine. Just go ahead. Really! We want to hear you talk, not ourselves."

I persisted. "Thank you, but I think I'll do better with my presentation if I first have a sense of who you are and what you're about. Since you're right next to me and you're the leader, why don't you begin? We'll each take just a minute. Tell me your name, how long you've been part of this leadership team, and something about your family."

Remember that you, the team leader, are the **Spiritual Shepherd**. No matter how great your inertia towards task accomplishment or dreaming up the vision, you must also provide for spiritual and emotional nurture to enable your team to grow.

The leader hesitated, then gave in. "Okay. My name is Nancy, and I'm married with two small children. I've been the leader of this team for ten months, and I joined it because I thought our women's ministry seemed old and tired and needed new energy and motivation. I've worked hard on that, as these women can tell you. We've done a new project every single month so far, and I've put them through their paces! Now it's your turn—only one minute each," she turned and reminded the older woman seated next to her.

There was a long pause, and Nancy tapped her pen on the table impatiently in the silence. Finally the next woman spoke slowly and hesitantly. "I'm Nadine." Another long pause. "My husband of forty-three years passed away a year ago this month, and I'm so lonely sometimes I don't think I can make it another day..."

The leader's head snapped as she turned to gaze at Nadine, her mouth open in surprise. "I, well…" she fumbled. "I didn't know that, about your husband passing away and all…."

The agenda of our morning together instantly changed, as Nadine shared more of her pain and ongoing struggle, and the women on the team surged together to support her and share honestly about their own lives. The leader Nancy was quiet at first, but she soon used her Systems/Task Organizer leadership component to begin organizing the group to surround Nadine with supportive initiatives: one would take her to the grief group that week, another invited her to join their family for Thanksgiving dinner. We closed at noon with prayer, going around the circle and praying specifically for each woman's personal needs. Nancy walked me to my car and thanked me. "I didn't realize. I just didn't realize," she said. "All I wanted to do was to help us make progress in our women's ministry."

So now you realize, too. Ultimately responsible leaders keep in mind that spiritual growth and great servanthood do not happen apart from community support from the body of Christ. Determining the concentration of community support in a team environment is an art that credible leaders learn. Pray daily for each of your team members, and follow up with them regularly. Motivation for the mission is a spiritual matter, fueled by community and care.

No Lone Rangers

Intentional leaders know that team leadership is not a lone ranger proposition. While leadership is certainly a specialized role, it serves best in conjunction and context with others—the body of Christ principle. It's not a healthy approach to think of yourself as the lone ranger way out ahead of your team, though it's easy to slide into this mentality. The best leaders bring the team along with them, share the load, and pull together according to who does what best.

In chapter 2, **Your North-Star Strategy**, participation in a personal/spiritual accountability group was named as a key need for every leader. The kind of accountability described in this section involves ministry leadership accountability rather than personal accountability.

In the spirit of avoiding the lone ranger leader syndrome, honestly ask yourself these two questions. You are not set up for true maturity in leadership until you've developed a strong and healthy answer to each.

To whom am I accountable?

Even though you may lead a team (paid or unpaid), it's dangerous if you do not have more extensive accountability than to your team members. How easy it is to drift off track into your own agenda without realizing it! Your team may not have the courage to tell you if this happens. Or you may not listen even if your team does tell you.

Stop and consider these questions: If you are the *pastor or senior pastor*, with whom do you practice active accountability on behalf of your ministry leadership? Is it the personnel committee of your church? A cluster of other clergy in the town or area with whom you meet regularly? Your district superintendent? A pastor at another church who is ahead of you in ministry size and sophistication, someone from whom you can learn and gain objective perspective, even if only by regular e-mail dialogue? Another pastor who faces similar ministry challenges, with whom you can share mutual accountability? It may be that no accountability route has ever been in place for whoever the pastor has been at your church—until now. Create one for yourself. Functioning as a leader in a vacuum, no matter how competent you believe yourself to be, is toxic.

If you're a *church staff member*, what type of regular accountability do you have in place with the senior pastor or other supervisor? If you're an *unpaid leader*, to whom are you accountable and how does feedback and conversation regularly take place? Again, take the initiative yourself to establish scheduled accountability touchpoints. Do not wait for someone else to think of it or set it up on your behalf.

Some leaders simply use the staff, team members, or congregation they lead for feedback and accountability. While certainly you need to listen to their feedback and understand you are accountable to them for providing great leadership, it's not healthy to be governed solely by those you lead. You'll gradually find yourself shaped by their opinions, trying to please them and gain their approval even when it compromises the direction you know would be true to the vision. Establishing accountability points for yourself outside the team ensures a balanced perspective.

Accountability is an active practice, not just something represented on paper by lines connecting circles on an organizational chart. Accountability is not about asking permission for every single ministry task you want to do. Think of your accountability practice like a sounding board. Your point of accountability comes best through a person whose feedback you are willing to listen, respect, and accept. Ministry leadership accountability happens through genuine dialogue around topics like these:

- How am I doing in my leadership role? Is there anything I could change or improve?
- Is what I am doing and planning with my team, ministry, or church in accordance with the overall vision of the church or ministry? Does it have a scriptural foundation?
- Am I paying attention to the components of Spiritual Shepherd, Systems/Task Organizer, and Vision Crier I need to bring to the team?
- What have been the demonstrated results of my team's ministry efforts? Have they accomplished the purpose of the team's existence?
- Here are the leadership challenges I'm facing (name them). What am I not seeing, or what do I need to do differently?

Craft what your accountability touchpoint topics will be, and use them to guide you in making worthwhile use of time shared in accountability conversations.

What if your church, staff, or ministry has designated a point person for your leadership accountability, and you do not find him or her to be credible, helpful, or even experienced enough to give you feedback? Honor and respect that individual, and at the same time pull together your own additional unofficial touchpoints of helpful accountability. Your willingness to be proactive and create a strong accountability network for yourself will be directly related to your leadership growth.

Who are my intentional strategic partners?

The next chapter, **Building a Team**, explains specifics on putting together a team that accomplishes ministry together. After you have the leadership basics well in mind, you'll be ready to think about how to choreograph the team around you.

In chapter 1 you learned that to be an intentional leader, you must grasp the primary leadership components of Spiritual Shepherd, Systems/Task Organizer, and Vision Crier. Intentional leaders also augment these by choosing strategic partners who have strengths and talents that exceed theirs in whatever particular areas their skills are most rudimentary. The impact of my own leadership altered dramatically for the better as I became aware of the synergism produced by strategic partnerships. Now I am constantly on the lookout, seeking to align myself in intentional strategic partnerships wherever possible. Some examples from teams I lead include:

- Kevin, whose ability to research and analyze necessary details puts seaworthy legs on many strategic ministry endeavors I propose
- Charlene, whose gifts for teaching brings inventive sophistication to adult Christian education curriculum I create
- Craig, whose contagious enthusiasm brings immediate activation to new ideas the team brainstorms for accomplishing the vision
- Michele, whose organizational talents keep vast detailed discipleship systems well structured and functional

While I am ultimately responsible for team success, strategic partnerships with team members help me to be more successful in my role. My strengths reciprocally partner with theirs, enabling individual team member success.

Strategic partnerships may seem logical and useful to you as you read this. Unfortunately, some leaders struggle with ego issues when it comes to actually creating such partnerships. The leader may think, *"After all, I'm the team leader, so I need to be better at everything than anyone on my team. To actually acknowledge that a team member is better than me at anything would be a sign of weakness…"*

If your ego strength resists allowing others on your team to be better than you in any area, beware—you are dealing with your own spiritual immaturity. The body of Christ principle unquestionably illustrates all believers as having particular talents and gifts of excellence they are to uniquely contribute. If you are unable to acquiesce to your team members' legitimate contributions in a given area, you effectively shut down the rich God-given resources they bring to the table. Strategic partnerships require a team mindset, a humble servant heart, and a spirit of respectful gratitude for how wondrously God has equipped those around you.

What Leaders Need: A Great Team

Even the most intentional leaders aren't fully effective without the right team to partner with them on the mission. Leaders who practice and demonstrate all ten leader credibility markers can mobilize any team to the fullest extent possible. But the best recipe for setting up success is to connect an intentional leader with the right combination of team members for true synergistic momentum.

Now that you understand the path to intentional leadership, let's move on to consider the basics of building a great team.

More on strategically creating a team with respect to individual capabilities is found in the next chapter, **Building a Team**.

ON THE DVD FOR CHAPTER 5:

-Leadership Styles/Credibility Markers Discussion Sheet

-"Rights Vs. Responsibilities" graphic to give to team members

-Video Story: Jane—"Mount Sequoyah"

"The signs of outstanding leadership appear
primarily among the followers. Are the followers
reaching their potential? Are they learning?
Serving? Do they achieve the required results?
Do they change with grace? Manage conflict?"
-Max Depree

6

BUILDING A TEAM

As the ultimately responsible leader in your setting, what kind of team do you lead? Is it an unpaid servant team or committee you inherited? A paid staff team of a few, or many? A team you have personally selected, or one that was gathered, chosen, or hired by someone else? Whatever your specifics, you can fuel your team to healthy and productive function by implementing the core practices of effective ministry teams.

Revitalizing Your Current Team—Paid or Unpaid

Customize and apply this section's information according to the unique committee, team, or staff composite surrounding you now. No matter how efficient or how challenging your present team, incorporate these steps to bring health and focus to your service together.

What the best leaders know is that they must begin by helping any team, paid or unpaid, define its purpose for existence and build its processes around that purpose. Unless this happens, a team drifts and struggles to accomplish and move forward. The team's purpose and resulting processes are primarily defined by answering the following **four core team questions.**

1. Why was our team created, and what is our "report card"?

In other words, someone decided that a team was needed to accomplish certain work for God's mission through your church or ministry. You now lead that team. You may know why the team exists, but do the team members know? Pause now and think about the church or ministry team for which you are responsible. How would you summarize in a sentence or two the specific reason for its creation? Share your summary with the team you lead. Do they agree? Work together to name the team's purpose succinctly. Don't bother spending hours on an abstract, complicated mission statement with main points and

A "Four Core Team Questions" worksheet is available on the *Ultimately Responsible* DVD, chapter 6. Print off copies for all team members, and work through these questions together for healthy teambuilding and preparation.

sub-points. Your purpose needs to be explainable in simple terms not only to the team itself but also to the constituency you serve—in a single uncomplicated sentence.

Your team also needs to clarify for itself what its own report card is, so it knows when success on behalf of Kingdom work has been reached. A ministry success report card for your team gives specific measurable or observable benchmarks that will be reached if the team works effectively and strategically. For example, the report card for a team of children's ministry workers might include items like:

- Excellent safety procedures and protection for the care of every child
- Quality classroom learning for every child, including good curriculum, trained servant teachers, creative arts, community-building, and prayer
- Continual recruitment and training of Sunday School classroom teachers so that we have our classrooms fully staffed every weekend
- Recruitment of plenty of experienced adult helpers to serve in our nursery so that parents attending worship services will have peace of mind
- Cleanliness and organization of our children's ministry classrooms or areas
- Active outreach to children of all ages to become involved in our children's ministry

Leadership by intention means that you coordinate the team to clarify its report card, review it regularly, and help guide any adjustments as necessary. If you as a leader have created the team, you may be the one who puts forth the report card terms of success. Give the team members opportunity to discuss and ask questions. They may recommend additional realistic measurables to add to the team report card.

If you inherit an existing team and need to establish a mutually-agreed-upon report card, your team can brainstorm together to create the report card. In the end, your job is to make certain the purpose for the team and its report card for success coordinate with the overall church or ministry's mission. Type up the report card items, and have them available at every team meeting for review: How are we doing? What grade do we give ourselves on each report card item? What do we need to do to improve? On what do we need to focus next?

An effective team leader does not proceed if team disagreement exists on what success will look like. No team can unify itself and mobilize for action without embracing this together. Think how to remind your team every time it meets about why the team was created and how it contributes to the overall mission of not only your ministry or church, but also the mission of Jesus.

2. Who is our "customer"?

Whom is our team called to serve? Is it the community, the church family, single parents, or teens? Clarifying the focus of the team's energy and efforts helps you, the leader, guide the team to stay on track. If your team isn't clear about whom it serves, your meeting agenda may fill with random ideas and suggestions that are outside the parameters of what your team originally united to do. When the customer has been clearly identified, however, it's much easier for you as leader to help team members' focus stay centered.

For example, at Ginghamsburg the Broken Chains Motorcyclists (biker outreach ministry) is centralized around one leadership team. This eight-person team exists to plan and coordinate weekend motorcycle rides for the purpose of community and outreach to bikers in our city and region. Every January, the biker ministry leadership initiates the new year of ministry by discussing and clarifying who its customers are: unchurched bikers in the community who can be invited on our rides and to our weekend worship celebrations; bikers in our congregation who are not yet connected into fellowship and service (both of these are Level 1, Prospectors); bikers who are already regular riders on our planned rides (Level 2, Regular Attendees); and bikers who are involved and committed to help serve in Broken Chains (Level 3, The Engaged). Everything planned for the coming year, then, is intentionally designed to reach, serve, and involve one, two, or all of these customer bases in order to create contagious ministry movement.

Even the Broken Chains ministry's Web site is geared for these three customer bases. Check it out at **www .ginghamsburg.org/ brokenchains**, and see if you can identify which features are intended to communicate with particular customers. Next, think about your own team and the customers it serves. How can you become more intentional in your strategy?

Knowing who their customers are keeps the Broken Chains leadership team on track and focused. "Let's have plenty of rides to our favorite restaurants around the county this season. That's fun—we get to spend time together!" one leader recommended at the February ride season planning meeting. "Well, that only might appeal to ourselves and to other bikers who have already established good friendships within our motorcycle ministry," another leader replied. "We've got to vary our schedule so that we also have longer rides for hard-core bikers who enjoy spending their whole Saturday riding and who might not enjoy a leisurely restaurant meal sitting around with what would feel to them like a group of strangers. Their connection to our ministry is riding, not eating together. We have to remember who we're trying to reach."

The Broken Chains leadership knows their motorcycles are only tools by which to connect with individuals who need the life transforming message, love, and invitation of Jesus. By first identifying who their customers are, they carefully customize and vary their ride season to appeal to their entire potential customer base.

Here's the blunt truth: If your team believes that it exists to simply serve itself, then it's not a ministry team. If the Broken Chains leadership team members only planned motorcycle rides on which they themselves wanted to go, their own needs would be met—but they wouldn't reach the customers their team was created to serve. A team with a self-focus is actually a small accountability (cell) group with a purpose to help its own members connect relationally and grow emotionally and spiritually. While ministry teams share spiritual growth and often develop valuable relationships between team members, keep the outward goal of service ever before the team so that it does not turn inward at the unfortunate expense of its intended purpose.

3. What are our core team agreements, and how will we get work done?

I had not selected the team myself. It was a five-person committee responsible for the church's soup kitchen ministry. I inherited responsibility for this team when another leader moved out of town. Our first meeting caught me off guard when it opened with an earnest argument among committee members about whether or not they would function by *Robert's Rules of Order* and, if so, whether committee members would have to purchase the pamphlets of Robert's Rules themselves, or whether the money for them would be taken out of the soup kitchen's sparse ministry budget. "Tell me why this is important to you?" I asked.

"Well, no one listens to each other when we meet. The arguments get tiring and loud! I just think if we had a protocol, timed our debate, and had a really strict system, it would help improve things," one earnest, opinionated servant leader shared. I looked around the small gathering of five. Was it possible to establish agreements among them that facilitated effective communication without imposing a stringent parliamentary procedure? I decided to find out.

I suggested to the committee that our first order of business was to create a set of agreements by which we would all abide in order to get our ministry work done. I gave them a few examples, then asked them to brainstorm others. Some of the committee members made critical remarks aimed personally at one another as we brainstormed, but I insisted on listing only task-related ideas on the board to focus on our mutual purpose: to accomplish ministry. I listed all suggestions on the white board, and then we streamlined and combined them until we reached what represented our final list of core team agreements—these specifically around team communication:

- We will create our agenda together at the beginning of each meeting, facilitated by the leader, and the leader will also facilitate the meeting times.
- No one interrupts the person speaking.
- We will stay on one agenda item until it's completed and action step(s) are established, then move to the next.
- All of our communication will be about our ministry work together; none will be aimed at anyone personally.
- Members will do what they have said they will do and will communicate with the rest of the committee when the tasks have been completed.
- If a task has not been completed as planned (for any reason, all judgmental attitudes withheld), members will also communicate that to each other.

Initially as we proceeded to practice these core agreements, it required me (the leader) to make a concentrated effort to guide the committee's meeting times. I had to carefully walk through meetings, calmly pointing out when we got off our agreements and then pulling us back on course. I made certain that the notes of the meetings simply provided the names of those present, a list of the agenda items covered, any decisions made and action steps established plus the day and time of the next meeting. What a streamlined change that made from the hours of copious labor one woman on the committee usually invested creating detailed verbatim minutes from every meeting!

These worked so well that later, this same committee created another set of core agreements about how they would function as they served at the soup kitchen itself when many servants were present to organize and deploy. This miraculously eliminated the customary chaos those serving often complained about, helped clear up who was responsible for what and brought the joy back into serving together.

Eventually we added one more core agreement to our original list that specified terms of service for committee members:

- Each committee member will serve a one-year term and then rotate off the committee for at least one year before potentially serving another term. This will allow new servants the same wonderful opportunity to be a part of this committee that we have each had.

One core agreement I recommend for teams (paid or unpaid) is this one: **"Take input from anyone, but take direction only from your team leader."** I've seen confusion dissipate with the implementation of this agreement, since it helps each team member stay open, yet focused.

No ministry team or committee should be without an upfront core agreement naming length of service terms!

This last core agreement was difficult for three people on the soup kitchen committee, since they had served for all five years since the committee's creation! Yet it was essential to share ministry ownership with others. Though it was initially painful to implement, this core agreement helped the soup kitchen ministry grow tremendously as new team leaders brought new ideas.

If you are the leader of a paid staff team, you may choose to create and provide a list of core agreements yourself. If you do, give time for discussion and clarification when you present them to your staff. Be willing to change or adjust the core agreements if useful improvements are suggested. Give each team member a copy of the agreements, and update it if any changes or additions are made. Then make sure you set the pace by honoring the core agreements yourself, as well as expecting everyone on the team to do the same. This core agreement list gives you permission to address a team member who is out of line, reminding him or her of what the team agreed upon. The core agreements are useless unless you, the leader, implement them as valuable and necessary for efficient team function.

A slightly different set of core agreements with teams I lead (paid or unpaid) helps define individual expectations for those on the team. I create the list of agreements and present them to the team itself, asking for feedback, changes, and discussion.

I once became the supervisor for a ministry staff team that included an individual with a reputation for immature, angry outbursts (like blowing up when servants were tardy). I created a "Great Ministry Leader" list of agreements specific to our church culture and staff expectations, brought them to the team's weekly meeting, and went over the list of agreements in order to let everyone know clear expectations. Periodically, we reviewed the list together. One example from the list of agreements was this:

- It is never appropriate for a ministry leader to blow up in rage, berate another team member or church attendee, yell at someone, stomp off when frustrated, or act out other forms of anger while on the job (on or off church grounds). All irritations must be handled in a professional manner, modeling mature leadership, no matter who is in the right or the wrong. Remember—other staff and servants will imitate whatever behavior we as leaders display.

A few weeks after I introduced the "Great Ministry Leader" agreement list, the leader with the angry reputation asked to visit with me privately. "I'm really, truly glad for the agreements you gave us. I didn't fully realize until now how damaging it is to my leadership when I act out my annoyance in front of others who are counting on me. It never occurred to me that my behavior wasn't in sync with my role—I just thought everyone gets mad sometimes. Now I know I have to rise above it if I want to be a godly leader. Somehow seeing it in writing woke me up."

Great teams also realize that not every decision can be made by consensus, with every team member in agreement. Unfortunately, it's common for teams and committees to dangle for an interminable length of time because not everyone is in agreement with a decision or direction. Often at each meeting, hours are spent talking and arguing over and over the same points of disagreement. While your team members' concerns are important to consider, and some of them may provide insightful, godly wisdom you need to hear, beware when disagreements become circular and stagnate urgent new work toward which your team needs to move. More than one church has split because the well-intended pastor kept trying and trying to get all the members to agree on a single issue (sometimes a trivial one!) until finally the entire congregation fell apart.

Sometimes it's the leader's fault when a decision gets deadlocked. It can happen when a leader brings to a team a potential decision on an issue about which team members have no training or background, particularly those of ministry strategy. In the business world, would the CEO assemble a group of employees who had never been to business school to help make important investment decisions? Yet in the church we occasionally set up a similar scenario, allowing good-hearted Christians with no background or experience in a subject to tangle up important decisions that need to happen—all in the well-intended spirit of seeking consensus.

Healthy teams—and growing churches, for that matter—make decisions by critical mass. Not everyone is going to agree with every important decision that you as the ultimately responsible leader must make. However, if key knowledgeable players on your team agree and support the direction, it does not violate Scripture, and it is aligned with the purpose of your team and church, then get the decision made and move ahead. No contagious ministry movement God has ever inspired has been characterized by complete consensus in everything. And if you are doing ministry right, not everyone will like or agree with what is happening—especially late adapters who struggle to adjust to change.

4. Who is good at what?

One of the great blessings of serving on a team is that each team member can become a specialist. Powerful teams embrace this approach and make it a priority to notice and acknowledge who among themselves

Spiritual Shepherds are particularly vulnerable to falling victim to consensus thinking when they need to choose the route of critical mass. Shape your pastoral proclivity to accommodate resolute decision-making when necessary, and remind yourself that God will use whatever resulting unhappiness in some members as tools for their spiritual growth.

shows abilities at what. This approach models the body of Christ principle, allows each individual to shine at what he or she is gifted to do, and sets the stage for persons to make their best contributions. It also gives them each permission not to be a generalist, not to be good at everything. A team member's privilege, and responsibility, is to make the best ministry effort possible in conjunction with the same offered up from the rest of the team. Synergistic teams like this realize they are better together.

Remember the Broken Chains Motorcyclists ministry that I described earlier? Its leadership team is a closely-partnered network of specialists who each bring their best to the table: Bob, who is adept at planning weekend ride routes and creating the necessary corresponding trip guide for the riders; John, who relishes the role of chaplain (Spiritual Shepherd) for the riders in the ministry; Felix, whose knack for photography and video faithfully documents for publicity and for our Web site all Broken Chains activities; Kathy, who shines in organization and logistics; Marno, whose eye for the ignored and the invisible newcomers on our rides sets the pace for making everyone feel welcome; Tim, whose passionate heart for those who don't yet know Christ motivates everyone to stay focused on the ministry's Level 1 outreach; Mark, whose enthusiasm and "git 'er done!" encouragement brings contagious energy; and Chuck, whose contagious ability to excite and recruit servants helps multiply Levels 2 and 3. Whenever the leadership team meets, a deep respect for each other's giftedness permeates the atmosphere. And when a new work project presents itself, team members quickly identify the parts they are best at owning. When talents and gifts (additional servant specialists) are needed for specific ministry tasks, Broken Chains forms smaller adjunct teams with others who bring additional abilities to the ministry movement.

See the video story about Mike, "Jack of All Trades," on the *Ultimately Responsible* DVD, chapter 6. Becoming a specialist around your talents when part of a team is empowering!

"But," you may be thinking, "how in the world can I get my team to think or organize like this?"

The way that the Broken Chains team formed itself around this perspective began through honest communication. They spent intentional time answering (and listening as the other team members answered) questions like these:

- What part of the ministry we serve do you love the most?
- What part of our team's work do you enjoy doing the most?
- What part of our team's work are you (or would you be) the least competent at doing?
- What part of our team's work do you think brings out your best?

- (And asked of the group as a whole about each team member) Where and how do you see this team member "shine"? In what do you see this team member being really competent?

You may not decide to discuss every one of these questions. Choose the one(s) that fit best for your team. But make sure you include the last one, where team members give each other feedback one by one on what others see as their "best stuff." This type of affirmation is what builds respect between team members who serve together.

When your team moves into planning time for ministry or work projects, pay attention to how the responsibilities are distributed and remind the team as necessary about who is good at what. Most teams have one or more persons who refuse to think according to their strengths and try to take on whatever assignments no one else wants. While it may seem admirable, this is not the pathway to an organically synergistic team. Keep guiding the team to sort their tasks according to who is best at what. You may discover a need to add members to your team in order to broaden the diversity of talents available. If you do, choose carefully according to what abilities your team yet needs. Your goal as leader is to gather the right set of persons with the gifts, experience, skills, and spiritual maturity to accomplish the purpose and mission. Do you notice someone failing in his or her tasks on your team? Assess whether the task fits the individual's gifts and experience, and be quick to rearrange responsibilities to set up that team member for better success.

Frank Tillapaugh, colleague in ministry, coined three definitions that may help you further as you discern with your team members who might be best suited for which role, applicable in both paid and unpaid servant settings. While they are general concepts, they can help shed light on each team member's best setting for contribution. Remember, God gives no divine extra credit for any of these. All have equal value in the mission of Jesus.

A ministry **Worker** enjoys joining in on a project with others. An individual who fits best in the Worker setting would rather not have to plan, rehearse, get up in front of a group, or prepare before coming to serve. Workers thrive by showing up and jumping in to help make happen what others have organized. Their time to invest in serving may be limited, but when they arrive to the project or task, they are fully present to the servant work at hand. Workers aren't looking to be in charge. They relish making a contribution as part of a team effort.

See the short **Worker** video story of Roland on the *Ultimately Responsible* DVD, chapter 6. Who on your team can relate to Roland's approach?

Typical examples of Worker servant roles might include distributing worship bulletins, answering the phone, pouring punch into the punch

See Terry's **Franchiser** short video story on the *Ultimately Responsible* DVD, chapter 6. Discuss with your team how Terry "franchised" the idea that grew into a significant servant ministry on behalf of the needy.

Norm's video story represents the approach of a ministry **Entrepreneur**, found on the *Ultimately Responsible* DVD, chapter 6.

bowl, shoveling snow from the church building's sidewalks, or stacking chairs after a gathering.

A ministry **Franchiser** relishes taking a ministry task or responsibility and customizing it to make it his or her own. The idea or initiative isn't original, but the Franchiser makes the approach to it unique. A Franchiser does not feel the need to do a ministry task exactly like anyone else. Rather, the energy comes from adopting a task or idea and fitting it to the Franchiser's personal skills and abilities, or the specialized needs of the constituency to be served. For example, team members or servants who are Franchisers may volunteer to serve as a classroom teacher and decide to customize the role to their own strengths and styles. Others might join a team serving the needs of ministry with teenagers and adapt the role to fit their own particular interests in ways that connect with youth—like starting a skateboard club or dodgeball group. The idea of serving teens is not new, but the way the Franchiser creates the approach and application is unique.

A ministry **Entrepreneur** enjoys inventing a completely original idea for ministry service and making it happen. Entrepreneurs aren't afraid of new possibilities and relish charting a path through the unknown. Your entire team may like thinking about and discussing new ministry dreams, but only the true Entrepreneur will embrace the venture and actively set out to make it happen. At times the Entrepreneur may forge a new initiative in response to a ministry need. On other occasions, a ministry Entrepreneur may set sail through motivation brought by an exciting new God-dream at the heart level. An Entrepreneur on your team loves to become the point person for new projects that are not yet invented and will become energized in driving them forward.

Some team leaders naively assume that anyone who suggests a new ministry idea is an Entrepreneur who is capable also of creating, then leading it. Be careful here! Ideas come from all kinds of sources, and not everyone who suggests one has the right strengths and wiring to make it happen. If God has motivated the idea, God will also draw together the right team of individuals who are capable of making it happen. The idea-provider may or may not be an Entrepreneur who can give it birth.

Building a New Unpaid Team

The first section of this chapter was designed to help you renew and revitalize the team that you currently lead. But if you have the privilege of assembling a brand new team, right from the beginning you can set the stage for mutual understanding, team compatibility, and gift mix. Here's how to get started.

What kind of team is needed?

First identify what type of team is necessary. Is it a team whose specific purpose is to serve or perform a task? Examples include a team to regularly weed the flowers along the front entrance of the sanctuary, change the oil for single mothers on Saturday mornings, or provide food for condolence dinners.

Or is it a team that will exist to provide leadership? The Broken Chains team is an example of a leadership team. It exists to organize and support the ministry as well as recruit and deploy servants for all phases of its seasonal motorcyclist outreach.

Perhaps it is a team to be formed for planning. For example, your church may desire to build a new classroom wing, so a planning team would assess feasibility, contact an architectural firm, enlist a builder, and map out a fundraising initiative that may need to be launched.

What qualifications are important for team members?

If it's a task team that will produce hands-on work, think of what skills would be helpful. A mission trip team that will build a home with an organization like Habitat for Humanity requires at least some of the team members to have house construction skills. If it's a leadership team whose responsibilities include recruiting and mobilizing servants for a specific ministry, some team members will need strong "people skills" and the ability to help connect with and train recruits. If it's a planning team convened to produce careful, well-researched strategies and guidelines to steer future ministry plans, professional maturity and competence in the relevant project areas would be essential.

Review the contagious ministry movement model in chapter 3 as you think from which levels to recruit for your new team.

Along with consideration of appropriate skills, pay attention to what levels of spiritual maturity are important for the work of the potential team. A task team may welcome members from Levels 1 and 2 as defined in the contagious ministry movement model. Leadership teams with high responsibility, however, perform poorly unless members are at Level 3 or 4.

Other attributes that generally define a good team member include open-mindedness, respect for others, a positive spirit without sarcasm or negativity, and a willingness to grow. Though your team's goal is productivity for God's work, an equally important by-product is the personal and spiritual growth of team members through their service together. In fact, this by-product may be more important to God than the actual amount of work produced.

What will be the terms of service?

Terms of service are basic team core agreements, created ahead of time. Those considering the invitation to serve on your new team will want to know the following:

- How long is the term of service—six months? A year? Longer? (Put a time frame on this; do not leave a term of service open. If there is no upcoming end of service term, it becomes difficult when a servant needs to rotate out.)
- How often will the team meet? How much time outside of meetings will the role require?
- What training will be offered to prepare?
- Are there any other team member expectations important to name ahead of time?

Creating terms of service that every new team member embraces is like establishing the foundation of the team's core agreements, right up front. It prevents misunderstandings later and allows the team to launch on track together.

Where can I find possible candidates for the team?

"I like your advice about building teams at my church," an adult education director told me. "And maybe it works at yours. But I'm sure you have really good people at your church to choose from. Here? Well, there just isn't anyone who is leadership team material, if you know what I mean. We just have regular folks with lots of problems, far from perfect."

Years ago when I made a similar complaint to a more seasoned ministry colleague, I heard a truth in reply that I've held close ever since: *We will do ministry with persons as we see them.* If all I think I see is a bunch of irresponsible, immature, small-town churchgoers who aren't capable of Kingdom-size dreaming, that is exactly what I'll find. But if I notice God's miraculous work occurring all around me in persons whose growth will be facilitated by what happens in a team environment, I become eager to bring groups of believers together to serve, to lead, and to plan. I become a Vision Crier, speaking pictures of what is possible when individuals grasp their God-given abilities and invest them collectively on behalf of servant-hearted priorities.

Look again, if at first you don't see the right individuals to invite onto the team you are building. If God has truly led you to form the team, God has prepared the right team members to join. I don't recommend passing around a sign-up sheet to enlist potential team members, although it's an acceptable practice for gathering Workers (see Workers,

Franchisers, and Entrepreneurs as defined earlier in this chapter) to help with a project or task.

If you don't know your congregation or ministry group well, another route for identifying likely team members is through interest/skill forms. Get to know interests and abilities by inviting attendees to complete a short, friendly, half-sheet form on which they may list their hobbies, interests, skills, and talents.

A third method is through references from trusted team members and leaders already in place. Or if your church offers a class through which individuals become church members, personally interview each new member to help place persons into service and recruit for teams as compatible.

When inviting a new team member to serve, remember what you've learned about recruiting a servant for any role. Explain the vision, and describe specifically how the team and each of its members will help accomplish it. Point out why you think the potential servant would be right for the team. Go over the terms of service and team member expectations including what training might be included.

Never complain that that you are short on team members, that you're struggling to find team members, that it's a thankless task, or certainly not that it would be a personal favor to you if the candidate would agree to serve! Always think about and speak out the privilege to serve that any team experience offers. Emphasize the opportunity to serve, the spiritual growth that it would bring, the value of learning to work together as a team, and your own excitement about what God has in store.

What's next after I have all the team members recruited?

Hold your first team gathering as soon as possible, while new team members still feel their initial enthusiasm. Review the terms of service together, restate the connection of the team to the overall vision, and reiterate the awesome chance to serve out the deep calling offered by team participation. Proceed to work through the four core-team questions together. Get the team launched into its work (tasks, leadership, or planning) right away. Implement your own leadership by intention, as you learned in the previous chapter.

As you lead your team, always stay sensitive to notice others whom God may be preparing to lead in the future. Intentional leaders perpetually seek to replicate themselves by raising up new leaders who are capable of multiplying the ministry movement. It's not as simple as just noticing who is your most responsible team member, however. Connecting with future leaders is an art you can learn.

Identifying Future Team Leaders

She was efficient, attentive, and loyal to the team. Candace never missed a team meeting, always showed up to serve, and had a perennially cheerful spirit. She never caused conflict, and the team could count on her predictable, supportive presence. It seemed logical to the team leader, whose term was ending, to nominate Candace as his successor. Candace was flattered at what felt like a servant role promotion, and she accepted.

Candace, however, quickly found that it took a different set of gifts and experience to lead the team than it did to serve on the team. Her passion and heart to be the hands and feet of Jesus—literal hands-on, front line servanthood—were not the ones the team leader role utilized. Instead, Candace now needed to recruit, train, and organize others to do the actual serving. Candace was shy and feared potential rejection when inviting persons to serve or asking her team members to perform ministry tasks. So she defaulted to doing most everything herself because, she reasoned, it was just easier. Soon her team members were idle as Candace floundered with too many action items accumulated on her own to-do list. Fewer and fewer servants helped support the ministry work that Candace's team existed to oversee and manage. By year's end, Candace's team meetings had spotty attendance, and the team's ministry efforts were staffed by only Candace herself, along with her two best friends. Candace rotated out of team leadership at year's end, embarrassed and disillusioned, and withdrew to become only an occasional attendee to weekend worship.

What happened? How did Candace go from the best member of her team to a struggling leader in such a short time frame? This scenario takes place in churches and ministries everywhere, even on paid church staffs: The leader in charge spots a loyal, faithful servant and assumes that team leadership is the individual's logical next step. After all, shouldn't the servant be rewarded with additional responsibility?

Unless you create specific criteria by which you will identify and select your next ministry leaders, you will make the same mistake that Candace's unfortunate story represents. A person who has the gifts and strengths of a faithful servant or team member does not necessarily have the right talents and experience to make that same servant an effective team leader. Team leadership requires a different giftedness zone. Keep in mind that a successful servant who is thriving in a certain niche is thriving because the work and the talents match. Moving the servant to a team leader role may inadvertently shift the person out of the unique setting in which those strengths had their ideal environment for fulfilling contribution.

Make a list of what the future team leader needs to possess. Does the specific leadership role you need require recruiting? Organizing? Specific, previous leadership experience? Does the new team leader need to be contagious? Have good people skills? Good social skills? What about regular worship attendance? Generous financial giving to the church? Congregational membership? A teachable and trainable attitude, not resistant to feedback and changes? Cleanliness and good hygiene? Make your list, and set your criteria.

While it's occasionally acceptable to choose a new team leader purely on potential, it's also risky. Your view of the individual's potential may be clouded because he or she is your close friend or relative, or because you are impressed with the person's spiritual growth—or other subjective reasons.

Review the contagious ministry movement model and its levels, described in chapter 3, **Anatomy of Contagious Ministry Movement**.

The best team leaders represent Level 3 or 4 commitment. Your strategy in building strong ministry initiatives requires team leaders who are deeply invested in your ministry or church vision and are capable of explaining and sharing it with others. The best candidates for assuming leadership have already demonstrated fruit in their ministry contributions and have cultivated the heart of a servant.

The best candidate may not volunteer for team leadership. You are not obligated to accept the most willing and available person who asks you about becoming the team leader. Be judicious; select and invite the right person instead of the most convenient person. Occasionally you may feel tempted to give in to an aggressive or pushy servant who is demanding a leadership role. But unless appropriate criteria support such a selection, resist the pressure. The future of your church or ministry is at stake with every team leader you recruit.

Some team leaders spend most of their time helping along and partnering with the weakest links on the team. While this may be necessary in order for team success, do not ignore the shining stars whom God may be preparing for eventual leadership. Through shared ministry experience plus time and training with potential leaders, you will successfully replicate yourself and strengthen your church or ministry's future.

Occasionally, leaders become addicted to the self-perceived importance of their roles and unconsciously hoard their leadership responsibilities so closely that they make themselves indispensable. While this may feed the human desire to feel valued and appreciated by others, it virtually guarantees that when they someday leave these leadership roles, the ministries or teams will crumble. Remember how Jesus invested himself in his close band of disciples, trained them, and modeled leadership for them? When Jesus left earth, his disciples continued so effectively that Christianity has persisted through two millennia. Now is the time to recast your thinking into a Kingdom perspective for the future. Every day is your next opportunity to invest in those who will rise up to lead after you. Drive the vision deep into those around you with potential to lead. Let God's dreams etch themselves onto the hearts of those in whom you are replicating your leadership.

The eight leadership styles described in chapter 5, **Leading a Team**, also manifest themselves when leading a paid staff. Study the leadership styles honestly, and identify which you represent. Is your leadership style part of the problem?

Building a Paid Staff Team

This section is for those who have the ultimate responsibility to supervise paid employees who work in ministry with you.

Roger, a pastor in his mid-forties, came close to tears as he shared his frustrations on this subject. "When I went to seminary, I took pastoral counseling courses that helped me learn how to support someone who is dealing with a difficult life issue or crisis. I remember also taking a required church administration class that gave me general information about setting up church committee structures and the importance of balancing the church budget. But nothing, nothing prepared me for what to do with paid church employees! I feel successful in every other area as a pastor. I can preach, the budget is balanced, and my board likes me. But this staff thing stumps me. Early on, my staff team was like a revolving door. I had four youth directors in two years! Now I hang on to everyone on our staff, even though I know a couple of them need to go. I guess I would rather keep someone whose issues I'm familiar with, instead of going though another hiring process—now, that's a real nightmare. How do you know who to hire, anyway? It's all a gamble, a guessing game. Some days I think all I can do when it comes to staff is just keep the train on the track. I even have moments when I'd rather just do it all myself, and wish I had no paid staff at all!"

Have you ever felt like Roger? Without any other training you, too, may default to pastoral counseling skills to manage your paid staff. The potential unsatisfactory results can be extensive:

- You bear with employees who don't get the job done much longer than it's worth spending the church's money on their salaries, reluctant to draw the line because it might upset the congregation (After all, you think, "It's the church—and we are called to practice forbearance!").

- You excuse inferior work performance, attributing it to the employee's personal issues that have little to do with the job, and invest your energy into counseling him or her.
- You do well at spiritually discipling those who are paid to be on your staff team, but ignore regularly training them for greater ministry competency.
- You fail to set up regular annual performance reviews (written measurables that reveal success or failure), schedule periodic feedback sessions, and maintain up-to-date job descriptions because these methods feel too much like a business for the church setting.
- You are guilty of trying over and over to train talent into employees as an effort to help them improve (ignoring the truth that though individuals can learn certain skills, training talent into someone is impossible).
- You may hire relatives without considering the impact nepotism might eventually bring to bear on paid church staff dynamics.
- Your instinct leads you to quickly hire your most faithful servant to fill an empty staff position, without evaluating whether the right gifts and abilities for a leadership role are actually present.

If I've painted a more dismal picture than your situation represents, it's because this aspect of building and leading a paid team is a pervasive struggle for many ultimately responsible leaders. The good news is that you can learn and improve. These are skills you can develop.

How Do I Know When I Need to Hire a Staff Person?

"Our moms group is growing like gangbusters!" Marsha told me. As pastor of her church, she supervised a small staff team: an office secretary, youth director, half-time choir director, and half-time children's worker. "I have one stay-at-home mom who has made jumpstarting the group her focus. She spends all day long, it seems, calling other young moms and getting them involved. You should have seen the swap sale they held for used baby clothes and toys! She can really organize, too. But I'm feeling guilty about all the time she's spending on this—it seems excessive. Shouldn't we start paying her or something? Maybe she's the next half-time position I need to lobby for my board to add to our staff."

I knew how Marsha felt. I have also often seen unpaid servants pour out their lives on behalf of a ministry that God blessed with phenomenal growth. "Is the young mom asking to be paid?" I asked. "Nope," Marsha replied. "Well, she's hinted around about it. But mostly she just seems happy with the success of the group. She says it makes her years at home with her children feel extra worthwhile."

Like Marsha, if you've wondered when and for what to hire your next staff person, ask yourself and your board or personnel committee this question: Could this be (or is it already) adequately accomplished by an unpaid worker or servant team?

Generally speaking, it's not worthwhile to hire staff to do the work that ministry servants can and should do. Hire only when it's necessary to enlist education, experience, expertise, or administrative support that is not otherwise available to help take your church or ministry to the next level. Remember that the goal of Kingdom building is unleashing the body of Christ for magnificent service. When unpaid servants find the niche in which they connect with their heart passions, their pay is the joy and fulfillment God brings through service. Do not mistakenly assume that money is necessary when a servant's calling is fulfilled through whole-life commitment. Working hard enough as a servant to finally get hired onto the staff is not a God-motivated goal. Becoming hired as a church staff member is not a reward or a move up the ladder. It is a move down into deeper service. And what happily-engaged servants may not realize is that by becoming paid staff members, they would have to give up what they love—their hands-on ministry work—to unpaid servants, and assume completely different staff responsibilities like ministry recruiting, organizing, and administrative oversight. A move from servant to staff might eliminate the specific ministry activity that gave the servant deep joy.

If you are not skilled in recruiting and deploying servants, you may tend to default to hiring someone to do the work that in other churches servants would do. Some pastors campaign for additional staff just to avoid improving their Systems/Task Organizer skills—which is all it might otherwise take to structure the work of the ministry so servants can participate more fully.

Be judicious when potential decisions about new staff hires are explored. Hire only when the work or leadership cannot be managed or accomplished through unpaid servant efforts, and clarify specifically what you need a new staff person to do. Otherwise, a whole batch of servants may lose their privilege to serve when a new staff person takes over what initiatives they could otherwise have supported—and your payroll grows without just cause.

See an example of a job description on the *Ultimately Responsible* DVD, chapter 6, to help get you started.

What Needs to Happen Before Interviewing?

If you and your board have agreed that a new staff hire is necessary—whether for a new position, or to fill an open position, think through these two steps as the start of your process:

1. Create a written job description.

2. Put on paper the qualifications for the position, the responsibilities it will involve, and the type of measurables or accomplishments expected (e.g. "Have twenty-five teens active in the youth group by the end of the first year," or "Launch ten new cell groups every six months."). A typical error made in job descriptions is to include only a laundry list of tasks and omit big-picture expectations. The ideal job description will help a potential candidate understand exactly what the position entails as well as what success looks like and will also enable you to use it as a structure for eventual performance reviews. (And by the way, a job description in the same format should exist for every paid position on your staff team—including pastors. If it doesn't, set this as an immediate goal.)

I believe in listing spiritual qualifications as an important part of a staff job description. Every paid staff position at a church is a leadership role, no matter whether it's for the custodial responsibilities or the preaching on Sundays. If you earn your living by working at a church, you are in the vocational ministry. And paid leaders of the church cannot take the congregation any further than they themselves have grown.

Everyone on the payroll (no matter what position) should practice these spiritual qualifications, as listed on their job descriptions:
- Profess Jesus Christ as Lord and Savior
- Be committed to personal spiritual growth and a healthy lifestyle
- Consider this position a ministry, not just a job
- Model standards and expectations of leaders within the church, including membership, worship attendance, cell group participation, a lifestyle of tithing and generosity, and serving out of call and giftedness

Before starting the interview process, establish what pay range is feasible for the position you have open. The Internet is a rich resource for research if you are looking for regional or national averages for most typical staff positions—for small, medium, and large attendance churches.

Membership, as listed in these spiritual qualifications, means membership at your congregation. The call to paid ministry means you have decided to fully become part of the mission of this church family, to make it both your place of work and your place of worship and service. If you work at one church but belong to and serve at another, you're a mercenary! Powerful paid staff teams—whether your staff numbers three or thirty or three hundred—unite to accomplish the mission to which God has called your church. Each must be fully present to the mission, both personally and professionally, and that includes making the church where you're employed your home congregation.

Another spiritual qualification is tithing, or giving 10 percent of your income to the church where you both work and belong. Giving is a spiritual matter, reflective of spiritual maturity. It's impossible for a pastor to preach every fall during a pledge drive about good stewardship and generous giving if that pastor and the church staff do not demonstrate what they want the congregation to do. Again, it's impossible to lead the church family further than you and your staff team have gone yourselves, including financially.

And a Christian healthy lifestyle qualification is included. Christian health includes celibacy in singleness, fidelity in marriage. Nothing other than the New Testament standards for lifestyle choices are appropriate for a paid church ministry leader.

Brainstorm what kind of candidate you're looking for before you start your search. Some churches work this process backwards: they interview potential candidates to see what they like and what appeals to them. But a better way is to decide first what you need in a candidate for the position before any interviewing begins. For example, if you need a new church secretary, you will naturally look for detail orientation, organizational ability, computer experience, and good social skills to relate to persons of all types. The right training, education, and expertise for the specific position are essential. But think what else might also be important in a great staff person, and make a list including qualities such as:

- Strong and active Christian faith
- Positive and cheerful attitude
- Self-motivated
- Enjoys productivity
- Good work ethic
- Team player
- Willing to do whatever it takes
- Self-confident
- Keeps confidential information
- Professional demeanor
- High energy
- Understanding and appreciation of the mission of your church
- Enough courage to make sure the right things happen

Do not finalize the hire of any new staff member until you have completed a background check. You need to know, for the safety of your congregation, whether the candidate has struggled in the past with child molestation, theft, or other crimes that would disqualify him or her for the position.

If you're unsure about qualities other than the needed professional qualifications you're looking for, think about what attributes your most successful current staff members (or unpaid leaders) possess that you admire. What about them do you appreciate the most? What qualities help them succeed in their roles? By starting your search process knowing what you want and need, you'll be wiser and more efficient as you interview, less likely to compromise.

How Do I Choose The Right Candidate?

Even if you are already acquainted with a candidate interested in the position, ask for a resume and three professional employment references. You'll be able to see quickly from a written resume the candidate's attention to detail, ability to write and to spell, and knack for written self-expression. Provide candidates with the job description ahead of time, so they will be familiar with the requirements of the position before a personal interview takes place.

Organize an interview team rather than conduct the interview alone. Possible interview team members might include staff who would be strategic partners with the as-yet-unfilled position, or leaders from your personnel committee or administrative board. It's not useful to overwhelm a candidate by facing an interview conducted by a whole roomful of persons. Choose no more than two or three others besides yourself. Before the interview session, provide your interview team with the written job description plus the other qualities for which you are looking in a successful candidate. Take time to discuss and answer any of the interview team's questions, then pray before the interview begins with a candidate.

Nepotism (hiring a relative) is an acceptable practice at some churches, and forbidden at others. If you're willing to employ relatives, it's never a good idea to have one relative supervise another. It may be difficult for the supervisor to be objective. And if one relative on a church staff becomes unhappy, leaves, or is let go, chances are good that other relatives on staff will follow suit.

When interviewing, include basic questions like these:

1. What is your relationship with this church?
2. What questions do you have about the written job description? What questions do you have about any of the qualifications or requirements?
3. What education/experience/expertise has prepared you for this position?

If you have included spiritual qualifications such as membership at your church, tithing, worship attendance, or other factors, then call the candidate's attention to that section of the job description. Explain each element, and do your best to make sure the candidate understands these expectations. Answer any questions raised. Include information for the candidate regarding the position's potential office hours, any regular required meetings, and any other specifics of the position.

To find out more about the qualities you desire in a future staff person, ask a question about each with a format similar to these examples:

1. On a scale of one (not very) to ten (highly), how self-motivated are you? Share an example with us about a time you showed high motivation in a workplace environment.
2. Would those you know best call you an optimistic person, a pessimistic person, or neutral? When specifically have you noticed this in yourself in a given situation? Tell us about it.

3. What happens when you see a problem that needs to be resolved? Would you ask your supervisor to deal with it, address it yourself, or go home and worry about it? Give an example of a workplace or ministry problem, and how you dealt with it.

4. What are your organizational skills like? Describe for us an occasion at work when your ability to organize came into play successfully.

When asking a candidate about an important quality you would like a staff person to have, invite him to share real-life examples that demonstrate or illustrate the quality. If a candidate cannot think of an example, it's likely the quality may not be present. Pay attention to the examples and stories that a candidate relates. If a candidate shares negativity during the interview in telling about a previous employer or a member of your church, take note. That same negativity will likely be brought into your work environment. If the candidate shares stories that paint herself as a victim in a past job, relationship, or church situation, chances are that same victim attitude will manifest itself if she's employed on your staff.

After you complete an interview with a candidate, debrief with the interview team about the following:

1. Did the candidate have the experience or education we want? What or how much additional training would be necessary, if we eventually hired this candidate? Do we have someone who could provide it?

2. Would this candidate become a strong strategic partner with our existing staff? Why or why not?

3. Does the candidate seem to understand or be receptive to the DNA of our church or ministry?

4. What evidence of spiritual maturity does the candidate display?

5. What of our needed qualities and qualifications did the candidate claim to have and verify with real-life examples?

6. Could this candidate be a capable leader in our congregation, building a healthy relationship with the church family?

7. Do we have any other tests, orientations, or information about the candidate that would help reveal more about whether the person is a good match for this position?

8. What careful and thorough further interviews do we need to schedule with the candidate (assuming the first interview was favorable), and with whom? What additional approval process is necessary in order to ascertain whether we feel led to make the candidate an offer of employment?

Some find it helpful to look at additional personality data provided by the candidate through online surveys like the Clifton StrengthsFinder, the Meyers-Briggs Type Indicator, the VIA Signature Strengths Questionnaire, or a spiritual gifts inventory. The purpose of interviewing is to get to know the potential candidate as well as possible, through as many means as possible. Check out what additional resources fit your needs.

If you and your team agree that the interview went satisfactorily, continue to pray for God's guidance. Contact the three professional references, and do your best to learn more about the candidate. Ask questions about strengths and weaknesses, attitude and work ethic, reasons for leaving. If you are unable to reach all three references, ask the candidate for more so that you are able to gain a context for the candidate's past employment (and ministry) history. Do not rely only on personal references.

What Happens After I Hire a New Staff Member?

The preferred first action step after a candidate has accepted a staff position is to prepare a letter or e-mail (and keep a copy on file) to send, summarizing the terms of the hire. This letter is a record of the agreed-upon plans, including job title, start date, salary, any benefits that accompany the position, and annual vacation time allotment. A copy of this letter the job description, and a document showing the candidate has undergone a clean background check are the first three items to place in the new employee's personnel file.

The first day your new employee is on the job, be prepared. Meet and review the job description, reminding the person that the measurables listed are the report card for success for the position. Itemize what needs to happen for a thorough orientation to employment at your church in learning how processes and systems work. Make a checklist if helpful for the employee to complete. Arrange details about workspace, office schedule, phone, computer use—whatever are essentials in your setting. Define any always/nevers that are important for the employee to know: always call in to the church office first thing in the morning if you are ill; never use the church phone for personal long-distance calls, and so forth.

On the first day, make sure you as supervisor also name your expectations about communication together. Do you want to touch base daily in person? At a staff meeting scheduled during each week? Through e-mail as necessary? What kind of ministry updates do you expect, and how often?

If your staff is small, all paid employees comprise the team that the newcomer is joining. If your staff is larger, you may have more than one paid team within the organizational structure. Help the new staffer meet and connect with his or her new ministry partners. Explain expectations of teamwork. Remember that great ministry happens through teams, not lone rangers. Every employee will be more likely to thrive if connected to a team. Your goal is ideally to perpetuate a flat organization, with teams empowered to make decisions and get work done. You as supervisor are like the hub of the wheel, the servant of all. Do not default into the opposite: a hierarchy where you are above everyone else instead, handing down edicts and commands! Leadership by intention embodies Jesus' model of servant leadership. Don't slow down the entire team and lower your expectations so that struggling employees can keep up. Rather, cultivate an environment for your employee team so that the best players will love it.

What Are The Basics of Supervision?

Refer to the ten leadership markers identified in chapter 5, "Leading a Team," as you hone your supervisory style. Whatever your plan for how you intend to supervise, keep reasonable proximity to your paid employees in order to provide leadership by intention. A regularly-scheduled staff meeting, even if your staff is small, is vital. It is here that you cast and explain the vision, work together to plan the systems and coordinate the tasks necessary to support the church or ministry, and give spiritual leadership to the team. The weekly staff meeting is not the place for personal counseling sessions. Keep the focus on your shared ministry goals and teamwork together.

It's helpful for every staff person who is responsible for frontline ministry to create a monthly staff report. These reports are useful not only for tracking progress and identifying goals but also for surfacing obstacles in ministry development. The monthly report is not long, usually a page or two. It covers the following:

- What were the measurable successes this month in my areas of responsibility? What new servants did I recruit and involve?
- What are my goals for next month, and how do I plan to accomplish them?
- With what challenges, if any, do I need assistance?

The monthly report is a record to help the employee stay self-aware of progress. It also helps you, the supervisor, track accomplishment of the job description. And occasionally you learn about challenges that you haven't heard from the staff person already, and can take action to help with training, advice, or teamwork. It provides you with an efficient way of keeping your Leadership Board informed about how your ministry productivity is going. And it also gives the personnel committee a written update on the work of your employees.

After three months of employment, it's a good idea to create a bulleted summary of what you have seen the new employee fulfill from the job description. Along with that summary, list adjustments or improvements that need to be made in order to better fulfill the role. Share this three-month progress review with the staff member, along with honest discussion about what his or her experience has been like and anything

Fully exercise all aspects of leading a team, as delineated in **chapter 5**. Whether paid or unpaid, teams function best when competent leadership is provided. Take your job seriously, and concentrate upon setting up your paid staff for ministry success.

that needs to be improved for better performance. Ask for feedback on how you can do a better job as supervisor: Have you provided what was needed in terms of the three primary leadership components? Have you piled on work that others are piling on you? Keep the three-month review on file, and provide a copy to the staff person.

Every year, each of your paid employees should receive an annual written performance review that you, or your personnel committee, has prepared. When it's time for an annual review:

1. Look back through the staff person's monthly reports, and note successes and accomplishments. List these first on the review. It's important to acknowledge what the employee has done well during the past year.
2. Title the second section of the review "Areas of Growth." List here unrealized requirements of the job description, goals you may have previously set together that may not have been completed, and any other areas of improvement necessary.
3. Name the third section of the review "This Year's Goals." List what needs to be accomplished during the coming twelve months, specific measurables rather than abstract concepts. This list of goals will be the basis of next year's review, so think and plan carefully.

Occasionally you might ask an employee to do a self-evaluation beforehand in each of these three categories. As appropriate, combine his or her lists with your own as you prepare the final review.

When delivering an annual performance review, no employee (if you've done well supervising through the year) should receive any surprises. Any area of growth or new goal should not be new news. Ideally, you have given regular feedback and input throughout the year (and made a note to yourself every time you have done so) so that the employee is well informed about how everything is going all along the way. Make two copies, and place yours in the employee's personnel file as part of your habit of keeping good records.

What if a Staff Person Isn't Working Out?

It's relatively easy to supervise a staff team on which everyone is doing well. But when someone on your team is struggling, how you handle the situation is crucial. And it's even more difficult if you inherit an unsuccessful employee your predecessor did not supervise well—a staff person who has not been functioning effectively for some length of time.

Remember Roger's story at the beginning of this section? It was in the area of supervising paid staff that he as senior pastor found his greatest learning curve. His habit was always first to ignore the problem employee, hoping that the situation would right itself. Then he would wait until he got so much negative feedback from church members or other staff that it became a necessity to act. As a kindhearted and pastoral person, he disliked holding an employee accountable for fear of hurting feelings or offending. Yet his conscience told him that it was a waste of money for the church to continue to pay an employee who was unproductive for the Kingdom.

Roger eventually learned a new strategy that he trained himself to follow. He began with Nadine, his church secretary, an employee who had served on the church staff longer than he. Complaints had been rampant about her attitude with phone callers, negligence with room scheduling details, and refusal to team well with other staff by delivering messages.

Meet with the employee and review the job description.

Roger found that Nadine had never been given a job description, so the first thing he did was to let her know he was working to develop one for everyone on the paid staff, including her. He asked her to make a list of every task she performed as part of her job on a regular basis. When she gave him the list, he put it into a standardized format that he had created for the other staff job descriptions and included the same section on spiritual requirements he had placed in them all. Next he scheduled an appointment with Nadine to review it.

As they looked over the new written job description together, Nadine objected to the section about teaming with all other staff as necessary to accomplish excellent communication. "I just don't like some of them," she stated flatly.

"Nadine, this is the job, and these are the expectations for it," Roger told her. "If you accept a paycheck from the church, we get to choose your attitude while you are here in the office of the congregation. And the attitude we choose is one that's cheerful, positive, and cooperative with everyone. Teamwork is required. It's not an option to refuse to communicate with one staff person or another. Everyone who calls our office will be received with hospitality and kindness. If a message is left for one of our staff, you will make sure it's delivered. That's what the position of church secretary is. That's what we pay you to do and to provide."

Roger ended his meeting with Nadine in prayer and hoped for the best. He made notes for himself about what he had told her, and put it in

Nadine's file. But Nadine refused to adjust to the newly-articulated requirements of her role. Everything seemed to get worse.

Continue to provide regular feedback.
Roger met with Nadine again after two weeks. He prayed ahead of time for the ability to be clear and honest, yet diplomatic. "Nadine, I see that you are still struggling to be friendly on the phone when our church members call, and I see your refusal to team with the rest of our staff 100 percent of the time," he began. "I've been here longer than you, and I'm old enough to be your mother!" Nadine shot back. "I know more folks in this church than you do! I've been this church's secretary for a long time, and I know how I'm going to do it. And that's all there is to it!"

"I hear that," Roger responded. He resisted his customary urge to give up and try to get back into her good graces. After all, everyone knew that when Nadine wasn't happy, no one in the church office was happy. "But I'm afraid we don't have a choice here. We are going to have to look at making sure teamwork is a priority. We need you to make this happen as part of your position."

If no improvement occurs, create and implement a performance plan.
Roger met with the personnel committee that weekend and showed them for their approval a four-week performance plan he had prepared for Nadine. It itemized specific workplace non-negotiables with which she would have to comply, or her employment would end at or before the four-week time frame expired. The items in the performance plan were taken directly from the responsibilities listed in the job description, and included correction of the issues Roger had already addressed with Nadine.

Roger asked to meet with Nadine the following Monday and tried not to shift into his familiar pastoral counseling skills as she glared at him across his desk. *Be loving,* he coached himself, *but be firm. You're her supervisor right now, not her personal counselor....*

"Nadine, today is the first day of an employee performance plan that the personnel committee and I are implementing to help you get on track with what needs to happen with your job. We want you here, and we want you on our staff team. This is your church family. But this is also your workplace, and in order for you to succeed at your paid job, we will have to make sure that you know exactly what is expected."

Roger carefully talked through the performance plan with Nadine. "Now, Nadine, I need you to sign both copies of this performance plan. I will sign them also—one copy for the church, one for you. It doesn't mean that you agree or disagree with it—only that it has been presented and discussed with you." Nadine was silent. Roger forced himself not to try to comfort and placate her, by staying the supervisor. "Every week you and I will touch base about how things are going, how you are doing with these non-negotiables. We will touch base daily if it becomes necessary. And if things just don't come together for you soon, we will have no choice but to agree that this position is not a good fit for you. We have up to four weeks for that to become clear, but it may clarify itself sooner than that."

Though his feelings weren't justified, Roger felt miserable and mean as he watched Nadine storm out of his office. But he also felt relieved. No longer was he ignoring the problems with Nadine's work. He had addressed them and had been perfectly clear with her what was expected. Now, he wondered what would come next. Would she resign? Cause even more upheaval on the staff?

Track and give careful feedback on performance plan success or failure, offering training or assistance as needed.

Nadine shifted her attitude from curt to cordial the very next day. Notes with messages left by church members began appearing regularly in the appropriate staff mailboxes. Room scheduling accuracy improved. Those who called the office on the phone were greeted with an amiable attitude. Roger was encouraged and gave her that feedback that Friday as promised. Perhaps Nadine could turn things around after all! But attempts at improvement lasted only another three days. When Nadine spent most of an afternoon pouting after arguing with a frustrated caller about how many times the phone had rung before she answered it, Roger knew what needed to happen. "Nadine, you've reverted to the workplace behavior that isn't acceptable," he told her before she went home from work that night. "Is there anything I can do to help you learn, or provide training in any area to assist you?" Nadine shook her head. "We'll see how it goes through the end of this week, and then we'll need to talk," he concluded.

Allow the right things to happen as positively as possible.

The next morning Roger found a neatly-typed letter of resignation on his desk from Nadine. *Dear Pastor Roger, I see that I'm not a good match for what you want in a church secretary. My last day will be two weeks from today. I hope you can find someone else in that time for the job.* As Roger read the letter, he winced. He resisted the inclination to simply e-mail Nadine an acknowledgement of her letter so he wouldn't have to deal with any potential negativity in person, and motioned for her to come into his office to talk.

"Nadine, I read your letter. I want to thank you for the season you have spent as our church secretary, and for honestly assessing whether or not you want to continue here. Thanks also for giving us two weeks' notice so that we can find our next secretary. I want to encourage you to finish well during these next two weeks. Let me tell you what I mean by that. Although you have worked here for years, the persons around you will remember you most by what you're like as you're finishing your time on staff here with them. You can choose a 'what the heck' approach and treat people poorly since, after all, you're leaving. Or you can choose to finish well and do your very best these last days. That, after all, honors your service to Christ and it honors your love for this church where you've been a member for so long."

Handle all personnel issues confidentially.
Nadine chose to finish well her final two weeks, and Roger was glad. He placed Nadine's letter in her file and notified the personnel committee immediately about her resignation, remembering how important communication is on such matters. He received a number of angry phone calls, however, from longtime church members who were friends of Nadine's. To each he gave the same explanation. "So, you ran Nadine out!" one aggressive caller accused, "What do you think she did wrong? She's more talented than anyone you've got up there in the church office!" Roger stayed calm as he answered. "The church is a workplace, and all employment personnel matters are confidential. I'm not at liberty to share any details about Nadine's work performance. But we do appreciate her long years of service, and we will miss her."

Keep the process healthy.
Roger was grateful for the work he'd done earlier to create a job description for the church secretary position, since now he needed it to proceed in his interview process for a replacement. This time around, he assured himself, he would practice the habits of a capable supervisor from the start. He worked quickly to recruit servants who could sit at the secretary's desk and answer the phone in the interim while a careful hiring process took place. He moved quickly to publicize the open position, and made available copies of the job description for prospective candidates to consider. For the first time, Roger felt pleased with his actions and management as staff supervisor. While not easy, he realized that he too could develop the right skills to support and lead his paid staff, even through the process of an individual staffing change.

Like Roger, intentional leaders learn that facilitating change is part of ultimate responsibility. Even when it's uncomfortable, the change process is the path upon which God leads you and your congregation or ministry to your future. Fortunately, the art of leading change is a skill you can learn. The final chapter will help you get started.

ON THE DVD FOR CHAPTER 6:

-Four Core Team Questions Worksheet

-Video Story: Mike—"Jack of All Trades"

-Video Story: Roland—"Worker"

-Video Story: Terry—"Franchiser"

-Video Story: Norm—"Entrepreneur"

-Job description example

"There are three stages in every great work of
God: first it is impossible, then it is difficult,
then it is done."
-J. Hudson Taylor

7

LEADING SUCCESSFUL CHANGE

"**I** see exactly what needs to happen in the ministry I now lead," Jeri told me. "All the right ingredients are present, it seems: we have a great facility, an adequate budget, and a decent attendance. There's just one thing to face: how to bring about the change necessary to get everyone to the next level, where I'm convinced God wants us to go. I wish I had a magic wand to wave. The process of change is so difficult! I know that's why my predecessor in this position quit. He said he just got tired of butting heads with the unpaid leadership, who were too stubborn and obstinate to agree to change the way they did things. I'm not so sure, though, if the barrier was really them—or him?"

Jeri is onto something. Whether it's bringing about change in your own personal life or leadership habits or in the direction of the committee, team, or church that you lead, the path of change can feel rough and uncomfortable to navigate. At times it seems those around you are impediments to forward progress. In other moments, you may become painfully aware that it's you who's slowing things down. The last step to igniting your church's ministry is learning how to effectively lead change—and how to manage both yourself and the constituency you serve as you go.

Leading successful ministry change is not about winning or losing. It is not about who personally gets his or her own way, should not be automatically dictated by who has been at the church the longest, and is certainly not change simply for the sake of change. It's all about how better to accomplish the work of Jesus—more effectively, more strategically, involving the most servants possible, serving the most needy possible, helping enhance the spiritual growth of everyone as much as possible. Let's begin by looking at both sides of the change process: first you as the leader and then the dynamic of your team, ministry, or church.

As you read this section of the chapter, ask yourself: What are the assets to maximize in my change leader approach? What about myself will I need to manage, so that I don't inadvertently become part of the problem?

You as a Leader of Change

You: a potential leader of ministry change. Whether you're a committee chair, team leader, pastor, or staff member, the same fundamental ingredients are necessary. Review chapter 5, "Leading a Team." Have you adopted the style of an intentional leader? (Leading change from one of the other seven dysfunctional leadership styles is a recipe for failure.) How about the credibility markers necessary for uniting and deploying your team or ministry? Have you established your own scope of ministry accountability, so you'll have an objective, safe space sounding board as you lead the journey of change to unfold? All change leaders begin with healthy leadership practices.

The tension of the adrenaline-filled atmosphere of change will bring out your primary leadership component: Systems/Task Organizer, Vision Crier, or Spiritual Shepherd. Your primary component will instinctively shape your approach. What impression will you leave with others?

Indiana Jones. Some change leaders, intent on utilizing their *Systems/Task Organizer* abilities, see where the ministry needs to go and step out ahead. Their focus is on accomplishing what's necessary in order to facilitate and organize the change process. "Indiana Jones" leaders appear to be loners, concentrating on their own tasks rather than ensuring that those in the congregation also have what they need for the journey: information, feedback, encouragement, and ownership. Without paying careful intention, you may lose sight of your group—and lose your influence as their leader.

Martha. Mary's sister and friend of Jesus was a classic *Systems/Task Organizer*, fond of seeing everything done in a certain manner. So when Jesus showed up at her home and change happened, she turned into a frustrated complainer, demanding certain behavior from her sister Mary. "Martha" leaders desire to accommodate change but try to control everyone and everything involved in the process. They become like army generals, barking out orders and losing focus when things don't go exactly as they have planned. If the environment of change brings out your "Martha," remind yourself that Jesus is the one to please in the process, not yourself.

John the Baptist. If *Vision Crier* is your primary ministry component, leading change might bring out your radical, distinctive side. You may find yourself relishing the opportunity to paint a new vision for your group, energized by unsettling them out of what you see as their complacency. "John the Baptist" leaders must pay attention not to explain the results of proposed change in terms that seem extreme or drastic to your group. Otherwise you may find yourself out in the wilderness by yourself.

Peter Pan. Another *Vision Crier* approach to leading change, the "Peter Pan" leader invites followers to "come dream with me...." The path toward change is painted in fairy tale finery, too good to really be true, perhaps too perfect a destination to actually reach. "Peter Pan" change leaders are magnetic, often irresistible as they charm their constituency forward. If this image fits you, make sure to tie the future dreams you portray to a reality that's attainable. Otherwise your group may end up disappointed and disillusioned.

Samson. Deeply committed to his religious heritage, Samson displayed an unmistakable anointing from God even as he bullied his way into control of every situation. "Samson" leaders are strong *Spiritual Shepherds* who tie themselves to a deep faith in God's miraculous power, subduing all critics by taking charge and ushering in a powerful movement of the Spirit in and through the change process. Take care not to overwhelm or intimidate those you lead. There's a borderline between anointed and annoying.

Mary. Also an approach of a *Spiritual Shepherd*, "Mary" leaders bring along their ministry attendees or team by encouraging them to be open and responsive to "how the Spirit leads." Rather than offering up a well-organized game plan, some "Mary" leaders prefer to wait, pray, and listen as they just go with the flow, recognizing the steps of progress as they present themselves. They're confident that the eventual next-level destination for the group will be God-designed. If this is your change leader approach, remember that planning is not a sin, and let the Marthas of your group contribute their organizational gifts as you move forward.

Did you identify yourself within these six change leader approaches? Now that you have some self-awareness of what you as leader bring to the process of change, read further to understand what potential obstacles to change may exist in your group.

Inertia Anchors

Whatever the specific circumstances, certain characteristics are common in churches or ministries of all sizes when it comes to facing change. Be open as you consider the following scenarios illustrating heavy anchors that weigh down a church or team facing a necessary change. These anchors contribute to the inertia that can paralyze God's work. Ask yourself: *Have I as the leader unintentionally contributed to the creation of an inertia anchor in my ministry?*

Anchor #1: Tug of War

Janice was thrilled to become the servant leader of the senior adult ministry at her church. Having become a widow only six months earlier, she dreamed of launching a grief support group as part of the senior adult activities and found a facilitator. Janice focused her time and energy into helping develop the grief group, personally attending it for her own healing as well as publicizing its existence in the community to draw more attendees. After a year, Janice told the senior adult leadership team that she believed their ministry purpose was to center themselves completely on the issues of grief recovery for the widowed, and that no other senior adult activities were necessary.

"But what about our social outings and bus trips?" one asked incredulously.

"Yes, and how about our senior adult Bible study and potluck dinner each month?" another pointed out. "And the long-time dream we've talked about: to offer computer and other life enrichment classes right here at our church?"

"No, none of those is nearly as important as helping people cope with loss," Janice maintained. "I know from personal experience that grief is our mission."

Janice's insistence upon her own agenda for her ministry set up the perfect conditions to birth a "Tug of War" anchor to change. The process of change can reach an impasse if differing agendas of the leader and the team or ministry create a standoff. When the leader attempts to impose an agenda upon the group based on personal needs and interests (sometimes mistakenly calling it the vision for the ministry), participants may become passive, sensing no ownership and having no buy-in. Or they might become passive aggressive, attempt to bypass the leader, and even stage a mutiny to go in a preferred direction.

Anchor #2: Opinion-Driven

Phillip, pleased to be named leader of the young adult ministry, always felt terrible if he inadvertently offended someone. So when it came time to plan the direction of the coming year in his ministry group, he was afraid to be the first to point out a next direction for growth, for fear others might think him bossy. Instead, he would hope that someone in the group would suggest it so he could agree. He always took the low-courage route.

"What do you all want to do; what direction do you want to go?" he would ask the attendees in general. Unfortunately, the most insistent and opinionated members usually spoke up according to their own likes and dislikes, not on behalf of best intentions for the group's growth and purpose. At other times when Phillip asked the same question, no one spoke up—which felt even worse. It became impossible to get the group off dead center, and it eventually shrunk to a small closed cell group of young adults, content to focus upon their own pursuits. Phillip had allowed the anchor of opinion-driven direction to prevent healthy ministry change and growth.

Anchor #3: Victim Mentality

"If only the senior pastor would support us, just think how we could truly evolve and grow!" one of the youth group sponsors complained. "And we haven't even been given an adequate budget for youth ministry! No wonder our outreach to teens will never be much. I vote we just do the same two projects as last year, no changes. How can we, when we're the underdog ministry of the church? No one cares about us!"

Melodie, the new youth group leader, was frustrated at the victim attitude of her team that stalemated any potential new goals she hoped to set for students in the coming year. She personally agreed that the senior pastor could certainly do more to spotlight youth ministry and make it more of a priority, but she chose not to openly admit that to her team of sponsors. The Victim Mentality was a challenging enough obstacle, and she rightly knew that if she as leader co-signed the negativity, it would become an inertia anchor and no potential path to successful growth and change would ever emerge.

Anchor #4: Loss of Openness

Louise loved the scrapbooking group she led. Who would have guessed a collection of women could be drawn together by a common hobby and end up becoming so close in the Lord? For the first time in her life, she felt mentored by more spiritually mature women every week when they brought their materials, photos, scissors and paper together for Bible study and scrapbook time. Louise knew her group could reach many more women in the neighborhood, but it was tough to want to change to an outward focus. The fellowship was rich, intimacy had developed as they prayed together about personal issues, and it was easy to talk about deep matters of the Spirit. When an occasional newcomer showed up, Louise and the others were initially courteous to her. But soon the regular attendees gravitated back to catching up with their friends. And sometimes when a visitor didn't know to bring along a Bible, no one offered to share. This was bothersome to Louise, but she thought, *After all, a lot would have to change if the group really decided to embrace everyone who came—and then our closeness would be sacrificed. Do we really want to lose that?* Without even realizing it, the anchor called "Loss of Openness" had begun to prevent all potential group evolution and growth.

Anchor #5: Problem Persons

William was proud to be selected as a church planter by his denomination, and he invested the first eighteen months working seven days a week in order to draw together his small, new congregation. Every new person counted, and he set as his personal goal not to lose a single one.

William sought to build close relationships with the individuals he had invited to be on his first leadership board and wanted each of them to feel ownership of the decisions made to help the church grow and develop, and to always reach consensus. Unfortunately, he didn't know Steven well before choosing him to be on the board. Steven criticized everything William did, opposed his suggestions, and appeared to take satisfaction at blackballing key decisions. When the board considered a crucial financial decision that would determine whether the church moved ahead to build its first building or stayed overcrowded in a local school gymnasium, the vote was favorably unanimous—except for Steven's. William stalled the bank month after month, pleading in vain with Steven both at board meetings and at frequent personal breakfast meetings for his support.

A **worksheet** to guide you and your team's discussion about **Change Leader styles and Inertia Anchors** can be found on the *Ultimately Responsible* DVD, chapter 7. Evaluate the dynamics of your obstacles to change. Are you a contributor to any of them?

Eventually the upstart congregation's growth died off due to space issues, and attendees drifted away. Within a year after presenting the crucial financial decision to his leadership board, William experienced the death of the church start and regretfully began the search for a new pastorate to serve. Why, he wondered, had he not sought critical mass rather than consensus on the board regarding that decision? Why had he not had the courage to disagree with Steven instead of placating him? William thought about Moses, a biblical figure he admired. When left to their own consensus-finding, the people of Israel always tried to turn back to Egypt. But Moses didn't let problem persons become an inertia anchor to stand in the way of God's direction. When it counted, Moses and his few key leaders led change forward with critical mass, not consensus. It was a painful lesson to learn about leading change—in hindsight.

These five inertia anchors represent some of the most common obstacles to change in the ministry setting. And, as you read, the leader in charge may exacerbate the weight of the obstacle. Like Janice, does your own personal healing process or spiritual growth journey bias the solutions you're willing to consider in pursuit of supporting change and growth with the group you lead? Or perhaps like Phillip, you struggle with leadership courage and are afraid to name a new direction. Maybe you're like Melodie, facing a victim mentality that makes it more comfortable for you to feel sorry for yourself and your group's underdog status than to go against the grain and speak positivity and possibilities. Louise believed theoretically in the growth and change potential of her group, but found the closed, cozy, predictable atmosphere preferable to the uncomfortable path of change. Or do you relate to William, who cherished the good will of his team so much that he sacrificed leading the change-creating decision necessary for the entire church to survive.

Launching the Change Process

Now that you have made certain you are practicing a healthy intentional leadership style, are mindful of the credibility markers necessary for effectiveness, have identified how your primary ministry component plays out as a change leader, and have investigated any potential inadvertent anchor-like contribution you have made to your constituency's inertia relative to change—let's move on to the tools you need to begin the actual process. By answering these questions, you'll gain what you need to see where you're going, overcome the inertia anchors, and make headway.

What needs to change?

What exactly needs a shift, according to your perspective? Is it:
- A total change of overall direction or core purpose?
- How one specific task should be carried out?
- Who is responsible for what?
- How decisions are made?
- In what ways servants are included and deployed?
- Something else specific to your environment?

Clarifying in your own mind what specifically you believe needs to change is your first job. Otherwise, you may find yourself openly criticizing the general state of affairs of your church or ministry without constructively identifying anything that is at the core of what needs to shift. Leaders who carp on their church or ministry are actually passing judgment on their own leadership ability, not on the group they lead. After all, the speed of the leader is the speed of the team.

Andrea, the new leader of her church's care ministry, was honored to have been chosen for the role. She was passionate about providing support to those in the congregation who were hospitalized. The care ministry was guided by a steering committee that met monthly. Most of its members had been active in the care ministry for years and were vigilant to guard the reputation of the care ministry's quick response and compassionate presence to those facing illness.

If the message of change is intended for one individual, sit down and talk personally with that person. Do not deliver to the entire group a message of change that's aimed specifically at one member. The hoped-for recipient may not recognize your message is for him or her, and others in the group may be confused, wondering how to apply your comments to themselves.

Andrea found herself wondering how else the care ministry could support church attendees in crisis, beyond its traditional focus upon those in the hospital. Right now the steering team included seven members, with another fourteen servants on the roster who also participated in the hospital visitation rotation. What would happen, she wondered, if the scope of the care ministry's purpose changed and broadened to include staffing the church's two small prayer rooms before, during, and after weekend worship services? Persons who desired prayer and support for any reason would be able to connect with a care ministry servant, not just if they were admitted to the hospital.

What are steps that could bring about the change?

Name these progress steps for yourself. Take time to settle down and examine the basic increments necessary to effect the change that's needed. Would it start by doing research about better ministry practices? By checking the church's scheduling calendar? By thinking of ideas for new servant recruits? Make a list for yourself, step by step.

Andrea began to ask God during her daily Bible study and devotional time to show her what might be possible for the care ministry's expansion. She kept a list in her Bible and added thoughts, ideas, and insights whenever they came to her. After a few weeks, she summarized them for herself in writing:
- Introduce the new possibility to the steering team.
- Double-check with the pastor to verify support of the structured use of the prayer rooms on weekends for this purpose.
- Set up bi-monthly training sessions for new care ministry servants, rather than just twice a year, to increase the ministry's resources.
- In addition to the current signup system for visiting those in the hospital, create a new system by which care ministry servants could sign up for specific weekends and times to staff the church's prayer room, and have available a ministry phone list to call a substitute if necessary.
- Allow servants to choose whether they feel led to serve in the prayer room, visit at the hospital, or both.
- Coordinate publicity information for the congregation to let them know of the expanded availability of the care ministry servants on weekends and when they will be available in the prayer rooms.
- Rearrange the furniture in the prayer rooms to be conducive to more than one person, adding a second chair and a wall rack to hold a Bible and devotional pamphlets.

Andrea knew that other steps would be involved, but those were the initial ideas God had brought to her mind. She was excited about how the potential change to broaden the care ministry's mission could help more individuals, bringing comfort and hope to many in emotional and spiritual crisis as well as to those in physical crisis.

With whom do I need to share my vision for change?

At this point, many leaders stumble. They begin to mention their hopes for change to good friends in the church or name it in casual conversations with attendees, forgetting that it needs to be brought first to those who would be most affected. Does a particular leadership team need to be in on the initial discussion of new ideas? Key leaders? Your staff? The entire church? A wayward servant? Take care with how you introduce your change-management ideas. Your goal is to build critical mass, not accidentally fuel resistant consensus.

Plan an appropriate occasion to introduce the possibility of change, rather than spontaneously blurting it out at an inopportune moment when there's no time for feedback and dialogue. This way you'll avoid what might feel like a hit and run approach to your group.

Andrea scheduled lunch with two of the newest, most positive members of the care ministry steering team a few days before the monthly team meeting. She chose them because she knew each had a commitment to active spiritual growth and personal prayer. She also knew that they each understood and embraced the church's overall mission of service to those in need and could see the care ministry's place within that mission. A few others on the steering team had been in care ministry leadership much longer, but Andrea strategically met ahead of time with those who had demonstrated a heart for openness to God's leading.

Andrea told the two steering team members that she sensed God had greater expectations of the care ministry, and she shared her ideas for growth and their connection to their ministry's purpose. Andrea gained perspective and insight from the ensuing discussion, and encouragement through their enthusiasm. She asked them to pray for the upcoming steering team meeting. And though her ideas were not confidential, she asked the two team members to allow her the privilege of being the first to share the possibility of this change with the others.

Vision Criers sometimes find talking about the potential vision of change so tempting that they overlook who needs to hear it first. Respect the change process enough to discipline yourself, and choose to start the conversation with those it primarily impacts.

What's the best way to present a proposal for change?

If you're bringing ideas for change to a team or group, prepare yourself by framing the intended change as progress. There's no need for you to take a derogatory tact when referring to the present reality in contrast to the future possibility. Instead, identify the ideas as potential ministry advancement, steps toward maximizing what you already share, raising the bar, or going to the next level.

Use your **Systems/Task Organizer** skills to keep the business of your team or ministry going even as you introduce conversation about change. This reassures your followers that nothing is coming to a standstill.

Andrea was excited and a little nervous as she arrived at the steering team meeting. As usual, the care ministry's agenda progressed predictably: review of how many hospital visits the ministry made during the last month; current status of members still hospitalized; report of days during the coming month on which care ministry servant signups to visit the hospital were still needed.

Andrea had added a final item, "New Ideas," to the typed agenda she had distributed at the beginning of the meeting. She hoped that way the steering team would not be caught off guard with the change in routine. When it was time, she smiled at her leaders and felt again her excitement.

"I wanted to add this monthly agenda item to our meetings," she began. "'New Ideas' are always important when we are involved in serving the mission of Jesus. You never know what inspiration the Spirit might bring to any of us about ways we could more effectively do our care ministry work, touch the lives of more individuals, and be used more fully ourselves."

"Well, we pretty much know what we're doing in this ministry," interrupted Thelma. "I've been on the care ministry team for nine years now, and we know the drill, so to speak. I don't imagine there's much different we could handle, with the number of servants we have. Everybody's happy right now, and we have our systems worked out. No changes needed, that's for sure!"

"I agree, we have no need to change any present system of making certain our members who are hospitalized get a visit of support from us," acknowledged Andrea. "Thank you, to all of you who give—and have given—such time and dedication to what we have going. It's a privilege to serve as a part of this."

What is important to emphasize first?

Couch all of what you propose to the team in the language of possibility. Do not arrive at the meeting with a typed, prepared summary of the potential change plans to distribute—this conveys top-down decision making, leaves no room for open discussion and sets the scene for the "Tug of War" inertia anchor to emerge in your group. Instead, present everything in the language of potential and possibilities. Remember that God may inspire someone in the group with an even better version of the ideas you bring, and avoid becoming defensive if that happens.

Affirm it! Be open, and visualize yourself as the player who only tees up the football. The proposal you share with the group ideally provides God's Spirit a playing field upon which to score the next victory. State up front the reason for the change you are proposing, tied into the big-picture purpose or mission of your ministry.

Andrea continued. "I was wondering the other day in my devotional time with God whether now is the time to enlarge our care-ministry scope on behalf of our church family. Our weekly worship attendance has grown; more and more are coming to our church. And we all know that it's not just those who are sick in the hospital who have cares and concerns, who need prayer. Just think what unspoken spiritual and emotional needs are represented every weekend in everyone sitting in the sanctuary pews. I wonder…how does God expect us to respond?"

When is it time to provide details?

Once your group has heard the headlines describing a new potential change, assist them by suggesting concrete steps that would need to happen in order for it to become reality. Explain in succinct terms how to you the change would better (more effectively, more efficiently) accomplish the purpose.

Andrea became specific. "I wonder—what would happen if we as the care ministry became proactive to make ourselves available on the weekends and staff the two prayer rooms just outside the sanctuary doors? We would have to get communication out, of course, to let everyone know we were there; put up signage outside the prayer room doors; and rearrange the prayer room furniture to accommodate the times when we would sit and talk and pray with a person or two. And, of course, we would need to offer our care ministry servant training more often, to add to our available servant pool. We would be able to involve many more who could help own this ministry and comfort those who need the love of this great church family."

How should I facilitate discussion about change?

Give care to the management of your instinctive change leader style at this point, and do your best to stay with the group's exploration of the change ideas. Allow healthy dialogue to occur, and do everything you can to keep the conversation about the potential change, not about the person who suggested it.

Andrea was eager to hear the team's reactions. "Well, what are your thoughts? Let's share discussion about this possible idea. Isn't it exciting to dream together about where God might be leading our care ministry and how God might want to use us and our passion to respond to those who need spiritual support?"

Utilize your **Spiritual Shepherd** leadership component skills during this phase of the change process. Be patient as individuals wrestle with new ideas, not impatiently trying to skip ahead with the vision.

Andrea prepared herself to respond neutrally to the feedback that came next. She made herself remember the team's commentary was about the idea, not about herself or her leadership. Andrea acknowledged each person's comments but did not personalize them or attempt to immediately address any of them. Instead she listened carefully, and she objectively summarized each on a whiteboard for everyone to see.

"I know for a fact that's a bad idea. We who serve in the care ministry don't have time to staff those prayer rooms. We would miss either Sunday School class or the worship service, one or the other. I'm not sacrificing my own Sunday morning to stand around waiting to see if anyone comes by the prayer rooms!"

Current care ministry servants don't have time to also staff the prayer rooms, Andrea wrote.

"Well, what would we do if no one came to the prayer room to ask for prayer, and one of us was stuck in there alone for a whole hour? A lot of wasted time!"

How would a servant use extra time while staffing a prayer room? The whiteboard list continued to grow.

"Wow, this is good. We are really thinking of all possible angles," Andrea encouraged the team. "What else?"

"I am thrilled by this idea, honestly," said one of the leaders whom Andrea had invited to lunch. "Just think how much more we could accomplish our mission, which is to provide care and support for those in crisis and in spiritual need! And we could involve so many more servants, too! After all, we need to think of cultivating the next generation of care ministry leaders to rise up behind us. Not that any of us are rotating off right now. But someday there will be a need for additional steering team leaders. We need to be mindful of that now, not later."

Would provide "bench depth" for development of future care ministry leadership—another whiteboard addition to the list.

"No, it would be way too much work to run the care ministry servant training more than twice each year. We have never done that before. I don't like your suggestion at all, Andrea."

Need to expand number of care ministry servant trainers to accommodate more frequent sessions, Andrea carefully reframed the complaint.

When is it time to move from dialogue to decision-making?

Pay attention to the discussion, and guide it so that everyone has an opportunity to share. Then simply summarize the observations made by the group. Objectively restate the observations, keeping them about the change and not about factions or personalities. As leader, this is your time to reply to each. Watch the pronouns you use. "We" and "us" imply a shared mission. The use of "I" and "you" draws a line and creates distance between the leader and those who are being led. Do everything you can in words to unite the group in the common cause of your church or ministry.

After each steering team member had opportunity to talk, Andrea focused them on the whiteboard list. "Let's take a look at the observations we've made and respond to each one. It seems to me that care ministry servants wouldn't have to sign up to serve both at the hospital and on the weekend prayer room duty, would they? So if a servant feels more comfortable just doing hospitals, that's fine. And it opens up the opportunity for new servants to staff the weekends. In fact, it might be better that way. We could involve more servants.

"Hmmmm…let's see. You know, it might be a godsend if a care ministry servant didn't have someone who needed prayer during the hour in the prayer room. It would leave time for the care ministry servant to pray for the worship service and for each member we know is in the hospital as well as to have a daily devotional time…."

Andrea and the team conversed as each point was revisited. The two team members who had heard Andrea's proposal beforehand added zeal that became contagious. Before long, five of the steering team members were in agreement to seriously explore the change of the care ministry's scope. Two others continued to scowl and shake their heads.

"We can't handle that much!" Paula protested. "I am already so busy trying to make phone calls and organize who is going to the hospital each day. I simply can't take on doing the same for the weekend prayer rooms! I refuse!"

When should I name the elephant in the room?

While grace-filled leaders may choose to overlook a certain amount for the sake of group progress, at times it's necessary to address on the spot the challenge that's being presented. Don't pick an argument. Do stay positive.

"**Wow,** we would never expect you to take that on also," Andrea responded to Paula. "If you still enjoy coordinating the hospital visits, you could continue that. We could enlist someone else to coordinate the weekend servants."

"But, but…" Paula was deeply offended. "Scheduling is what I do; it's my responsibility. Are you saying that you are trying to take that away from me? Am I not doing it well enough for you or something? I couldn't share scheduling. How would I know who is doing what, when?"

Andrea made herself ignore Paula's personal challenge. "You know, hopefully this will be good news for you, Paula. All that scheduling doesn't have to be done by just one person. You could keep doing the part you do for us now, and the weekend schedule really could be handled by others."

"No! I don't agree with you! I will do this ministry's scheduling, period. I always have. But I won't do it for something like weekend prayer rooms." Paula's face was flushed.

Andrea stayed calm. "You know, Paula, why don't you give this some time; think about it and pray about it. Who knows—God may be directing you in the midst of this care ministry change. It may well be that you have done the scheduling for so long that your frustration is coming from fatigue and from needing a break. It's also possible that you could enjoy a season of functioning simply as a care ministry servant, without any scheduling responsibilities at all. That would give you a rest. You must be tired. And it would also give someone else the fulfillment of that responsibility you have enjoyed."

How will everyone notice this change as it happens?

Once the momentum begins to build toward change, it is helpful to clarify what won't happen anymore when change is implemented and what will occur instead. Name what will be different. Then when everything comes to pass, no surprises are in store. Emphasize collective ownership for what is about to take place.

Andrea turned to the whole team. "One of the effects of this change would be that no longer would everyone on our steering team know every single detail about everything happening. As we diversify our servant responsibilities and include others, this team would still oversee the big picture. But our season of functioning like a mom-and-pop shop would be over. That is what would change in order for us to go to the next level. It would be a trade-off, but it is one we cannot afford to refuse."

Andrea knew the steering team had the necessary critical mass to move forward with the change. She closed the meeting with prayer, but beforehand she gave the team one last reminder: "Today we decided to be open to expanding the care ministry, and we assigned ourselves tasks to explore the idea of staffing the prayer rooms on weekends. We discussed the pros and cons of this idea, and have decided to see where it leads.

"This group decision belongs to us all. If you as an individual cannot own the decision yet, you have three options. First, take it to God in your daily devotional time, and ask God through prayer for wisdom and discernment on behalf of our ministry. Second, bring your concerns to me, and we'll continue to dialogue about what changes we would need to make and how those changes would impact what we are doing. Third, bring your insights to our next meeting at which we'll update each other on our research and planning. We will continue to seek God's guidance together for this next step.

"As a steering team member, I encourage you to exercise any or all of these three options. Taking negativity or concerns out to process among our care ministry servants would not be fitting for a steering team leader. It would definitely pull their servant focus off what they feel called to do, which is to provide presence and support as they care for others. Let's stick together as the steering team in good stewardship of the responsibility we have to guide God's ministry."

How do I handle the "casualties" of the change?

If you are an intentional leader who is effectively taking your team or ministry forward, not everyone will agree with or like what is going on. Some may even choose to leave. View this not as failure but as God's redirection for some of the lives involved. Help others share this perspective.

Six months later, Andrea could tell that the monthly care ministry steering team meeting had a different feel. After two care ministry servant training sessions and three months of weekend prayer room staffing, the care ministry servant roster was growing and the results were inspiring. Andrea opened the meeting with prayer, then invited steering team members to share stories from the new prayer room outreach.

"I talked with and prayed for a young single mom who was trusting God to help her find a job. I shared Scripture with her, and she cried as she thanked me. She said she's so happy she found a church that truly cares about people."

Some leaders and teams struggle with **procrastination** when it comes to the change process. Do you tend to know what needs to change, but struggle to get started (either personally or in ministry)? View a short segment of Mike Slaughter's powerful message, "Purging Procrastination," on the *Ultimately Responsible* DVD, chapter 7, to get a jumpstart.

"I prayed with a man who just found out the day before that his father has cancer. What a time to help him remember the hope God can provide, even in the darkest hours!"

"I had a pretty shy teenage girl come for prayer. Turned out she had a bad argument with her mother and felt guilty about how she'd treated her. After we prayed, she said she had some forgiveness to ask of her mom, then left. I really felt like God was using me that morning!"

Andrea had also planned a special "thank you" for Paula, whose disagreement with the care ministry change had led her to quit the steering team and the entire ministry in protest. Rather than allowing her to leave harboring negativity, Andrea invited her to one last steering team meeting for a time of recognition along with cake and punch.

"Paula, you have been a pioneer in this care ministry!" Andrea said. "Thank you so much for all you have contributed. It's a privilege to celebrate your many years serving in the care ministry. Now let's all lay hands on Paula, and I'll pray for her as God leads her to the next place where she'll serve."

The steering team gathered around Paula as Andrea prayed. Afterwards during the refreshments, each steering team member shared a memory of one contribution Paula had made that they especially appreciated. Paula left before the rest of the meeting's agenda, visibly moved. Rather than feeling rejected, she felt launched into her own personal, spiritual change process as God would lead.

Final Wisdom About Change

Now you're ready. This is your season, your time of intentional leadership in the strong name of Jesus! Your change process may not be as simple (or as complicated) as Andrea's. But no matter how multi-layered and lengthy your church or ministry's process of change may appear, you'll lead the way by sticking to the basic steps listed above. And as you embrace the gift of change, remember:

- The larger your constituency, the slower the pace of change. Think big ship, tiny rudder. A big ship must turn slowly; otherwise it may capsize. Move steadily, yet carefully.
- Even though you may be focused upon the future, the next level that will result through the change process, remember to enjoy and value the present. God is at work now. Don't miss the joy.
- Validate the worth of the individuals you lead, not their dysfunction or entrenchment. That way you'll stay connected to the significance of their potential, and expect the best from them.

- Stay concentrated on your sphere of responsibility, that which you can affect, rather than your sphere of concern, that which you may worry about but over which you have no control.
- Expect to be changed yourself. God will amaze leaders who are open to the practice of healthy personal change along the way. And you'll gain wisdom on how to help others do the same.

In chapter 1, the "Ministry Success" equation was defined as:

[Awareness of/leverage of your primary ministry components/strengths]
+
[Your daily living and growing relationship with God]
+
[Your contagious, ministry-movement strategy and communication]
+
[Your full embrace of the "Body of Christ" approach to Kingdom work]
+
[Your ability to develop strategic partnerships and teams]
+
[Your skills as a leader of change]

= Ministry "Success"

Step-by-step, chapter-by-chapter, you've learned about each element of the equation. You've viewed the accompanying stories on the DVD, and utilized worksheets with your team, staff, or committee.

Share your victories and your challenges with other ultimately responsible leaders at www.ultimately responsible.com, and find new ideas and resources to help your ministry flourish!

So now you have learned why this book is called *Ultimately Responsible.* That's the extent to which true leaders in the making take serious ownership of every part of their call to lead and ignite their ministries. You are God's hope for intentional leadership right where you are with the individuals you serve. You're the right person at the right time, with the right gifts fueled by the right passion. Have courage! Purge procrastination, rise up, and get rolling on what needs to happen. Your greatest season of leadership lies before you.

ON THE DVD FOR CHAPTER 7:

-Change Process Worksheet

-Mike Slaughter video segment on "Purging Procrastination"

APPENDIX

USING THE DVD-ROM

Playing the DVD on a set-top player

Set-top DVD players are connected to a TV. If you have previously played a DVD motion picture, you will see that the *Ultimately Responsible* DVD behaves in much the same way. Once inserted, the disk will begin playing automatically, beginning with the copyright notice and logos. After these have played, the **Main Menu** will appear, and you may then use the menu to choose what you would like to view.

To navigate through the DVD menus, use the **Up** and **Down** arrow keys on your remote to move the pointer to the menu item that you wish to play. After an item is highlighted, press **Play** or **Enter** to move to the next screen or to begin playing an item such as a video. Clicking on the **Title** button will take you back to the very beginning of the disk.

Volume is adjusted in the normal way for your DVD player. Other buttons on the remote, like **Fast Forward**, will allow you to quickly move through a video. Many of the screens also have embedded graphical buttons, such as **Menu**, to help you navigate. Selecting the graphical **Menu** button will take you back one level in the menu structure, depending on where you are. To go back to the **Main Menu**, you will need to click the **Title** button on your remote. Selecting the **Back** or **Next** button will move you through the other menus at the same level.

Playing the DVD on a computer
System requirements
Windows
- Windows 98 and higher (ME or higher recommended)
- At least 600 MHz processor (1Ghz or higher recommended)
- 128 MB of memory (256 recommended)
- DVD-ROM drive with appropriate drivers and software

Macintosh
- OS 9 or higher
- G3 processor (600 Mhz or higher)
- At least 128 MB of memory (256 recommended)
- DVD-ROM drive with appropriate drivers and software

If you have the capability to hook a computer with a DVD player to a projector, you may choose to use this method to display the video components. Every computer will have a different type of proprietary software that comes with the DVD-ROM drive, and the controls on each will vary slightly.

Many of the buttons on the software interface will act just like the buttons on a DVD remote, though there will be some variation. Using the **Up** and **Down** arrow buttons on your software remote will cycle through and highlight each of the buttons, functioning just as they do on a set-top DVD player. (**Up** and **Left** will move through the buttons clockwise; **Down** and **Right** will move through the buttons counterclockwise.) Once you have highlighted the button you want, hit the **Enter** key to activate the button. The advantage, however, of the computer navigation over the DVD set-top player is your ability to use the mouse to easily select the item you want by clicking it.

In general, clicking the **Menu** button will take you back one step: if you are simply in a menu, it will take you up one level to the previous one; if you are playing a video, it will stop the video and take you back to the sub-menu. You can also use the **Menu** button to exit out of a video and return to the menu. Depending on where you are, you may have several choices when you click the **Menu** button. **Title** takes you back to the very beginning; **Root** takes you back to the previous menu (if this is your only other choice).

Clicking the **Title** button will take you back to the very beginning of the disk. The **Fast Forward** and **Rewind** buttons will allow you to advance or rewind the video.

Accessing the resources on the DVD

To access the printable worksheets included on the DVD, you will need to place it in a computer DVD-ROM drive. To browse to these data folders in Windows, open **Windows Explorer** and find the **Ultimately Responsible** disk icon. Double-click the DVD icon for a listing of the contents. (Be patient; it may take several seconds for this list to appear.) You may also use **My Computer** to get a listing of the data folders. However, you will probably need to right-click the DVD icon and choose **Explore** rather than double-click since this might cause the

DVD to begin playing. On a Macintosh, simply double-click the DVD icon to view the contents of the disk.

Once you have located the file you need, either copy the file to your hard drive or double-click the file to open it from the disk. If you open the file from the disk, remember that manipulating the file this way may be slower than copying it to your hard drive.